OP 90

30 -

B

Grass Roots Private Welfare

Grass Roots Private Welfare

Winning essays of the 1956 National Awards Competition
of The Foundation for Voluntary Welfare

ALFRED de GRAZIA, *Editor*

New York University Press
Washington Square   New York
1957

Foreword

We can recall when most Americans believed that every welfare need could be supplied by the voluntary work of individuals and communities. We have more recently lived in a period when prevailing opinion has exalted governmental (and therefore compulsory) action as the normal means of doing welfare work. Indeed this may be called the welfare ideology of our times.

As history so amply demonstrates, a successful ideology indiscriminately stamps out both good and evil of the past. Often only the good sense and skill of a country's leaders, at the grass roots and at the seats of power, will make the difference between a destructive and a constructive ideology. Our leaders require these qualities today, because a dogmatic belief in a fully secular, mechanistic, bureaucratized, and compulsory system of social welfare may produce not only a poor system of welfare but also an attendant deterioration of our whole way of life.

We believe that the contemporary philosophy of social welfare, as it may be discovered in public and private welfare agencies, in universities, and in the political forums of the country, needs reassessment on two levels. It needs first of all an inquiry into our welfare goals. Our goals should include, we believe, an insistence upon the utmost of personal liberty and choice, in the fields of welfare as in other fields. Our goals should include also a profound concern with and attention to our people who suffer misfortunes beyond their control. But as the insistence upon liberty should not encourage irresponsibility to suffering, so neither should concern for the unfortunate foster irresponsibility toward freedom.

The reassessment of welfare philosophy should inquire into techniques as well as goals. A general set of principles, like a map, will orient our thought and direction, but the actual navigation demands a more complex mingling of ideas and practices. Some welfare workers—both volunteer and professional—will subscribe to goals such as we have stated above, but at the same time engage from day to day in contradictory behavior. They will, for instance, develop a private welfare project and "sell" it to the government as a matter of course; they will take directions from public authorities without heeding the implications of their subordination; and they will identify themselves with those they serve to the exclusion of those whose resources make them able to serve others. They will separate themselves from the world of humanitarian ideals by a wall of red tape and scientism in order to pursue a cut-and-dried ideal of professionalism.

A major cause of this contradictory behavior is poor leadership. Leadership in social welfare work is not keenly aware of its goals. If professional, it is too professional; if volunteer, it is too often gullible; if financial and civic, it too rarely concerns itself with anything but fiscal problems; if political, it is too busy with temporary expedients. How few philanthropists there are who ask, while giving, whether their funds are supporting a truly private rather than an incipient public project. How few consider, as they should, not only whether the supported *act* is good, but also whether the *frame* or *context* of the act is appropriate to their goals of liberty and voluntarism. Current activities and proposals for new programs receive little theoretical consideration. The "New Dealism" of the thirties plus the "professionalism" of the forties sum up much of the philosophy of leadership in social welfare.

Meanwhile in many other fields the country has gone ahead: the sciences have been very dynamic; business has undergone remarkable changes of attitude, organization, and leadership; the income and tax structures of the country have been altered; many new ideas and practices have agitated the field of public administration. Yet social welfare philosophy, we believe, has not addressed itself adequately to its operational problems; it is still too concerned with its personal problems and is too subjective, whereas it should be more conscious of the objective problems of conducting innumerable welfare enterprises in a swiftly moving economy and society.

It is with these thoughts in mind that we are pleased to introduce the winning essays of the National Awards Competition of the Foundation for Voluntary Welfare. The intent of the Competition was not to seek a general philosophy of social welfare so much as it was to uncover examples of welfare activities that, if extended, might strengthen private and voluntary welfare in America. Many of the essays seem to us to afford such constructive suggestion; some seem still to bear the marks of the several conditions in the field to which we referred adversely above. A number describe inspiring episodes of Americanism at work. All together, they take an important step toward calling attention to the operating theory of social work. We hope that the essays will excite imitation in many communities throughout the land, and that they will recruit many private citizens for the unending task of voluntary constructive efforts in social welfare.

The Foundation for Voluntary Welfare

Contents

12. THE AGING

13. RECREATION

14. SPECIAL FINANCING METHODS

15. THE GENERAL SPIRIT OF VOLUNTARISM

Introduction

The Foundation for Voluntary Welfare is a nonprofit corporation organized under the laws of the State of California. It seeks to advance education and to encourage private activities and organizations in the field of social welfare.

The United States has a long and vigorous tradition of private welfare work organized and backed by private citizens and groups, both professional and lay. Yet voluntary welfare always needs new ideas, a stronger morale, more workers and money, better organization, and a greater public appreciation. There is no end to the possibilities of new devices and techniques for private welfare activities and of new organizational forms for administering them (including that ingenious creation for administering to his welfare, the individual person). In spite of considerable public apathy regarding private welfare, there is a great field for social invention. The more voluntarism in welfare, too, the less likely that any government can obtain an excess of power over its citizens.

As one step toward its goals the Foundation established the National Awards Competition. Through the Competition, the Foundation offered a total of $13,250 in awards for the best essays on the subject: "A Way to Extend Voluntary Activity and Organization in Social Welfare." The First Grand Award was $2,000; the Second Grand Award was $1,000. Twenty-eight awards of either $500 or $250 were also made. The essays were to be from 1,200 to 2,500 words long and were to deal with one of the following areas of social welfare: juvenile delinquency, mental health, basic medical research, the aging, rehabilitation, alcoholism, the blind, child welfare, chronic illness, the crippled, the deaf, medical care, migrant workers, or recreation. If an entrant did not wish to write on any of these, believing himself more competent in some other area, he might contribute an essay on that area, or perhaps one about the general field of social welfare; such essays were placed in a category termed "general." In order that each essay might be evaluated without the judges' knowing the author's name, the entrant was directed not to place his name on any page of the essay.

The rules of the Competition provided that any person who was, or ever had been, a salaried employee or an unpaid volunteer worker in any social welfare agency, public or private, for a period of one year or more, was qualified to participate.

Each entry was judged, following accepted principles of content analysis, according to three criteria: (1) how well it depicted a clear and practical method for extending private, voluntary efforts and operations in social welfare, in either a large or a small field; (2) how precisely it detailed the experiences of the author that led him to endorse the method he proposed; and (3) how fully it recounted the experiences of other persons, and of agencies, with similar objectives. Entries were judged upon their content, not their literary style. The Foundation had the assistance of an Advisory Council of nine members in administering the Competition. The chairman of the Council is the Honorable Herbert Hoover, thirty-first President of the United States. Other members of the Council are: Dr. Frank G. Dickinson, Director of the Bureau of Medical Economic Research, the American Medical Association; Dr. Sheldon Glueck, Roscoe Pound Professor of Law at Harvard University Law School; Mr. A. C. Mattei, President of the Honolulu Oil Company; Monsignor John O'Grady, Secretary of the National Conference of Catholic Charities; Reverend Norman Vincent Peale, Minister, Marble Collegiate Church; Dr. Henning Webb Prentis, Jr., Chairman of the Board of Armstrong Cork Company; Mrs. Henry P. Russell, distinguished civic and philanthropic organization worker in San Francisco; and Dr. Franklyn Bliss Snyder, President Emeritus of Northwestern University and President of the Board of Managers of Presbyterian Hospital in Chicago.

Judges of the prize-winning essays of the Competition were Dr. George W. Bachman, Director of Medical Studies, The Brookings Institution (retired); Reverend Asa J. Davis, Pastor of the Pilgrim Community Church, San Francisco; and Mr. Robert H. MacRae, Director, Welfare Council of Metropolitan Chicago. They were assisted by the staff of the Foundation, under the direct supervision of Mr. Thomas H. Stevenson.

President of the Foundation and director of the Competition is Dr. Alfred de Grazia, political scientist and author. Vice President is Mr. John L. Dupree, Vice President of the Hawaiian Pineapple Company. Mr. Richard C. Cornuelle, Vice President of the Princeton Panel, Inc., is Secretary-Treasurer.

More will be said in the last pages of this book about the approximately five hundred participants who made the Competition a success. With these introductory remarks, it is time to read the stories told by the thirty award winners and by nineteen additional workers whose essays the Foundation is also pleased to publish. Each essay stands by itself, as does, in fact, every part of this book. Although the Foundation hopes that a general impression favorable to its goals may emerge from considering the separate parts, it cannot claim nor wishes to claim any consensus among the independent authors.

1
Mental Health

1. Developing a Community Mental Health Program

MRS. CHARLOTTE S. HIRSCH

How to obtain adequate mental health facilities has long been a problem besetting almost every community, large or small. With recognition finally being given to the vast scope of the problem of mental illness, with our mental hospitals so terrifically overcrowded, some areas have been taking their first good look at what their community provides for the treatment and prevention of mental illness.

Private agencies, mental health groups, and public agencies are looking for ways of obtaining the general public's understanding and support for mental health services. The need is so great, and the cost of psychiatric treatment so high, that without broad support an adequate program cannot be realized, even on a small local level. Family Service, a "first-aid station" in mental health services, has found it difficult to extend its service to meet the need. Psychiatric clinics are pitifully few. Millions are being spent to build more and larger state hospitals. This staggering figure could be reduced by local voluntary efforts to make available early treatment to citizens while they are still members of the community.

One method through which clinics, casework agencies, and private and public agencies, could extend their services is described in this paper. It is a way of securing broad support through a process of organization within a community, which not only sets up the machinery for extending services and creating new ones, but educates and involves the community in mental health in the process.

Agencies already established and working together in a community welcome this joint over-all approach, because it is a method whereby a balance of services is obtained.

This paper will describe from personal experience the step by step process of the method, showing how there was developed in one community a program of education and action for mental health services, and the establishment of a voluntary organization, representative of the total commu-

3

nity, for the over-all purpose of developing and implementing mental health services and activities.

First a description of the community, referred to here as the Valley. This community, a fast growing, large area of over 500,000 population, is typical of many others throughout the country. Lying outside the metropolitan area, it grew too fast for services to keep pace. Agencies such as Family Service and Red Cross made attempts to extend their services but did not meet the need. There were no psychiatric clinic facilities, except for a school guidance center for school referrals, with long waiting lists. A mental health group of lay citizens was struggling to gain recognition but it was for the most part composed of a small group of interested people fairly isolated from the community. A previous attempt to obtain clinic service by a group of professional agency people who felt the need failed.

Because of the large geographic spread of this area, 250 square miles, the community has smaller community areas within it, identifiable by post office name. There are eight of these smaller areas, each with its own chamber of commerce, service clubs, women's clubs, etc. In each of these communities there also exists a coordinating council, an autonomous, loosely organized group made up of organizations within the area, including private and public agencies, schools, PTA's, church groups, and civic organizations. Membership in some of these councils consists of two hundred or more organizations—a true cross section of the community, generally interested in the welfare of their community. These organizations are usually found in all areas, some brought together through coordinated efforts, others through business councils, chambers of commerce, church councils, federation, and still others existing side by side.

In one of these coordinating councils, a health committee examining possibilities for a program recognized the lack of mental health facilities as a major need for the entire Valley. Also recognizing the need for joint effort, representatives from the seven other councils were invited to establish a unified health committee to coordinate efforts to obtain needed mental health services for the entire Valley. One can easily imagine the results if any one of these smaller areas attempted to bring services to its own area. It started bringing together, for the advantage of the whole, areas that had primary interest within their own boundaries.

In accordance with the recommendations of a research study previously made of the entire county, it was established that the Valley would require five clinics to adequately meet its needs. The Unified Health Committee then launched an intensive educational campaign to make the community aware of its critical needs. It proceeded on the premise that to be most effective it must involve the greatest number of people within their own organizations. Therefore, existing community structure was utilized, in this case the coordinating councils, so that the lack of mental health facilities became the problem and the program of all types of organizations, rather than the vested problem of a sole group.

The uniqueness of this educational and organizational program was that it involved in a very active manner all organizations whose primary interest was not necessarily health, to an extent that practically every organization supported the program for extension of mental health facilities for the Valley.

The educational program had several extremely effective methods for stimulating and involving individuals and groups. One means of informing the community was the publication of a fact sheet which received wide distribution. To suggest the scope of the method, it involved the following titles:

"Mental Health Clinics for the Valley"
"Facts and Figures for a Program of Action"
"Why Do We Need Mental Health Clinics?" (statistics of the problem)
"What Is a Mental Health Clinic?"
"Where Is Clinic Service Available Now?"
"How Can the Valley Obtain Mental Health Clinics?"
　Details of the plans for extension of existing clinics
　Possibilities for additional clinics
"What Can You and Your Organization Do?"
　Enlisting Support
　Contacts—Letter Writing

As each coordinating council planned a program, or had a speaker, these fact sheets were distributed. In turn, as member organizations of the council were stimulated to plan a mental health program, these sheets were distributed.

A press conference involving every community newspaper in the Valley was planned with the purpose of stimulating the interest of the press itself in the problem. At this conference, every agency, public and private, along with school representatives and others, told of their firsthand experiences with the lack of clinic services in conjunction with their own work.

Public and private groups charged with the purpose of planning and supporting such clinic services were invited to public meetings. The problem was there presented, not only to inform them of the need and of the community's readiness, but also to explore such groups as possible implements for the extension of services. By this method, each organization, including those operating and supporting clinics, became involved and the problem became theirs as one of action rather than observation. In other words, they became the "ball carriers," and not only the rooting section, which is the key to the success of this type of program.

When a newly formed Welfare Planning Council for the area, the planning agency of Community Chest, came into existence, the problem of the lack of mental health services was referred to it. With its staff, a study committee of this group was able to augment the work with current research, and followed through with assistance in the formation of a Mental Health Services Board composed of a representative cross section of community leaders. The functions of this Board are:

1. To develop needed mental health services.
2. To strengthen and increase services of family agencies, which are first line of defense.
3. To coordinate mental health services and activities.
4. To conduct research, public relations, legislation, and education.
5. To develop structure for cooperative private–public joint operation.

This method of stimulating voluntary activity and organization in the field of mental health has had the additional result of actually establishing, at present, a part-time extension of clinic services to the area on a joint private–public basis. The community is contributing funds to this effort, which provides a focal point of a tangible nature for further development and participation by the community. This method is applicable to other communities, large or small, either for the purpose of creating new mental health facilities, or for extending the services of already existing agencies. In communities less well organized, the same method can be utilized by any agency, committee, council, or group willing to take responsibility for looking at the community as a whole, and forming a primary community structure for mental health at the place where it belongs, with the community.

2. A Church Mental Health Clinic

DORTHEA M. LANE

INTRODUCTION

The Mental Health Clinic of the Westwood Community Methodist Church [1] which opened in February 1955 has proved to be a tremendously interesting experiment in the extension of voluntary services in mental health. It is staffed and operated by volunteer psychiatrists, clinical psychologists, and psychiatric social workers with the church providing the setting, clerical help, and considerable sympathy for mental health principles. The suggestions to be made in this paper result from two years' experience in developing such a clinic as a volunteer in cooperation with other professional people.

We are all aware of the dearth of psychiatric treatment facilities, particularly for individuals in the middle or low income groups. Nation wide there are waiting lists of as long as two years for even an initial interview. As an example of the local need I have recently been asked to help the West Area Welfare Planning Council establish a low cost clinic in the West Los Angeles area; as a result of this I have learned that there are about 300 hours of therapy weekly available to a population of roughly 800,000.

It seems to me that there is an opportunity for churches to be of service today in providing treatment for the many individuals who need help to cope with their emotional problems. This idea can be used in various ways: several churches could support one clinic; a traveling clinic could be organized to serve several churches in rural areas; clinics could originate from staffs in outlying state hospitals and in large cities. This is the only church clinic of which I know that has been established on a completely professional basis comparable to national standards for mental hygiene clinics.

It was of utmost importance that the psychotherapy offered a patient did not arouse any conflict with his religious faith. Sound psychiatric concepts and religious convictions are not incompatible, since both lead toward con-

[1] Address: Dr. Melvin E. Wheatley, Jr., Westwood Community Methodist Church, 10497 Wilshire Blvd., Los Angeles 24, California.

sideration of oneself. It was found that selection of therapists depended on their respect for the religious principles of others. It was not possible—and probably was inadvisable—to secure church members as volunteers; hence religious affiliation did not enter into the selection of therapists.

BACKGROUND

The possibility of a counseling service in the church had been discussed for some time prior to 1954. At this time the impetus to establish the clinic originated with the ministerial staff, particularly Dr. Melvin E. Wheatley, Jr., of the Westwood Community Methodist Church, in cooperation with the Church Welfare Bureau of the Church Federation of Los Angeles. Mrs. Frances Poynter, Casework Director of the agency, was most encouraging. The leadership of Dr. Richard G. Johnson and James F. T. Bugental, Ph.D., provided the professional stimulation, judgment, and direction to give life to the idea. There were many meetings with church members and the principles of organization were developed which served as a future guide for the professional staff and the sponsoring group, the Church Mental Health Committee.

I was invited to participate as the chief psychiatric social worker in establishing this clinic a few months before it opened and also to serve on the Church Mental Health Committee. My initial contribution was in formulating and executing plans for intake, relationships with community agencies, the contribution scale, procedures, office equipment, and recruitment of volunteer social workers. There were conferences with the chief psychiatrist and chief clinical psychologist about types of cases to be accepted and the general clinic program.

Because of the enthusiasm of the initial lay and professional Mental Health Committee, the clinic opened its doors with a minimum of financial support. One church group had secured some donations of furniture and purchased some chairs, another arranged telephone service, and Sunday school rooms were made available. Applicants were referred by ministers, members of the church congregation, and by the community in general inasmuch as there were no restrictions of religion, color, or place of residence. The first year was difficult and real financial backing came only after the congregation recognized the value of the clinic as a result of publicity and closer acquaintance with its facilities. Because many church members and even some of the supporting committees had questions about the advisability of the venture, our chief problem was to educate the congregation about the meaning of emotional disturbances. This was fundamental in securing necessary financial support and was handled mainly by the chief psychiatrist.

After clinic hours were established on three evenings and one afternoon weekly, I spent one evening a week at the clinic handling applications, referrals to other agencies, and social studies, and arranging social work assignments on other clinic hours.

During this initial period the therapists selected their cases from those with which they were involved in the intake study. At the end of four months, nine therapists were carrying 27 patients in treatment. I continued with intake and tried to cope with problems of communication and recording for the next few months.

Five months after opening, the Church Welfare Bureau contributed the services of a psychiatric social worker from their staff for half-time work at the clinic under my supervision. Continuity in the program emerged, communication between various therapists who gave time at different hours was possible when the social worker could provide this channel, and the clinic began to be integrated. Since then, my affiliation with the clinic has been general responsibility for the social work aspects of the program.

During the first year we moved furniture, contributed office supplies, wrote out interviews in long hand, and generally functioned in a somewhat archaic fashion. Each of the original professional people recruited friends and colleagues only to be somewhat embarrassed by our expecting them to contribute other than professional services. For instance, the psychologists furnished their own test materials, and the psychiatrist found himself volunteering three times the amount of time he had planned because of the number of psychiatric evaluations necessary as well as the need to interpret clinic function to the church. Within two months a waiting list developed and we felt completely overwhelmed. At the risk of being sacrilegious I will say that God must have felt our discomfort because the next two volunteers joining our staff were interested in doing group psychotherapy. Although there was not a closely defined intake policy we learned we could accept no patients who presented problems of psychiatric emergencies. One development that we had not anticipated was requests by various groups within the church that certain therapists offer lectures to the young married groups and sit in on the training courses for Sunday school teachers. During the first eighteen months of operation there were approximately 1,500 hours of therapy for 125 patients. A paid secretary was added after the clinic had been in operation almost a year.

A MODEL PLAN

The ingredients for success in establishing a clinic in a church setting are enthusiasm, conviction of the importance of the project, and patience.

I. First, there must be at least one important member of the church interested in extending a professional mental health program to the congregation and the community. The founding group should ultimately include the minister, chairman of the finance committee, public relations director, chairmen of the youth and Sunday school programs, and director of the women's program.

II. Interest can best be developed by a professional person within the congregation. The need for a mental health clinic can be demonstrated in a number of ways:

a. A psychiatrist could talk to small church groups and clubs about treatment of emotional disturbances. Through acquaintance with the psychiatrist certain fears are dispelled, and individuals come to see that personal problems can be ameliorated through psychotherapy.

b. A clinical psychologist might talk with a mothers' group about normal growth and development of children. The mothers become aware of deviations in their own children and the availability of help at an early point.

c. A professional person participating in training sessions for Sunday school teachers helps them, through group discussion, to see how their own attitudes affect their ability to teach.

d. For a concrete demonstration of treatment in a church setting a psychiatric social worker could volunteer his services to help the minister with problems of marital discord brought to him. Either by direct casework service to a few families or by effective referrals to community agencies, the extent of the need and the soundness of professional help becomes clarified.

III. The interested church group is formalized as a committee composed of the above-mentioned members and adds the three persons who will have professional responsibilities—psychiatrist, psychiatric social worker, and clinical psychologist—from the church or community. The lay church members and professional people can get well acquainted in developing a set of principles as a base for the clinic operation. Through this experience (probably a number of sessions will be needed), the principles of organization should emerge, and include the following points:

a. A general statement of purpose in which the compatibility of psychiatric treatment and religious principles is clearly stated,

b. Responsibilities of the church, as represented by the committee, for financial support, publicity, space, and equipment,

c. Qualifications of the clinic volunteer professional staff,

d. Relationship between the church and the clinic,

e. Appointment of a liaison person who takes responsibility for business management of the clinic.

IV. The group considers space for clinic offices that can be used for church purposes as well. Sunday school rooms are usually decorative, light, and cheerful. The office where equipment and confidential records are kept should be the only one not for duplicate use. A desk and two chairs fit into corners of other rooms so that a minimum of rearrangement of furniture is necessary. Rooms for both individual and group therapy according to number of volunteers are necessary.

V. Equipment includes desks, chairs, and lamps for therapists, dictation equipment, locked files, and supply cabinets for clerical operation. Telephone and message service is needed. If reasons for equipment are made known, clubs and other church groups enjoy collecting things or raising funds to purchase them. We found that desks and lamps could be donated but that appropriate chairs and cabinets should be new items.

VI. Effective recruitment of qualified professional staff depends upon thoughtful planning. Among the most important elements is the caliber of professional people in the founding group, maintenance of high professional standards, stimulation, and opportunities for research and for preventive work not possible in private practice. To secure good therapists the eligibility standards must be carefully listed in the principles of organization. Arrangements for affiliation and consultation with good psychoanalysts, clinical psychologists, and psychiatric social workers can be arranged if their interest is evoked by high-caliber staff and program. For this reason as well as for maintenance of standards each volunteer therapist must qualify through his own professional organization. The clinic can offer stimulation for trainees in the various disciplines who will volunteer their services in a setting such as this. The clinic will benefit and the trainees will be furthering their own training. The volunteer therapist should be required to give a minimum of three hours per week for therapy, supervision, and staff meetings.

VII. The church should be prepared to hire a nucleus of paid staff to provide continuity and consistency as well as clerical assistance to the volunteer staff. This nucleus is composed of a psychiatric social worker with at least three years' experience to handle intake and cooperative work with the church, and a secretary for transcription and office management. Janitorial service should also be available.

VIII. Treatment offered.

a. *Individual Psychotherapy* should be arranged in accordance with needs of applicants.

b. *Group Psychotherapy* would be offered both to applicants in need of this kind of treatment and as support to relatives of patients in treatment.

c. *Prophylactic Treatment.* Prevention is always stressed—there is lots of talk about it; but most clinics are usually so busy handling acute emotional difficulties that it is not possible to really get to preventive work, hence we continue to think that activity groups, the Scouts, the YMCA, the YWCA, the Camera Clubs and dancing groups, meet this need by providing healthy social relationships. And they do. These groups meet important needs in youngsters who are looking for such activities and who are aggressive enough to join them and submissive enough to continue in them.

But here in a church we have a natural setting for preventive work—all the age groups from tots to oldsters are organized in classes or clubs; the social relationships are obvious in the Young Marrieds, the Young Adults, and the Christian Endeavor. In addition, the ministerial staff may include pastors who devote themselves to training interested members for leadership in the church. The congregation wants knowledge about mental health. I say, let's use these interests!

I propose this: a plan for a therapist to talk with some of the ministers and the group leaders about the possibility of starting some discussion groups—such as socio-drama with young parents, engaged couples, adolescents, Sunday school teachers—around the general topic of mental health.

The young parents will be interested in the emotional development of children, for instance, and—as in every group with whom I've ever talked, regardless of size—the questions that arise reflect the personal concerns, problems and difficulties of each parent. Instead of answering generally, the therapist can use this as an opportunity to help each member share his problems and concerns. In these groups role playing would be the therapeutic technique of choice because sound interpersonal relationships can develop through this method; individuals are able to crystallize for themselves those forces against which they are struggling. Also, this technique requires a minimum of interpretation—a parent taking the role of the unhappy child can see the child's problem for himself. Calling this socio-drama makes it more acceptable to groups of so-called normal individuals who are naïve on the therapeutic level; to call it group psychotherapy or psycho-drama would be frightening and unnecessary. In a group such as this shy, quiet people learn to verbalize and socialize; and there are great values for adolescents, as Zelda Wolpe has found, in a socio-drama group of adolescent youngsters who have no particular emotional disturbances but meet with her because their parents requested it. These adolescents are gaining tremendous insight into their own feelings at a particularly turbulent age, and as a result they should become better parents and better citizens.

A step I foresee from this involvement of church members in learning about mental health principles is that individuals who are emotionally disturbed can be identified and offered help in the clinic on a personal individual basis as they recognize the need for it. I think this would have far reaching effects in relieving the stigma some people still attach to psychiatric treatment. It would also be possible to reach youngsters and young parents at a point when treatment could be brief and wholly successful rather than late, lengthy, and only partially successful.

SUMMARY AND CONCLUSIONS

Because a church is a natural meeting place for people as well as a recognized source of help, churches could offer a tremendous service to humanity by fostering a mental health clinic and a prophylactic mental health program under church auspices. The plan I suggest encompasses stimulation of the minister and key people in the church concerning an awareness of the need, using the experience in the Westwood Community Methodist Church as an example. The clinic should actually open its doors only when a church will provide a nucleus of staff, space, and equipment. Adequate records for research and public relations should be kept from the very beginning because of the impact this has on public opinion and acceptance as well as for future research needs. I would follow the same high professional standards established in the Westwood Church because this policy has engendered great respect in the nearby community and in the entire church group of Los Angeles. Interpretation of clinical function and discussion of mental health principles with church groups should be initiated at the time the clinic first offers individual service. If this were done the preventive program of socio-drama and discussion groups would be more a part of the entire clinic structure than is true in the Westwood clinic.

A high professional contribution to the field of mental health can be made through a plan such as this so that we can reduce the gross deficiencies in mental health resources that are so obvious in our society today.

3. Pennsylvania's Fountain House

MARCELLA I. SCHMOEGER

"It is not wisdom to be only wise
And on the inward vision close the eyes;
It is wisdom to believe the heart."
GEORGE SANTAYANA

In life, suffering and happiness, pain and joy, defeat and accomplishment are almost always inextricably bound up in the same object or event. This I have come to know experimentally as the result of twenty-seven days spent in a psychiatric hospital, an experience that changed the course of my life. This paper is the story of the results of that experience. It is not the story of the experience itself. It is the story of Pennsylvania's Fountain House, Inc.: (1) its beginning, (2) its volunteer structure, (3) its volunteer organization, and (4) its objectives.

ITS BEGINNING

I say that the experience changed the course of my life because before going to the hospital I had been teaching kindergarten and had just applied for a scholarship to qualify further for this work. When I returned from the hospital, the scholarship was waiting for me together with a small sum of money I had inherited. Without hesitation I returned the scholarship check. I had to do something constructive about the suffering I had witnessed and had shared. I had to make sense out of my hospital experience. There was with me both a deep sense of vocation and of guidance.

Then, too, the doctor's question at the hospital had both startled and stirred me: "Where will you go? Who will take you?" she had asked. Though I could answer it satisfactorily, it made me realize that there are many people who cannot. These are the people delayed at hospitals—sometimes days, sometimes months, sometimes years—who could get out if they had a place to go where there would be minimal supervision. It is a tragic thing to find yourself in a hospital, to feel caught behind bars, and not to know if and when you will get out. It could make you ill all over again!

In 1956 the Pennsylvania Commissioner of Mental Health wrote, on the basis of a survey in seventeen State hospitals, that "out of 40,000 patients, hospital superintendents felt that 5,000, or one in eight, could be returned to the community under various degrees of supervision." In 1952 I had wanted to get a house where people who were being delayed in hospitals, either because they had nowhere to go or because of lack of social service workers, could go temporarily while they and/or their social workers worked out permanent arrangements. This idea met mostly with discouragement; some hospital personnel would not commit themselves. During 1952 I spent most of the money I had inherited trying to do something about it— and that was how Fountain House in Philadelphia got started.

Fountain House is a truly grass-roots organization. It is dedicated to supporting a rehabilitation program for former psychiatric patients. Because of its beginning, its volunteer nature, and structure, Pennsylvania's Fountain House could well serve as a way to extend voluntary organization in this mental health sphere. It must be remembered, however, that the reason why it works is that it is centered on something specific and vital, namely our Fountain House Fellowship program (which is what we call our social rehabilitation program, after the one in New York). The director of the Mental Health Association had suggested that I visit the New York Fountain House which serves as a former patient activities' center, not living quarters. It was founded in 1948, after a group of former patients were discovered meeting on the Public Library steps.

It soon became apparent that if anything was to be done in Pennsylvania in this way, it would have to be done through a newly organized group. It was then I met someone who agreed to be chairman of a committee to discuss this. She was receptive to the idea because she had been a psychiatric social worker. I found several others who agreed to come to the first meeting in March 1952. From then to January 1953 a fluctuating group—but with a permanent nucleus—met monthly to discuss the philosophy of Fountain House. A lawyer volunteered to write the articles of incorporation. I had received over thirty letters of endorsement from prominent psychiatrists, and armed with these was able to get twenty people to give $100 apiece. On January 5, 1953, when Fountain House received its State charter, it had $2,000 with which to begin.

The board of directors, drawn from the committee that had been meeting throughout 1952, continued monthly meetings. At the February 1953 board meeting I was hired as Development Secretary. My job was to get the support of the community and to raise the money to start a program.

The New York Fountain House was first supported by a few wealthy people and a State grant. Unlike New York we had no individual source of finance, and no State grant. Though we could copy the Fellowship idea, we had to work out our own way to get community support. We now have a voluntary foundation, manifested in our contributing members, our Women's Auxiliary, four Friends of Fountain House groups, and numerous other volunteers. The way in which this foundation for our Fellowship program was built offers a pattern to extend voluntary activity.

Its Volunteer Structure

We had bylaws; we had a State charter; we had a board of directors. We needed community support. We started to build our contributing membership by developing a prospective mailing list. We got the names from other agencies, medical directories, friends, and newspapers. We sent out a magazine reprint about the New York Fountain House program with an educational, fund-raising letter signed by a prominent psychiatrist. The next year we printed our own descriptive leaflet inviting contributing members and volunteers. An artist, printer, and typographer donated the first 5,000 copies. Our contributing membership grew. We now have 700 contributing members and a constantly changing prospective mailing list of 3,000. Contributing members give $5 to $99 and/or volunteer services. We called the people who had contributed $100 or more a Citizens Council. We used their names, together with the names of well-known psychiatrists, for recommendation purposes.

We find that to follow a regular, yearly pattern of community educational activity creates a definite sense of purpose and steadiness. We have two community meetings a year to further the Fountain House message: our Annual Contributing Membership dinner meeting in October, to which board and staff members report; and our Annual Community Meeting in May, open to everyone. To help attract our good attendance we have such speakers as Dr. and Mrs. Harry Overstreet, Pearl Buck, and Dr. M. F. Ashley Montagu. In most cases they have served without an honorarium. There is no charge for either meeting.

We have a September annual fund-raising mailing, and a biannual Newsletter serving a double purpose. One goes out in November to follow up the fund-raising letter, and to give news of developments. The second Newsletter, in April, serves as an invitation to the May Annual Community Meeting.

We use posters, car cards in subways, buses, and trains (space donated free), newspapers, and TV and radio stations. The radio stations give us spot announcements. Each year we have had a benefit, which in addition to giving financial help also creates interest.

Our first benefit, given voluntarily by a prominent 'cellist in February 1954, netted $500, enabling us to start our Fellowship program. We hired a psychiatric social worker for one evening a week. A central city church donated a meeting room. The first former patients came as a result of reading about Fountain House in the newspapers. They had called to say what a good idea it was, how much they wanted to help. Many felt that though they did not need it for themselves they would like to volunteer to help others. And this is truly one of Fountain House's creative aspects, for there are always a few who though they no longer need it voluntarily stay on in the Fellowship to help others.

Fourteen former patients came to the first Fellowship meeting, including three nonpatient volunteers. The group selected its own officers and drafted its own constitution. Although it always meets with a qualified professional person, the group plans its own activities. As in New York skilled volunteers in games, dramatics, etc., are used. In time there may be a volunteer committee of Fellowship members and others who will visit patients in the hospitals. They do visit individually now, write letters and send cards. At present we have a two-room apartment which serves as a day-time office, and a meeting place for our Fellowship two evenings a week.

The Fellowship is not something the former patient is expected to adjust to permanently. It is a bridge from the hospital to the community, helping one through the first lonely days of uncertainty. As the program expands, the director will interpret it to the hospitals and develop our referral procedure. We will also have a printed "Letter of Invitation" addressed to former patients, or those about to be discharged, written by Fellowship members themselves.

Fountain House can be more than a social agency. It is an opportunity to create a healthful atmosphere, an opportunity for channeling creative reaction to this very serious social problem of our time. The core of Fountain House is our fellowship program, but the ground and spring for this program is the wider fellowship that is being built up through our contributing membership.

Its Volunteer Organization

The four Friends of Fountain House groups, located in the city and suburban area, came about through speaking at church meetings. These groups function through a Liaison Chairman, who calls on the individual members when we have specific needs such as volunteers for crafts, mailings and officework, or to furnish and serve refreshments at our Annual Community Meetings, or usher and serve at our Annual Contributing Membership dinner and meeting. As we carry our message to additional community organizations the number of Friends of Fountain House groups will increase.

Our Women's Auxiliary of 72 members seeks financial backing, as its first purpose. After meeting less than a year, through its voluntary activities the Women's Auxiliary contributed $1,000. We started it by finding one key person to be the first temporary chairman, announcing the first meeting in our April 1955 Newsletter, and then introducing the chairman and announcing the first meeting again at our May 1955 Annual Community Meeting. Eighteen attended the first meeting. The first year was a struggle, but the Women's Auxiliary now has very capable officers and its own constitution. In her report to our 1956 Annual Contributing Membership meeting, the president of the Women's Auxiliary said:

> Our purpose is many-sided. Apart from our fund-raising activities . . . we are also missionaries in community understanding. . . . In this we have been most successful. Through word-of-mouth contacts and local publicity, we have helped to bring the name of Fountain House to the attention of many. Our organization offers a channel of expression to those who wish to do something in the field of mental health because of an illness of a friend, or a member of the family . . . or because they just want to help. They come to us knowing we are understanding. This, too, is an important part of our work. Our Board of Directors have planned stimulating educational and social meetings. . . .

Its Objectives

As we strive to achieve the following present and possible objectives, we will continue to involve an increasing number of volunteers:

First, we need a full-time rehabilitation program. However, our present quarters are inadequate. I would like to see Fountain House get a house, but keep its present office as a promotional, educational center: a place for volunteers to work; committees to meet; and where the Fellowship members can come at their own pace when they are ready to work with other volunteers in furthering common objectives. In this way the former patients will get a greater sense of security through feeling that the program is theirs. Their house would not be overrun with volunteers. Another reason for keeping a central office would be that we could think of ourselves as a clearinghouse for development throughout the State, and could plant the seed for similar developments in other cities. We would plant the seed and suggest the pattern, but it would be nourished and shaped by local volunteers.

Second, we need a Room-Finding Committee. Because of its voluntary nature, Fountain House is closer to people in the community than nonvoluntary organizations are. Among our contributing members are people who, through their own social, club, and church associations, could help to open up rooms and jobs. These volunteers would be oriented by a professional. We would then keep a file of addresses that would be available to all social workers. The social workers themselves would evaluate the rooms and would do the placing of the patients. I would hope that our room-finding activity might ultimately lead to the decision that when we get a house we should have a few temporary rooms.

Third, we will set up a job adjustment program. At present we give an opportunity for former patients to work in the office, to brush up on clerical skills and gain confidence. Also we act as a referral agency. I would hope that in time we might take an active part in locating and informing employers.

We are developing a sense of community responsibility by bringing people of all faiths, races, nationalities, and vocations together to work on a mutual problem and interest. In "In the Name of Sanity," Lewis Mumford writes, "No part of man's life has value except in terms of the person and the community he is in process of actualizing and realizing. The very essence of human character, indeed of morality itself, is purposeful action in terms of an ever-emerging and ever-enlarging whole." That which makes for well-being in man can also be applied to a society. As a society becomes involved in something greater than itself, it is well on the road to developing sound mental health. So, too, Fountain House is being built on the premise that its sphere of helpful influence is an ever expanding one. I see Fountain House symbolically as a circle within a circle—a fellowship within a fellowship—and this has wide community-integrating implications for us all, both here in and around Philadelphia, State-wide and nationwide.

2
Alcoholism

1. Uniting a City's Skills

ROBERT STEVENSON

Three men play important new roles in turning a Tom Thumb volunteer activity into a Paul Bunyan operation in the Upper Midwest area as part of a "Minneapolis Experiment."

They are "The Man in the Gray Flannel Suit," "The Guy in the Bartender's Apron," and "The Man in the Blue Uniform."

Underpinning these three are some old but fundamental approaches to extend voluntary activity and organization in the field of alcohol sickness in Ivy League garb.

Net result: Tom Thumb has become a virile giant of Paul Bunyan proportions employing the experience, skills, techniques, and time of over 1,000 volunteers.

How did such a diminutive volunteer activity grow up?

Simply by:

1. Educational forums and seminars, large and small, within business, which wiped off the scowls of the businessman at alcoholism and replaced them with thoughtful understanding and aid; substituted the frozen mien of the teacher and the pulpit-pounding of the parson with enthusiastic cooperation born of scientific facts; replaced the shrugs of trade-unions with teamwork.

2. Giving the area a Foundation on Problem Drinking, Inc., which serves all segments in matters pertaining to abnormal drinking, thus bringing alcoholism out of shameful hiding into the open of "do-somethingness."

3. Setting up an Alcohol Clinic utilizing the medical, psychological and social welfare skills instead of continuing with the punitive measures of the snake pits, bull pens, and workhouse sentences.

Before the volunteer movement in behalf of the alcoholic was given vitamins and measured for the new attitudes of activity, the nonalcoholic more or less shunned any responsibility for the vagaries of the inebriate. Such volunteer tasks were left to the mission worker and the temperance crusaders. Indeed the "squares" and solid citizens thought that any general

23

activity on their part either implied that they had the dark secret of alcoholism hidden in their family closet, had a close friend that tippled too much, or (horrors!) that they themselves were cursed with such a malady. The people who served gladly on such popular boards as Sister Kenny, Heart Fund, and others, generally bypassed alcoholism as once they had avoided service for tuberculosis.

The beginning point of volunteer activity, then, in the Minneapolis Experiment was to call in the Man in the Gray Flannel Suit. He knew how to get started as a high diver knows how to take off from a fifty-foot tower. It was necessary for the gray flannel suiters to set up a framework of volunteer help and one that would not come tumbling down with the leaves at the end of the year.

The boys from the creative departments of the advertising agencies were smart. They voted for an initial all-out educational project to trigger their plans. Calling in similar skills of professional reporters and writers on the one large metropolitan newspaper, they set their sights on a Civic Forum on Alcoholism that would have all the appeal of a Hollywood première.

This author had been trained as a newspaperman, and as the promoter of the entire volunteer effort he saw the wisdom coming out of the hucksters' cute, shiny brief cases. Hence the first approach toward extending volunteer activity was given an Ivy League garb.

The flannel suiters loosened their narrow ties, took off their slim coats, and went to work with an overwhelming barrage of news releases, editorials, television programs, and posters. They even tried for such celebrities as Lillian Roth, and although not able to produce her in person, they succeeded in getting her on their broadcasts. *I'll Cry Tomorrow* became as popular as a political button before election. A mobile truck offering alcohol literature and showing movies made its rounds advertising the Civic Forum on Alcoholism. It was manned by a doctor and nurse who talked about vitamin deficiency and cirrhosis of the liver. "Thirteen Steps to Alcoholism" in pamphlet form was generously distributed. From the ivy-covered towers of Yale University to spark the Civic Forum on Alcoholism came the fast-talking Dr. Selden Bacon, head of Yale's world-famous school on alcoholism; and Dr. Leon A. Greenberg, head of applied physiology. From Sweden's brilliant Karolinska Institute in Stockholm, there came the impeccable Dr. Leonard Goldberg, leader of all chemical testing for drunken driving; from world-known Mayo Clinic, Dr. Charles Mayo himself; and many others.

But the men in the gray flannel suits were just beginning to get warmed up. They wanted Top Drawer Brass, and they wanted it in a big way. They decided on a "cards-on-the-table" Echelon Appeal to set the plateau of community thinking. No longer was inebriacy to be allowed such a humble setting as Skid Row. Our smart young men blew up huge research bulletins showing that 85 per cent of the entire alcoholic population was to be found in the plants, firms, small business places, lodges, clubs, colleges, and schools—yes, and swiftly infiltrating into the ranks of housewifery.

No longer was Top Drawer Brass to sit in ivory towers and order termination of employees with a drinking problem. A vast amount of literature was circulated prior to the Civic Forum showing how termination for overindulgence is an added burden to the community and an unprofitable act for the industrialist. The gray suiters set a goal of 100 Top Drawer Brass drafted on the project. These executives were charged with the responsibility of registering 300 industrialists in the foreman and supervisor class who could attend their Civic Forum on Alcoholism.

Let me interject a warning at this point. To build a solid volunteer organization, and one that will last, you must secure the interest, approval, and participation of top management. If your steering machine is made up of subordinates, you will be playing in the bush leagues. I do not mean a polite or grudging nod from the president or owner of big business. He must be there in person at your first dramatic bid to secure community attention and support for voluntary action on a large scale, especially in the field of a controversial welfare program such as alcoholism. He must be at your first civic luncheon either as a guest, a presiding chairman, or a featured speaker; he and plenty of other Brass. Running this kind of show (Civic Forum on Alcoholism) with department heads is like putting your second team on the field in a championship game. The odds are all against you. The gray suiters knew this, and they leaned on it hard.

Now the Top Drawer Brass in the Minneapolis Experiment picked 300 industrialists from strategic positions. They did so by personal call, letter, secretary, or forum phone committee. It was surprising how many actually made the calls themselves. The gray suiters stood behind them until they accomplished this. If your first team is active enough, they figured, you will have no trouble in getting your secondary team who are your chief pupils. The Brass picked the 300 with swiftness and sureness once they were warmed up over the idea. All calls, of course, were made in the name of Higher Echelon and had its blessing.

The gray suiters knew how to put on a show. They ran employers' panels, alcometers, experiments with white rats, and women's discussions, and they highlighted the two-day blast with the Yale headliners and the experts from the Mayo Clinic. They even ran in governmental alcohol leaders from the provinces of Canada. The Civic Forum was a big success and a permanent one. In the spring of 1957, the fifth annual Civic Forum on

Alcoholism will include a high school seminar with 500 students, public and parochial, participating.

The objective of these forums is to set up smaller seminars within the plants and to create a functioning public relations committee which will have as its particular goal the breaking down of the social stigma surrounding alcoholism or problem drinking.

The gray suiters were smart enough to set up a long-range program. They secured the backing of the Chamber of Commerce to plan and set up a Foundation on Problem Drinking, Inc. This was the second approach. Such a foundation now functions as a screening place for problem drinkers and their families, with an extensive library on alcoholism. Once the foundation was established, industries as well as small firms and private families began to send their problem cases in abnormal drinking for referral to existing treatment facilities.

After the foundation was properly incorporated and endowed, the churches were asked to furnish a counseling ring of pastors who had shown some ability to interpret the Alcoholics Anonymous program and study on other therapies relevant to the disease of alcoholism. Another panel of AA counselors was enrolled to be on 24-hour call.

A foundation office in a metropolitan area should be staffed with an executive secretary who has a public relations background and can solicit firms for financial support, and an office secretary with some experience in alcohol counseling. These should be salaried workers, but the remainder of your assistance should and will come from volunteers. All these aids come after your educational plateaus have been established.

Once established and known in adequate offices equipped with counseling rooms, emergency beds, and a detoxication room, the foundation was able to offer short-term courses on alcohol studies to foremen and supervisors within industry. The purpose of such courses was not only to indoctrinate "immediate bosses" on alcoholism but to create a bridge between personnel offices and the foundation, thus initiating a preventive program.

As referrals on alcoholism increased, the foundation found it was necessary to go into the third phase of volunteer aid; namely, expediting treatment and rehabilitation. A home was provided offering a few beds for alcoholic women, whose numbers seemed to be increasing. It was simple to organize a Women's Corps to serve this home on a volunteer basis. Then a Motor Corps was enlisted that would stand ready day or night to transport acutely sick alcoholics to the State institution, fifty miles away, when the screening seemed to indicate such treatment; or to drive them to rest homes or to privately endowed rehabilitation sanitariums. A few doctors were picked to give part-pay treatments. A clinic was set up for psychotherapy within the foundation. Psychologists from the State university were used on a voluntary basis. Experience here proved that if the time of young psychologists, doctors from the staffs of the large hospitals, and social workers can be meshed into one center and their hours staggered on a part-time basis, such a plan offers results. In the Minneapolis experiment, the foundation used the services of three part-time doctors, a psychologist who employed the Minnesota Multiphasic Personality Inventory, and a graduate nurse. All gave their aid in return for experience gained. AA counselors and the volunteer Motor Corps worked the clock around.

So far the Minneapolis experiment in securing volunteer organization for alcoholism had proceeded along proved promotional lines. Public attention had been gained, social stigma lessened, the Civic Forum had become a fixed community event, and a Foundation on Problem Drinking, Inc., had been organized and perfected to operate a counseling bureau and an alcohol clinic.

But the experts wanted to further extend voluntary activity and they looked around for a new source. They found such a source in, of all things, "The Guy in the Bartender's Apron"! They said, "After all, who knows more about alcoholism than the humble bartender? These men see the loss of health and the family crackups brought on by overindulgence every day of their lives and are sympathetic. They also see the threat to the manufacturers of brewed and distilled beverages in the rising toll of alcoholism. They also see what might happen to their jobs." Truly this was a volunteer service arising from an unexpected source. But you don't look a gift horse in the mouth, even if that horse is wearing an apron and a cigar, and is polishing glasses.

Therefore, the bartender was enrolled as a volunteer and supplied with information and a card admitting his prospect to the foundation. We soon found that the man with the apron was a real crusader. Often he would call the foundation, take keys away from a drunken driver, transport him in his own personal car, and generally devote time, thought, and physical aid to get an intemperate customer inspired with doing something about his problem. Indeed, the man with the apron worked out so well that we added his boss, the innkeeper, and the distributor to our list of volunteers. One of these not only gave the foundation a generous contribution but took a place on the sponsoring board where he spent time and energy in enlisting other volunteers and helping the general educational plan.

Another new type of volunteer enlisted by the planning committee was the police officer. "Why," the gray suiters asked, "should this man's efforts be confined to punitive measures and why should he not understand that alcoholism is a sickness?" "The Man in the Blue Uniform" needed some education, and a little volunteer service was the best way to get it. Let him put away his badge and his nightstick and regard the "drunk" with an open mind. Therefore, classes in early detection were started for policemen. An officer was acquainted with the work of the foundation to which he would in the future refer drinkers instead of carting them off to jail.

At this point it might be well to interject the author's experiences as an alcohol consultant as well as a promoter and organizer of the volunteer effort. To enlist the services of more than 1,000 volunteers in a field as controversial as alcoholism presents many problems. Conflicting areas and cliques make it difficult at times to obtain rapport and uniform enthusiasm. A lunatic fringe appears including the rabid "drys," the equally rabid "wets," and the sin-haters who would help you send all bartenders straight to Hell; the long-suffering wives who have "given the best years of their lives"; the skeptic medics, the teachers who believe all parents should be re-educated; the wildly enthusiastic AA'er who wants to ditch all therapies but the "magic" of AA; and the boss who states, "We got no problem here; if they get drunk, we fire 'em!"

Alcoholism is a comparatively new field of social welfare and therefore offers only limited experiences in the volunteer field. Probably the most notable is in Chicago, where a social agency known as Portal House enlisted in their behalf the Chicago Committee on Alcoholism. Portal House offered psychotherapy cures and went out directly to secure the support of industry. Their method of securing voluntary activity was comparable to the Minneapolis experiment; the committee first used the newspaper to attract the attention of the public and then set up industrial seminars to acquaint business and industry more directly with the problem. As in Minneapolis, the leaders concentrated on top management to gain approval and support. The Chicago committee secured responsible company executives to call in outside agencies or individuals to supply educational material and answer questions for management. The supervisory personnel received short lectures explaining why industry should be concerned, and by a slow and gradual process acquired volunteer interest and help.

This author has attended and graduated from the Yale School of Alcohol Studies and the Utah School of Alcohol Studies. Social workers, the clergy, the AA group, and even the manufacturers of distilled liquors are studying at these schools, but thus far the voluntary effort in this field is newborn.

In conclusion, then, let me sum it up. Get voluntary activity started by using the special services of skilled newspaper and advertising persons. Allow them to help you create and popularize a large-scale Civic Forum on Alcoholism. Next follow through with a continuing series of smaller seminars in plants, schools, and churches. Enlist the social worker, sociologist, psychologist, and doctor among your volunteers; employ a speakers' bureau and motor corps. Enroll the experience and sympathy of bartenders and police officers.

Alcoholism and its study is a highly specialized field of health and a new one. The volunteer who enters it must be well indoctrinated with literature, films, lectures, and know-how to be effective.

Most of all, he or she must be more or less dedicated.

2. Contents of a Comprehensive Program

KENNETH A. GREEN

This is a paper written about a major contribution to the treatment of alcoholism by a private social agency. To be able to write about this program is a matter of real pride to those of us in this part of social welfare work. The heightened professional standards of social workers, the professional quality of the work being done, the leadership and direction that have given social welfare its present high status, enable those who create welfare programs to undertake the solution of larger and more complex problems.

Certainly, by whatever yardstick used, the problem of alcoholism is one that is most complex and destructive in our present society. It is also a problem that has received recognition as a problem for centuries. It becomes all the more impressive, therefore, that programs for and prevention of this illness have so often tried and failed to help. Many have become discouraged. Families, doctors, social agencies, and industry have frequently thrown up their hands and tried to pass the responsibility for the solution of the problem to someone else. The result has been that the problem drinker, aware of his own inability to make a positive decision about abstinence that will help him, is all the more discouraged by the rejection and ineffectual help he receives when he turns to others. It is often said of the alcoholic that he lacks a desire to get well. Through increasing experience we now know the problem drinker does want help, and can be rehabilitated. It is my feeling that such a program is beginning to develop in the Los Angeles area, and is an expression of voluntary activity and organization in social welfare that will have great benefit in this community.

I make this statement as a result of six years' work with problem drinkers. I began my career in psychiatric social work in the alcoholic clinic operated in conjunction with the Alameda County Prison Farm in California. Two years later I became director of Social Services at the Sierra Madre Lodge in Southern California, and have worked consistently with alcoholics in that capacity. A year ago I accepted a half-time position with the Volunteers of America in their Family Counselling Service, with the purpose of integrating that service with the new Alcoholic Clinic. Having thus been associated with private agencies for five years in the treatment of this problem I feel that most treatment programs to date have not dealt with the total problem, but tried to work with parts of the problem. It is with this in mind that I have such optimism about the present program.

With rare exceptions, all effective programs developed to help the problem drinker are State-operated. The remaining few are privately owned or endowed. The States of Connecticut, New Jersey, and North Carolina have programs in operation. California has begun to develop a program by establishing the Alcoholic Rehabilitation Commission. There are a few private sanitariums which have developed effective plans patterned after the suggested plan of the Yale Institute of Alcohol Studies. Almost without exception these private clinics are not endowed, and must charge full rates for their services. Quite understandably, therefore, they cannot hope to reach many who suffer from this problem.

An effective program must offer several fundamental kinds of treatment, because of the complexity of the alcoholic problem. First there must be medical treatment, because most problem drinkers are not in good physical condition, and good health is essential to abstinence. Fatigue and physical depletion are most frequently a major cause in relapses and periodic drinking bouts. It is also necessary to provide for the acutely intoxicated individual a facility where he can be detoxified promptly and without the use of other habit-forming drugs. Such medical attention is possible today. No rehabilitation process can begin until the patient is sober.

Second, there must be psychological help as well as assistance toward obtaining employment and renewed social status. Individual and group psychotherapy aimed at helping the alcoholic grow up is most important. We know that regardless of the extent of the problem, all alcoholics have had trouble with themselves and their emotional life long before the drinking began. Although abstinence is of immediate importance, therapy is the tool that reaps the lasting results.

Third, it is necessary to reach the family, whose own emotions have become involved with those of the problem drinker. This is also accomplished through social casework, with particular attention to the spouse and teenage children.

Fourth, the continuity of the program must be safeguarded. The main change takes place as the individual re-evaluates himself and his relation to his environment while not drinking. If, during this time, he has help in understanding the underlying reasons for his behavior, great growth takes place. It is during this period that the treatment problems become acute. The problem drinker is by all odds the most shortsighted of individuals and the most prone to fantasy thinking. Inclined as he is, from long experience, to think that wishing will make it so, he frequently withdraws from treatment before receiving much help. In accepting this trait of the problem drinker, we can also see how essential it is that a total program include a concerted effort on the part of the staff to see that this withdrawal is checked and prevented. If we accept his rationalizations and do not enforce the program, we actually reject him.

The fifth aspect of our program is the need for education of those in the community on the nature, extent, and treatment of alcoholism. Whereas increasing attention is given to this subject in newspapers and periodicals, compared to the coverage given heart trouble, cancer, and other major illnesses, alcoholism remains a relatively unknown illness.

The particular program under consideration in this paper is operated by the Volunteers of America in Los Angeles, who have long been cognizant of the skid row problem in that city. Several years ago they established a Men's Service Club in the skid row area and offered limited service and shelter to indigent men through that facility. At the same time an advisory committee of interested citizens was formed, and through their concern with the total problem of alcoholism the main impetus for the new program has come. In March 1956 an alcoholic clinic was founded to deal comprehensively with the problem.

Since it was clear that any halfhearted or stopgap measures were doomed to early failure, the groundwork for the clinic followed closely the five-point program already discussed. The medical director of a private sanitarium where a comprehensive program for alcoholics was in existence was asked to become medical director of the new program, where he continues to volunteer his time. He is assisted in the medical program by a registered nurse. A psychiatric social worker, formerly head of the Detroit Commission on Alcoholism, was appointed full time to coordinate all functions of the clinic. He also represents the program by his membership on the Welfare Planning Council of Los Angeles. In addition, he is in charge of the individual and group psychotherapy. A chaplain is available for counseling and spiritual guidance.

Several of the large pharmaceutical houses have made volunteer donations of valuable medications, including antabus. The Welfare Information Center of Los Angeles has begun to direct inquiries made by those seeking help to the clinic. Alcoholics Anonymous information centers send persons to be helped through the initial stages of sobriety, then have them return to AA for sustaining help.

The Volunteers of America also contracts with a private sanitarium to detoxify those who cannot be treated without hospital treatment. However, with the present medical knowledge about intoxication, the number needing hospitalization is diminishing.

Therapy, both individual and group, is carried on at the clinic. Also important to the long-range planning of the program is the continuation of counseling and follow-up work by other agencies. Most important in this respect is the Family Counselling Service of the Volunteers, which is the Community Chest agency for family counseling in northeast Los Angeles. It is increasingly helpful for those starting on a total rehabilitative program with the clinic to continue the followup and counseling in their own locale. From the district counseling office, problem drinkers are referred to the clinic for full evaluation and initiation into the program. They then return home and may continue their psychotherapy either in the district office or at the main clinic. Their families are seen in one or the other office as well, and their response has been gratifying. Followup is facilitated by this closer, more comprehensive contact made possible by the branch offices. At the present time, after the initial review at the downtown clinic, about one half are seen regularly there, about one fourth go to the district offices, and about one fourth return to AA for continuing support.

In addition to the staff of the clinic, the staff in the local offices do essential public relations and education within their areas. As workers in both offices have worked largely with problem drinkers in previous jobs, they are able to enhance the program by talks at club meetings, coordinating council meetings, and other gatherings.

This is a unique and a comprehensive program, sponsored by a private agency and utilizing volunteer people in certain spheres. Yet it is a program that can be duplicated, as it does not consist of unique components. The validity of the program lies in the interrelation of services, which are important enough to repeat. First, there is the medical care and facilities for detoxification. Second, a great emphasis in individual and group psychotherapy. Third, services to help readjustment of the patient's family. Fourth, coordinated followup so that the benefits of treatment can be realized. Fifth, community education and information about the problem.

The clinic has not made available its first run of statistics, in the compilation of which they are being assisted by the Alcoholic Clinic staff at the U.C.L.A. School of Medicine, but we know that the response of patients has been gratifying. Further expansion of facilities and services at both the clinic and local offices is necessary and imminent.

With increasing success this comprehensive plan for the treatment of problem drinkers will continue to have a real impact on the community. For many years there has been a feeling of dejection and hopelessness about any successful treatment of the drinking problem. Those who stopped drinking often did so without help, which gave rise to the idea that will power was the main ingredient of the cure. The problem drinker, although often deserted and abused, was usually tolerated and pitied, without the realization that such overprotection perpetuated the problem. Various treatments were developed, but all focused on a particular part of the problem instead of the whole. The program outlined above now adds its support to the total comprehensive and scientific effort to control the major medical, psychiatric, and social problem of alcoholism.

3. First Steps in Organizing Against Alcoholism

GEORGE H. GIBB

Me, I'm just an imaginary figure. Call me Dr. Les Jones. I'm a physician in a community of 50,000 population.

Our city is located on the main line of the railroad in a thriving business and industrial area. I, like others, am proud of our city with its fine school systems, including excellent public and parochial schools and also one of the leading older colleges in the state. The social organizations of our community are noteworthy. Many groups participate in our social program. Organizations such as two large hospitals, the YWCA and YMCA, Family-Children's Service, The Salvation Army, Boy and Girl Scouts, Boys Club, American Red Cross, Community Center, and other smaller groups all work to help the people of the area. We have an outstanding Community Chest Organization, of which I am a director, and our clubs, societies, fraternities, and places of recreation are adequate. Five service clubs are active in our city with projects galore to challenge the imagination and keep alive community interest.

I'd like to relate a very significant incident that happened to me and affected our community life just one year and a half ago. One of my patients called me that day. We'll call her "Helen." She and Jack had been married for eleven years. Their only son, John, had come home from school that afternoon to find Helen weeping bitterly.

"What's cookin', Ma," he said as he entered the living room of their home. The house was a six-room bungalow, neatly furnished and in a fairly fashionable neighborhood. Helen turned to the boy and though he was only ten he knew that Daddy was drinking again and had got into some kind of difficulty.

This time he had lost his job. It seemed that there were just too many "days off" in the past few months. When he came to work that morning, one hour late, and with a "real good jag on" as the boys said, Mr. Pellington, his foreman, told him that he was laid off until further notice. On

35

leaving the plant he spent the rest of the day making the rounds of the taverns around town, where his friends had continued to warn him about the dangers of excessive drinking, but Jack couldn't be told.

When Helen, through her friend Joyce, found out about the incident she and Joyce tracked Jack down, brought him home and put him to bed. Jack was a sick man, and Helen, realizing this, called me to her home. As I hung up the phone I thought of the ten or twelve other somewhat similar cases I had treated recently. Certainly other physicians in town had had similar experiences.

When I arrived I was greeted at the door by Reverend Jorgusen, the pastor of a local church. After administering treatment and making Jack as comfortable as possible, I sat in the living room chatting with Reverend Jorgusen. His first remark was, "Isn't it a shame that with all the modern conveniences and methods at our disposal in the community we do not have any way of dealing with the alcoholic problem?" Of course Reverend Jorgusen recognized the activities of the church and other groups who had worked with many individuals who were alcoholics, but the problem was facing us. What was the community doing to combat alcoholism?

This, too, was the first mention of the word "alcoholic." Yes, Jack was an alcoholic. He had started his drinking when in the service. He had an excellent service record, but when he came out of the service his alcohol problem was different from that of his friends. He continued to drink socially for a while, but within the past years his drinking habits had changed. He would sneak drinks on many occasions; he almost always had to have a drink the first thing in the morning. His drinking was now a problem that he could not control.

We talked quite a bit about Jack's problem and the problems of others whom we knew. Then Joyce, Helen's friend, entered the room from the kitchen where she had been preparing dinner for John and Helen. Joyce was a social worker with one of the local agencies. Having a knowledge of what we were talking about she said, "In many dealings with families and their problems, I find that alcohol is a factor in the problem and that some mothers and fathers are alcoholics or potential alcoholics."

Then Reverend Jorgusen said: "Cooperative community effort is needed to provide facts about alcohol. Families of alcoholics need assistance to meet their problems. I believe that cooperative community effort can be a spiritual and social experience in which the cooperation of the churches and social agencies in our community can be expected."

Here was an opportunity presenting itself to us. "Why can't we do something about the problem?" I suggested. Joyce then said that the State had recently passed a legislative act making it possible to study the problem of alcoholism, and she presumed that we might be able to get some aid. I offered to write to the State committee and find out what assistance could be given.

We were pleasantly surprised to receive word within a week from the director saying that a community organization representative would come to the community to see us the following week, and that I should arrange for our group of three to meet with him at my office.

Mr. Charles Watt, the representative, arrived in my office on schedule. Needless to say we were all alive with anticipation of what might be done. He outlined what had been accomplished in other communities and suggested that we communicate with about twenty local residents who have a keen interest in the problem of alcoholism. The proposed members of the group or committee were to be outstanding community leaders. He left a good deal of information from the State Division of Alcohol Studies and Rehabilitation, The Yale Summer School of Alcohol Studies, The National Committee on Alcoholism, and Alcoholics Anonymous. He then assured us of the government's interest and cooperation in the local program.

By the middle of the next month we were ready to call our second meeting. Included as members on our committee on alcoholism were a county judge, an AA member, an attorney, two clergymen, two social welfare workers, two physicians, a manufacturer, a retail merchant, the executive from the council of social agencies, a union representative, a high school principal, a personnel counselor, a public health nurse, a housewife, a banker, a college professor, a hospital administrator, and a wholesaler. I was elected the first chairman. The chairman was to be succeeded the following year by the vice-chairman; a secretary and treasurer were also appointed. The membership was to be a three-year rotation plan. The chairman was to be elected yearly. We affiliated with the National Committee on Alcoholism and put into force a set of bylaws suggested by it, with some minor changes to suit our needs.

The interest of the entire group surprised me. There were representatives of industry concerned with the loss of time therein as well as the loss of good men who had given years of service in their particular industry. Other members of the group wanted to develop a program of public education on alcoholism. Others expressed interest in the long- and short-term treatment of alcoholics, their rehabilitation, the transient alcoholic, and many other phases of the problem. As we progressed, we appointed committees to take care of various aspects of the program. I remember well that not all was easy, for some people misinterpreted our motives and others just insisted it was a hopeless cause and would not cooperate. But on the whole, the program advanced quite rapidly.

Through the medium of pamphlets we started an educational program. The speakers' bureau committee gleaned much information from available literature and we started, through the council of social agencies, an information center. At the end of a year the center was on its own, financed by gifts from interested citizens. We are now working on a plan whereby we might be able to set up larger facilities and have a full-time staff with a trained administrator.

We have also conducted two public forums on alcoholism. The newspapers have been more than generous with editorial comment and news articles regarding our work. The radio station gave us a twelve-week program without charge, and we have had a few appearances on television programs. We have given lectures in schools, churches, and to many groups in the area.

An outstanding development is our future plan for an out-patient clinic at the local hospital. We will be assigned twelve beds for an alcoholic clinic with a complete clinical staff. All the details on the project are being worked out at the present time. The patients will stay for a seven-day period for treatment and study and a program of rehabilitation.

We have already referred some patients to private institutions for care and have had some treated at our State-operated clinic. One of the most helpful groups has been Alcoholics Anonymous. It seems their membership has doubled since we started our program, and we must commend them for their participation in the program. We have had excellent cooperation from ministers, welfare organizations, industries, and government health agencies. It seems that everyone has taken an interest in this public health program.

To sum this up, Jack is back in his job again. His foreman, Mr. Pellington, is now a member of our committee. Jack is an active member of AA and has been very helpful with our work at the information center. Helen, his wife, has devoted many hours to counseling wives of alcoholics and carrying on other voluntary duties within the center. The community is recognizing that the alcoholic is a sick person and needs assistance. I look back today and say it would all be impossible without cooperative community planning. In looking forward I can predict a great benefit to the community as a result of this cooperative enterprise.

3
Juvenile Delinquency

1. The Berkeley Big Brother Project

WILLIAM J. DAVIS

The varied resources of a college or university community can be highly useful in extending voluntary activity and organization in social welfare. This fact becomes increasingly important as the number of colleges multiply across the nation and as their enrollments swell.

The young men and women who constitute the student bodies of America are vast reservoirs of community service *if* means can be found to capture and hold their interest, to channel their naturally generous impulses, and to utilize their qualities of leadership and intelligence.

In a small way, this has been done in Berkeley, California. Although it is true that the conditions in Berkeley appear almost ideal for the type of program that is to be described, it also seems evident that these conditions could be re-created in almost any college community in the land, if there were a will to do it. To be sure, the particular arrangement of sponsoring organizations might differ somewhat, but the chief elements of such a program are probably inherent in almost any four-year college community of 50,000 population or more.

The program to which we refer is the Berkeley Big Brother Project—a Specialized Program in Juvenile Guidance.[1] This is a unique combination of three diverse types of organizations that have pooled their resources so that Berkeley boys in need of the friendship and guidance of an older male companion might have it under as effective circumstances as possible.[2]

The effect of this program is to enlarge substantially the amount of personal supervision that can be given to juveniles by the Juvenile Bureau of the Berkeley Police Department, but to do it on a private, voluntary basis. The actual work with the juveniles is done by carefully selected University men students under the supervision of Juvenile Bureau officers. Funds with which these students are paid (at the modest rate of $1 per

[1] This is the title of a full report on the project recently published by the University YMCA.

[2] The Berkeley project is not part of the national Big Brothers of America movement, from which it differs in several important respects.

hour) are provided by fellow students who are members of fraternities surrounding the campus. Most of the administration of the project is assumed by Stiles Hall, the University YMCA, a privately supported agency.

What is the record of the Berkeley Big Brother Project? Although it started originally as a non-paid program in 1932, it was reorganized on its present basis in late 1946. In that year the Junior Chamber of Commerce undertook to subsidize the student workers and in the ensuing two years invested about $3,800 in the project. Beginning in the fall of 1948 the fraternity men at the Berkeley campus assumed the financing burden and have carried it ever since. Records have been kept since 1946. The following statistics cover the ten-year period to June 1956.

During this period there have been 68 Big Brothers who have worked a total of approximately 13,000 hours. The average number of hours worked by each was 191.4 over an average period of twelve months. On the other hand, there have been 117 Little Brothers on the project. The average time spent with each of these boys was 111.2 hours. They received individual help of a kind that is not available from any other agency.

Of the 117 boys who had Big Brothers, nine (7.7 per cent) were committed to Juvenile Court while on the project because they had got into serious difficulties. Thus 92.3 per cent (108) can be presumed to have made a more or less satisfactory adjustment. Furthermore, it would be quite incorrect to assume that the 7.7 per cent committed to the Juvenile Court all became hardened criminals. Case histories can be cited to the contrary.

Of course, those associated with the project know that these figures are in no way definitive. Neither the success nor the degree of success of the project can, with present methods, be accurately measured. But each year adds to the general evidence that the program works. And it works in a variety of ways—some of which were not anticipated by those who initiated it.

First, there is the obvious and primary value that it has for the boys—youngsters in need of the friendship and guidance of an older person, in this case the student. At its best, the project creates a relationship that, in the great majority of instances, enables the boy to realign his attitudes and actions to bring them into conformity with those of his new friend whom he has come to trust and admire. The Juvenile Bureau is confident that many boys, destined for a career of delinquency and probably adult crime, have been helped by their Big Brothers to become good citizens.

Second, there is the less obvious but also important effect on the student workers. A high percentage of these men are now working professionally in related fields. In many instances their participation in the project opened to them the possibilities of such work. In every case, it seems safe to say, the quality of their performance has been greatly improved by their experience with the Big Brother Project. And in every case it provided them, as students, with socially constructive part-time employment.

Third, there is the value for the fraternities that contribute funds to pay the Big Brothers. In the six years that they have assumed this responsibility, they have given $8,818. They have done this with the express understanding that they are *not* to receive publicity in the newspapers (since this is felt to be harmful to the program), or special consideration for any of their members who may apply (since the jobs are for the best qualified, regardless of their affiliations). In the process of being "educated to give" they have learned something of the community and its problems. They have gained a little practice, perhaps, in the "art of giving."

Fourth, there is the aid to the Juvenile Bureau. Like many such agencies it is understaffed. The project enables it to work closely with boys with whom it otherwise could have only a cursory relation at best.

Fifth, there is the saving in tax funds for the community at large. In 1956 Citizens Advisory Committee on Youth Activities of the Berkeley Council of Social Welfare published these figures: "The cost of a delinquent in Juvenile Hall is $7.00 per day. Probation costs $150 per year. The cost of a boy given over to the custodial care of the California Youth Authority varies. In forestry camps the cost is $1,981 per year. Costs in other Youth Authority institutions range from $2,473 per year to $3,131 per year." The cost of helping a boy through the Big Brother Project (in terms of pay to his Big Brother) is roughly $111 per boy—and it is provided by students! There is no doubt that the project has kept many boys from becoming public charges at one or more of these levels, not to mention the costs of institutionalizing adult offenders!

Sixth, there is the value for parents of the boys in trouble. Often the Big Brother proves to be a key factor in improving an entire family situation. Sometimes he finds that his job is not so much with the boy as with those the boy lives with. In many instances he brings relief to distraught parents or guardians who have "reached the end of their rope."

Seventh, the Big Brother sometimes makes a valuable contribution to a school situation, particularly if the juvenile's problem is such that he is a "troublemaker" who disrupts classroom and playground.

The effectiveness of the Berkeley Big Brother Project was recognized afresh only a few months ago when the Berkeley Mayor's Committee on Children and Youth, in its report to the Governor, recommended that some means be found to extend the scope of the Big Brother idea as it has been operating in Berkeley.

And this leads to a variation on the plan as it has operated up to the present—a variation that Stiles Hall is currently seeking to implement in response to the committee's recommendation.

Whereas in the present project a boy is usually given a Big Brother only after he has officially come to the attention of the Juvenile Bureau, it is now proposed that a parallel program be operated out of the University YMCA to which youngsters would be referred directly from schools, other social agencies, or parents. The cooperation of agencies accustomed to working with family and youth problems would be solicited in order to ensure expert "screening" and "matching" of the juveniles with the students. Stiles Hall would undertake to provide supervision for the Big Brothers. One of the local service clubs has expressed a tentative interest in helping to underwrite the cost of this supervision. Nonfraternity student groups may be solicited to finance the time of additional student workers.

In short, there seems to be a fair possibility that, with a slight rearrangement of resources, the Big Brother idea can be extended to provide an even more truly preventive type of service—to help the youngster who has not yet come under the supervision of the Juvenile Bureau. But whereas Stiles Hall entertains high hopes for this extension of a proved idea it cannot yet put it forth as a working scheme. It is mentioned here only to demonstrate the earlier statement that in other communities some realignment of resources may be necessary or desirable to make the primary idea work.

But as it is now operating, the Berkeley Big Brother Project is a going concern with well-established patterns of operation. Its recorded experience is certainly sufficient to justify describing it as "a clear and practical method for extending private, voluntary efforts" in the field of prevention of juvenile delinquency.

Some words of caution are necessary. Great care must be exercised in selecting students to serve as Big Brothers, in "matching" the students with the boys, and in supervising the students. Berkeley has been fortunate in the quality both of its students and its Juvenile Division officers. Any effort to extend this program to other communities should concern itself, first, with finding competent supervision and, second, with recruiting student workers who have the necessary qualities of personal adjustment and maturity. Given these requirements, the other factors can, somehow, be supplied and a project undertaken.

The University YMCA will be glad to furnish copies of the report to any communities or agencies requesting them.

2. Youth Anonymous

MILTON J. HUBER

This is the story of Youth Anonymous, an experimental program of mutual help among delinquent youth under the voluntary leadership of reformed men with previously well-defined histories of delinquency of their own. Two fresh ideas, both somewhat revolutionary, are being tested in this program for rehabilitating delinquent youth.

One idea is that a rehabilitated man with a criminal record of his own has a unique contribution to bring to bear in work among delinquent youth. He has been through the mill. He knows their "beefs." He knows how they "tick." He's from their side of the tracks. Stigma, rejection, guilt, defiance, bitterness, and all the other terms applicable to boys in trouble are more than professional phrases to such a man.

The other idea is that association among delinquent youth, more specifically among institutionalized delinquents, can be beneficial. This idea challenges the traditional conviction in the field of delinquency and crime that association among law violators is destructive and to be discouraged. Parolees are ordered to refrain from any association with one another since one law violator's weakness or pathology seems to serve as a fuse for another's and the result is recidivism. In contrast to this prevailing idea, Youth Anonymous is employing some of the techniques of Alcoholics Anonymous. Two in particular are in operation: one, that some fellows in trouble are more receptive to help from another in trouble than from others since they both are in the same boat; and, second, that the challenges and temptations of life can be met a day at a time when support is forthcoming from others similarly committed.

Youth Anonymous took form in the office of Boys Republic, a private training school for delinquent boys in suburban Detroit in December 1954. Three men brought their experiences and ideas together and Youth Anonymous was born. I was one of the three. My contribution was a "hunch" that reformed ex-cons with a sense of mission in their lives could turn previous adversity to advantage in establishing rapport with institutionalized delinquents, particularly gang boys—an asset not obtainable through professional training. This, coupled with a willingness to put the idea to the test among my own boys at Boys Republic, constitutes the essence of my contribution.

More important were the contributions of the other two men, Dr. Albert Eglash and Ernest "Tip" Rumsby. At that time Dr. Eglash was a psychologist on the staff of the Detroit Youth Commission, having come to that position after serving on the staff of the Mayor's Rehabilitation Committee on Skid Row Problems in the same city. Through the latter experience he observed time and time again the simple program of Alcoholics Anonymous bring to an end the supposedly fixated behavior of compulsive drinking. Transferred to the Youth Commission, the idea came to him over a period of time that there would appear to be a compulsive element among some boys to commit delinquent acts that continued to manifest itself in spite of disciplining. Perhaps such compulsive behavior also could be stopped by applying the principles of Alcoholics Anonymous mentioned earlier.

The credit and responsibility for putting these ideas to the test in the form of a concrete program go unreservedly to the third founder, Ernest "Tip" Rumsby. A brute of a man, Tip appeared in the office of the Mayor's Commission on Youth in the midst of an outbreak of violence among delinquent youth in the city with the simple inquiry, "What can I do to help?" Several such persistent inquiries over a period of months resulted in the December 1954 meeting at Boys Republic. Tip has served as the inspiration and leader of Youth Anonymous ever since, first as a "forty-hour week" volunteer, and then as its professionally employed executive-director since August 1956, when we persuaded the Detroit Downtown Rotary Club to set aside $10,000 for Tip Rumsby to expand the program on a trial basis for a year.

Tip Rumsby has a magnetic personality that can turn adversity to advantage. Born in the Purple Gang district of Detroit, he was well known to the police at the age of thirteen for drunkenness and other charges. At seventeen he joined the Navy and at eighteen received a bad conduct discharge. Next came armed robbery and Jackson Prison. Three months after his release he was sent to Leavenworth for stolen cars, attempted murder, and kidnapping. While there he led a riot, and was charged with insurrection and placed in the "pit"—hence his nickname, "Pit" spelled backwards. After this discharge, another armed robbery and Jackson for seven and a half to fifteen years. While serving his last year of that sentence at the Detroit House of Corrections he became attracted to Alcoholics Anonymous, mainly because he could find no "gimmicks" in it. He has been one of its missionaries ever since.

The actual program got off the ground the first Thursday in January

1955. On that evening Tip told his story from the time he was thirteen years old, in all its tragic details, to the delinquent boys under commitment at Boys Republic. After a spasm of spontaneous questions following his presentation, which delved into everything from the kind of "rod" he had used on his "jobs" to the kind of "ole lady he had," Tip informed the boys he would be at the Republic every Thursday to meet with those who would be interested in continuing the discussion. The group has met regularly since that time without interruption or interference from the administration, as initially agreed, under the guidance of Tip or one of his other volunteers of similar background.

About one third of the Republic boys take part in the program each week. Initially they called themselves "Delinquents Anonymous" but they soon changed that with the comment: "After all, alcoholics haven't organized under the title of "Drunks Anonymous"! Every other week the boys discuss under their own leadership the meaning and relevance of one of the "Twelve Steps" of Alcoholics Anonymous for their situations. On alternate weeks they invite as guests and as speakers persons who have struggled with problems similar to theirs. Court officials and police officers— off-duty, on their own time—have been invited to present their slant on things.

Other groups have since been organized at other institutions. The various units exchange ideas, programs, and problems with one another. Alcoholics Anonymous meetings are attended periodically by some of the boys. More recently, the first of a number of neighborhood groups has been organized.

This last-named step was a natural and necessary step to round out the Youth Anonymous movement. Boys being released from Boys Republic after having been part of the program felt a need to continue the association. As time passed and the members involved accumulated, it became impracticable for them to return to the Republic each week for the program. Personal conference and associations with Tip on an individual basis were helpful but overburdening on a truck driver doing all this in his spare time.

The next step was obvious and the Detroit Rotary Club responded to the challenge. Youth Anonymous was formally organized with an operating budget of $10,000 and Tip Rumsby was appointed executive-director. An office and secretarial service have been provided in downtown Detroit. A board of directors made up of members of the Rotary Club and professional men in the child welfare field determine the policies of the organization. I am vice president of the board of directors.

The present emphasis is on the establishment of neighborhood groups under the guidance of volunteers with backgrounds similar to Tip's. The nucleus for each group is usually a "graduate" or two of Boys Republic, but increasingly older teen-age "delinquency-prone-or-undetected" boys are being attracted either out of curiosity or anxiety for their own situations. The main problem to date has been to circumscribe the limits of the program. The attention the press has given to the program has brought every type of personal tragedy and problem to its doorstep, from infidelity to Federal parole violation, and the energy exerted in directing these people to the proper agencies is taxing. There seem to be strong reservations among some citizens against seeking help for their personal problems from the professionally recognized and highly specialized agencies established to meet their particular needs. Moreover, the answering of inquiries about the program from other cities and from countries as far away as Italy has been time-consuming.

In closing, as administrator of Boys Republic, which has profited from the Youth Anonymous program, I would like to make a few random observations. First, and most interesting, the program appears to appeal to boys who otherwise make only marginal adjustments within the institutional program itself. Boys so alienated from society and so distrustful of authority that they cannot bring themselves genuinely to accept placement have often become leaders within the Youth Anonymous program. Indeed, occasionally a boy returned to court after nine months of institutionalization and placed on probation as a "poor risk" remains active in the Youth Anonymous program and eventually matures beyond the juvenile age without having become a recidivist as might have been expected. Furthermore, socially rejected boys with a background of gang membership seem to find a satisfying and constructive substitute for their previous associations in the Youth Anonymous program.

To date, then, it can be said that boys who have difficulty in forming a positive identification with people are receiving the most help from the Youth Anonymous program. Possibly Tip and his fellow workers epitomize this type of boy's underlying feelings of rebelliousness toward society and accordingly such a boy is attracted and identifies himself initially with the negative or criminal past of Tip and the others. Over a period of time through continuous association the relationships of these boys are strengthened, and gradually the socially commendable values for which Youth Anonymous stands are assimilated and become an integral part of their personalities.

Finally, the number of reformed "no-collar" men with prison records and social and economic backgrounds comparable to those of many of the boys here, who have come forward to volunteer their services both to the school and the Youth Anonymous program at large, has been most rewarding.

These men, largely of limited income, work with Tip regularly at considerable financial loss to themselves. Three in the course of time have been employed as members of the Boys Republic staff as housemasters and maintenance men, and one, a three-time loser, has earned his teacher's credentials and now is a vocational shop teacher in charge of the arts and crafts program. Typical of the men attracted by the program is this one who recently wrote:

Dear Tip,

Like you, I too am a graduate of Jackson, a 4-time loser. I too have wondered what I could do to help others keep out of there. But never tried to approach the authorities, because I figured those bastards aren't interested in helping. Tip, I guess I was wrong.

3. Observations on Recruiting Volunteers

DR. ALBERT MORRIS

It is assumed that it is desirable to extend voluntary activity and organization in social welfare only if the volunteers are worth their salt. This requires that they either be persons who have had successful experience related to the activity in which their services are to be contributed, or that they be willing to serve long enough and continuously enough under competent guidance to become useful. The amount and nature of the previous experience needed or the length of service required to obtain it will necessarily vary with the nature of the contribution that the volunteers are expected to make. Experienced volunteers might be former professional men or women now retired or former professional married women whose children have grown up or who are childless. There are of course excellent volunteers to be obtained from almost every level of the general population; also, it should be remembered that retired professional welfare workers sometimes find it difficult to collaborate effectively with younger active professional workers who may have found it necessary to use a fresh approach to new and different conditions, or who may define their activities in terms of a new vocabulary if not in terms of fundamentally new techniques. Married women without children sometimes prefer paid opportunities for service but they may volunteer with the thought that the experience will be a steppingstone to a paid position. Such workers are highly motivated and may be most helpful, and so also may be the married women wishing to devote themselves to some community service after their children have grown up. Some of these are dedicated persons and if they are reasonably well informed they can be most useful. Occasionally they bring to their efforts the disadvantage of a certain rigidity. Intelligent, trainable college students and graduates are also a good potential source of volunteers, and because of their youthfulness and abundance of physical energy they may be particularly valuable in working with actual and potential juvenile delinquents. Their chief handicap is that the amount of time that they can devote to service is likely to be limited by their scholastic and work obligations.

How then can one obtain the most useful volunteers from all of these sources? Obviously, by making people aware of what needs to be done and by giving them a high degree of motivation toward doing it. Knowledge of what needs to be done can of course be extended into the community by all of the conventional public relations methods, including newspaper publicity, television advertising, and motion picture films made available to a variety of organizations. There is, however, no substitute for a much more direct and personal type of recruiting through the approach by agencies to individuals with the right qualifications who are recommended by clergymen, university instructors, and other people who are in a position to know where such talents lie. In many instances, volunteers can best be obtained by a direct approach to groups or to individuals as members of groups such as the Boy Scouts, church schools, service clubs, veterans organizations, and the like.

Motivation to serve may be induced (*a*) by bringing about a coincidence of the interests of the volunteers with those of the agencies with which they will serve and by making the volunteers conscious of the value of their service in terms of its personal satisfactions; (*b*) by providing for each volunteer a reasonably clear-cut and definite place and function in the structure of social welfare; (*c*) by providing him with such in-service training supervision, guidance, and support as he may need to give him self-confidence in his work; (*d*) by recognizing and accepting in fact and not merely at a verbal level the value and need of volunteers as part of the total organization of welfare work. This last will require that professionals themselves take stock of their dependence upon the community and of the importance of the volunteer as a liaison between themselves and the community.

Because juvenile delinquency in its most serious and persistent form is associated chiefly with members of the lower socioeconomic group in deteriorated urban areas, volunteers are needed who can effectively develop rapport with people whose patterns of life and whose values may be in some degree different from those with middle-class bias. Volunteers who have never experienced life in such an area may have some difficulty in dealing with its people effectively; on the other hand, those brought up in such an area may be too deeply involved in it emotionally to work in it effectively, even if they have outgrown it and acquired education and a position outside of it. With these cautions in mind, one might expect to find the most serviceable volunteers among those who have been brought up in modest circumstances and under some hardships, but under conditions peripheral to those that obtain in high-rate delinquency areas. This is not to overlook, however, the important and valuable resource in the people who live in delinquency areas, but who have assimilated and accepted the essential values of the larger community to which it is desirable for young people to conform.

There are two particularly good sources of volunteers in the field of juvenile delinquency: The first includes graduate students in universities for whom volunteer service would be a useful experience preparatory to their life work, and whose fields of study are such as to give them both interest and training in human relations. These would include theological students, graduate students in sociology and psychology, and perhaps some in such fields as political science, education, public relations, and journalism. This source of volunteers, though used, is not at all adequately exploited. Many of these students are in limited financial circumstances, and even small additional expenses strain their means. If agencies which can provide rooms and possibly some meals and take care of minor expenses such as carfare would do so, they might find this would have a surprising effect, since students are apt to be more reluctant to ask for these lesser forms of support than to ask for a paid position. Moreover, most students in this category, though aware in a general way of the opportunities for volunteers, are not acquainted with specific situations or the specific contributions they might make to them. They are also not fully apprised of what such service can contribute to them by way of enriching their experience and of giving them a deeper and broader understanding of people and conditions outside of their own social class.

The current practice of agencies that seek volunteers is to send notices or letters to university department heads, but these letters do not tell the student what he needs to know if he is going to be brought to the point of taking the initiative in offering his services. What is needed is a personal recruiting effort, well organized in cooperation with the academic staff and comparable to that done by business firms recruiting college graduates for careers in industry.

The second major source of good volunteers, specifically for work in the field of delinquency, is the people who are directly affected by the behavior of delinquents. In the deteriorated sections of cities where persistent delinquency is most common, neighborhoods suffer perhaps more from social unorganization than from social disorganization, and the lack of channels of communication among the residents coupled with their limited skill in social organization makes it difficult either to identify, or to enlist the help of, local leaders. The experience of those engaged in urban renewal projects, and in such delinquency control projects as the Back of The Yards Program in Chicago and the Special Youth Program in Roxbury, Massachusetts, suggests that fruitful and successful ways of organizing neighborhoods and communities to deal more effectively with delinquency are built on the strongly felt needs that are common to many as yet unrelated and unorganized individuals. These may be the small shop owners in an area, all of whom suffer from vandalism; or they may be the people living anonymously side by side, each of whom worries alone about the behavior of his own child, or they may be unconcerned about their children's behavior but be disturbed by the lack of such community services as street repair, trash collection, or snow removal.

It is possible, under these circumstances, for the representative of some appropriate welfare organization to arrange a meeting of a group of shopkeepers or neighbors to air their complaints about municipal services, for example. Out of this and through the connections of the professional worker, there may come a meeting with responsible city officials or with their local political representative which can result in the early remedy of such direct and simply handled matters as street repair or trash collection. This experience of working together and of getting something done, with its accompanying feeling of hope and power, are the most important results of such gatherings. Properly directed, they can develop to the point where such groups begin to take an interest in other local situations, including juvenile delinquency. A psychological sense of community begins to arise, accompanied by a measure of local pride and a feeling of satisfaction in the accomplishment and in the growing confidence that something can be done. The organization of such a group of local volunteers may be on a neighborhood basis, or it may be developed around a church or athletic group or almost any common interest. Such an organization will provide a forum for the exchange of information and ideas and a source of local action under the leadership of local people, guided perhaps by outside professionals called in as consultants.

In less disadvantaged areas than the deteriorated zones of cities, a psychological sense of community can be built around a natural area, which may be a neighborhood in a city or the entire township if it is a small community. The assumption here is that if leadership is available to bring people together on the basis of some common and keenly felt interest, such as concern about the behavior of young people in the community, an organized volunteer welfare group as well as individual volunteers for specific jobs will quickly emerge. The experience of PTA's in the presence of a school crisis, or the experience of one-industry communities in organizing to save their economic life when such an industry is shut down, are both cases in point and illustrations of what can be done when a community becomes aroused about delinquency.

In the small communities of the nation, therefore, or in the less deteriorated neighborhoods of larger cities, such natural local leaders as clergymen, editors, school officials, public welfare officers, and others (depending on the local situation and the leadership qualities of the individuals who comprise such professional classes) would be expected to take the initiative in giving rise to voluntary organizations for the prevention and control of delinquency. The initial impetus to do something would come from whatever person or persons first became conscious of and sufficiently disturbed by the delinquency problem, be it the editor of the local paper, the school principal, or a clergyman. His activities would lead to an initial informal meeting; out of this would come in time, it is hoped, a community council, a youth project, or some other type of volunteer effort to which the editor, the clergyman, the school officials, and others would lend their special kinds of support, in the form of editorials, sermons, the organization of forums, youth canteens, youth work projects, Little Leagues, or recreational activities, depending on what each with his special talents and opportunities could encourage or provide.

All of these things have been done successfully in one or more places. All could be both extended and intensified, as well as improved. Some procedures that on paper look like those suggested are far from it in practice, because there is lacking the specific know-how with reference to organizational details or of the psychological approach to the problem of obtaining volunteers that makes all the difference between success and failure in securing the right people for the worthwhile job. It is these subtleties of method that defy adequate brief verbal description. Nevertheless, many years of professional work, specifically in criminology, and including teaching in several major universities in the United States and other countries, of consulting work in connection with delinquency control projects, of services on the boards of a community council and a variety of welfare agencies, and including the task of assisting in the recruiting of volunteers as well as the employment of professional people, specifically in the field of delinquency control, have persuaded me of the essential validity of the general observations herein set forth.

4
Neighborhood Rehabilitation

1. A Neighborhood Council

RALPH M. KRAMER

In spite of the millions of volunteers and the hundreds of thousands of voluntary associations active in American life, there seems to be a growing uneasiness regarding the role of the volunteer in social welfare. Behind the community organizer's interest in "citizen participation," or the agency executive's emphasis on the "partnership between Board and Staff" is a continual struggle to retain the flavor and color of voluntarism in our social welfare system.

Actually, the concern for extending voluntary activity and organization in social welfare stems from two related and interacting forces:

I. *The changing character of American society as it evolves more and more toward a "mass society."* Social scientists have analyzed for us the effects of urbanization and industrialization in bringing about a radical dehumanization of life. They have decried the increasing sense of meaninglessness, of being lost and insignificant in a world growing more complicated and threatening, and less comprehensible.

Consequently, there is a real need to strengthen the aspects of social living from which the individual can get the feeling that *he counts,* that he can have a share in influencing the future character of life in his neighborhood or community. As Erich Fromm has said, ". . . the only criterion for the realization of freedom is whether the individual actively participates in determining his life and that of society, and this not only by the formal act of voting, but in his daily activity, in his work and in his relation to others."

We begin to get a clue leading to one of the major, but often neglected, ways in which we can extend the force of the individual acting in a voluntary capacity (which will be elaborated in this paper) from the following statement of Arthur J. Altmeyer:

> Today the social evils confronting us are . . . more subtle, more pervasive, and more difficult to attack—because to a considerable extent they grow out of our changing way of life.

World wars, increasing urbanization and industrialization, increasing population, increasing mobility of people, commercialized recreation have all created problems which we are far from having solved. Moreover, they cannot be solved simply by legislation, but must be solved largely by *better social planning and better social organization* in our towns, cities and states where people must learn how to live and work together for the common good under rapidly changing and increasingly difficult conditions.[1]

II. *The changing character of social welfare services and their growing complexity, specialization, and professionalization.* During the last twenty-five years, the sheer numerical increase in the number of agencies, size of budgets, and number of clients, members, patients, or constituents is almost staggering. Along with these quantitative changes, there has been a con-current increase in specialization and, probably most important of all, the gradual professionalization of most social welfare services. Whereas these trends have undoubtedly raised the level of effectiveness of these services, it has also resulted in removing them and making them seem remote from the ken of experience of most people.

What Can Be Done?

In the face of these special needs for increased voluntary activity, and in view of the limitations imposed by society and the social welfare system on citizen participation, what can be done? It is suggested here that certain concepts and methods of community organization—particularly those pertaining to decentralization through Neighborhood Councils—provide the most suitable tools ever devised for citizens, their organizations and agencies, to participate in the shaping of their own community life.

Why Neighborhood Councils?

In actual experience, much community organization has foundered because it violated the fundamental social work principle of self-determination by planning *for* people and not *with* them. This has special implications in considering the place of Neighborhood Councils, because the various social forces and programs that are regarded as separate specializations at the city or national level merge indissolubly in the neighborhood—where they directly affect the lives of people. Here such concerns as health, delinquency, recreation, housing, family and child welfare, liquor control,

---

[1] "The Dynamics of Social Work," *Social Work,* I, No. 2 (April 1956), 3.

street lights, employment, and zoning make up the interrelated and inseparable pattern of life of the family and individuals. Although these problems are handled by separate agencies, in the neighborhood they become so intertwined that they cannot be solved by separate groups, but require interrelated planning.

The Neighborhood Council, based on the experience of the cities where they are in existence, seems to be the best way to stimulate individuals and groups on the neighborhood level to involve themselves in their community affairs. It occupies a unique position in that its scope of work is all-embracing and is not limited to particular problems; it is an autonomous, self-governing movement from a small area outward, controlled and operated by the people of the area for their immediate benefit.

What Is a Neighborhood Council?

A Neighborhood Council has been defined as:

A voluntary association of organizations and individuals, the purpose of which is to improve conditions of community life in a specified geographical area. Its membership includes a broad cross section of community interests, drawn together on a non-sectarian, non-partisan, and non-commercial basis, by a desire to achieve united community action on problems of common concern.[2]

Since the Neighborhood Council envisages a broad outlook without a slanted attitude, it is only fitting that it should be started by a voluntary group dedicated to the welfare of the whole community. It has been found that local suspicion of attempts to organize a Neighborhood Council are best allayed when these attempts are under the auspices of a voluntary, nonpolitical and nonprofit group such as a Community Welfare Council. This facilitates the development of a two-way channel between the neighborhood and city-wide planning needs; it keeps neighborhoods aware of over-all community objectives and prevents extremes of local self-interest. It serves to temper city-wide planning with the expressed needs and attitudes of local citizens.

Nationally, this movement is active in many metropolitan areas including Chicago, Cleveland, Philadelphia, Detroit, Boston, Washington, Kansas City, Los Angeles, and Baltimore. Neighborhood Councils receive staff service from a Community Welfare Council in over fifty cities.

[2] "Neighbors Unite for Better Communities," Community Chests & Councils of America, 1956.

What Do Neighborhood Councils Do?

Here are some of the major projects of Councils affiliated with Cleveland's Welfare Federation: a clean-up campaign, children's needs, parent education, social hygiene, day-care centers, interpretation of health and welfare services, public safety, rat control, referrals to social agencies, traffic control, community studies, and legislative action. Neighborhood Councils elsewhere work for better housing, the use of school buildings as community centers, TB case finding, health institutes, improved race relations, courses on family life, counseling services, day-care centers and playgrounds, improvement in such city services as police and fire protection, garbage disposal, street and traffic lights, transportation facilities, enforcement of zoning regulations, and securing volunteers for youth-serving agencies.

All this is accomplished by a working partnership among citizens, social workers, and public officials, who engage in a process of defining the problem, getting all the facts about it, considering all opinions and all possible solutions, reaching agreement among all concerned upon a plan of action, and then following through to see that action is taken.

How Do Neighborhood Councils Start?

Usually there is an opportunity for forming a Council when local citizen leaders or organizations have been aroused by a crisis or a specific situation calling for agency coordination, public support for legislation, etc. The importance of motivation cannot be overstressed; there must be some active discontent with the status quo, even if it is a vague feeling that "something ought to be done." In this way, a Neighborhood Council becomes a way of bringing together people who want to improve their community, and a way of doing something effective about the need. This does not always happen by itself; a catalyst is needed to bring these community groups together. Experience has shown the importance of having a professionally trained staff—preferably related to a Community Welfare Council —available to help neighborhood leaders develop studies, seek out appropriate resources, coordinate competing activities, educate citizens about services and standards, and take responsible action to bring about needed changes.

The Story of One Neighborhood Council

The following is an account of how one Neighborhood Council emerged within a period of less than a year in Richmond, California.

The neighborhood. North Richmond is an area of sixty blocks partly within and partly outside the city limits. It was the only land available for purchase by Negroes who came from the South to work in the ship-yards during World War II. It is separated both psychologically and geographically by two main railroad lines and a strip of heavy industry. Because bank credit was unobtainable and building codes were not enforced, most of the homes, stores, and churches were actually constructed by the residents themselves. Today it is a community of 4,500, nearly all Negro; most are employed in unskilled jobs throughout the San Francisco Bay area, and there is frequent and extensive unemployment.

Like many substandard areas on the fringe of cities, North Richmond is notorious for gambling, narcotics, and prostitution. Delinquency, both adult and juvenile, is high in North Richmond.

Concern for North Richmond by the wider community has wavered between total disregard and sporadic attempts to "clean it up."

The method. Under the impetus of a 1954 survey, the Group Work and Recreation Section of the West Contra Costa Community Welfare Council embarked on the "North Richmond Neighborhood Demonstration Project"—a coordinated effort to provide more effective health, welfare, and recreation services to this "less chance" neighborhood. This group (composed of agency staff members and a few volunteers) soon realized it could not bring about improvements in agency services unless the project secured the participation of people living in North Richmond.

A group of fifteen residents were invited, and began attending the meetings of the Group Work and Recreation Section. For the first time in the history of the community, Negro and white citizens—professionals and volunteers—began working together for the improvement of North Richmond in an organized and democratic manner.

Through direct interviewing by teams of two or three persons, three surveys were completed:

1. *Existing services* offered by health, welfare and recreational agencies
2. *Activities, interests, and attitudes* regarding the needs of all organizations and clubs in North Richmond
3. *Present services* and needed improvements of all City and County departments serving North Richmond [3]

[3] In the course of these surveys, an issue arose over the proposed construction of a new elementary school in North Richmond, regarded by the residents as a segregated school. Because of the intensity of feelings involved, the Welfare Council asked the Board of Education to defer its decision—which it did—and arranged a public meeting to clarify this problem by providing accurate information and an opportunity for a full expression of opinion. This meeting was attended by nearly 200 people, and it was a first experience in developing a public meeting on an explosive issue.

The organization. As a means of bringing the information gained through these surveys to a larger group, two town meetings were organized by committees headed by residents of North Richmond. This was a significant development, because in the beginning most of the Negro members of the section were silent, passive, and suspicious. They gradually moved toward active participation on an equal partnership basis in all of the agreed-upon tasks. Several influential Negro ministers took leadership roles and encouraged their congregations to participate. Gradually a social climate was created that encouraged participation from people not accustomed to taking responsibility for improving their community.

Several hundred people attended the town meetings, which tackled the many problems of the area: schools, recreation, parks, sewers and streets, drainage and flood control, fire and police protection, buildings and housing, planning and zoning, health and sanitation, job security, and law enforcement. All this was presented by North Richmond residents; there was also discussion of how individuals and groups can work together to improve their community through the organization of a Neighborhood Council.

At the second town meeting, it was unanimously voted to organize a Neighborhood Council under the auspices of the Community Welfare Council. A temporary steering committee was elected and empowered to draw up bylaws. Four study committees were appointed. The North Richmond Neighborhood Council was launched with a membership consisting of representatives of the twenty-five organizations (churches, clubs, and agencies) then present, plus interested individuals.

The progress made by this unprecedented activity was sufficiently impressive for a local philanthropic foundation to grant funds enabling the employment of an additional staff person in the Welfare Council to assist the North Richmond Neighborhood Council, and organize others in this area.

Volunteers learn it pays. Possibly for the first time in their lives, citizens in North Richmond have learned what voluntary citizen participation can do. In only two months, North Richmond Neighborhood Council has accomplished the following: The Committee to Study Hensley Tract (a blighted area scheduled for industrialization), instead of merely gathering names on a vaguely formulated petition, has undertaken a study of the redevelopment process and the sources of help. The Committee on Teen-Age Recreation arranged meetings involving teenagers, parents, volunteer leaders, the school principal, the City Recreation Director, and the Sheriff's Office, and initiated a weekly social program at the school. The Committee on Planning and Zoning attended a meeting of the County Board of Supervisors, arranged two meetings to publicize their findings, and plans to represent North Richmond in future civic planning. The Committee on Traffic Lights for a busy intersection has completed its work, which is a symbol and a beacon of the effectiveness of voluntary citizen activity.

The future. Immediate plans include carrying out a clean-up campaign, and securing more park and recreation space and more volunteer leaders for youth-serving organizations.

The North Richmond Neighborhood Council can be the key that opens the door to a better community in which to live, more and better public facilities, an opportunity to be heard in governing bodies, and an opportunity to make better use of the social services offered—to give as well as to receive.

This particular experience is illustrative of the unique role of the Neighborhood Council as a way of extending voluntary activity and organization in social work.

As Norman Shaw [4] has expressed it:

Community Councils represent a signal development in the field of human relations. The discovery of this mechanism, through which people can work together for common causes, is as basic as the technological discoveries of the atom bomb. . . . Councils are the mechanism for improving neighborhood conditions in metropolitan areas and are most important because they are the means through which standards of neighborhood living can be raised. Councils mean that citizens are no longer alone in their efforts; they can speak and act jointly. Neighborhood people through their councils have renewed hopes in their efforts to maintain decent values for neighborhood living.

[4] Associate Editor, *The Cleveland Press,* in "Neighbors Unite for Better Communities."

2. Civic Cooperation in Miami

MRS. VLADIMIR E. VIRRICK

AND

MRS. FRANKLIN JOHNSON

Coconut Grove, one of the earliest settlements in South Florida, maintained its own municipal government for many years. Reluctantly, in 1928, it became part of the city of Miami, but it has never changed its character. The natural beauty of its subtropical growth along winding, narrow streets has attracted residents who prefer its quiet dignity. They are, for the most part, individuals of background, education, and quiet tastes; some retired, others artists, writers, and professional people.

There are actually two parts to Coconut Grove—one is "Colored Town," some fifty-odd blocks with over 6,000 inhabitants. These are Negroes, mostly employed in menial work and as domestics and gardeners. There are no professional people except a few teachers and ministers. The other is the white area known as "the Village," which covers an area several times as large as the Negro section with a much lower population density.

If the white citizens knew of the conditions under which the Negroes lived, it was only a subconscious awareness. The wooden shacks in Colored Town were surrounded by luxuriant foliage and shaded by huge banyan and mango trees. The old grandmothers rocked on the front porches and watched the children playing in the sun. At first glance, the scene was quaint and picturesque. No one ever looked behind the scenes. This was in 1948.

By chance, we had a look behind the scenes, and found, among other things, 482 outdoor toilets, with, in one case, 24 families using the same one; outdoor pumps, located only a few feet from these privies, the only source of water; eleven bars (as compared with two in the white section), which caused almost nightly brawls and knifings; unbelievably crowded living conditions. We met one of the Negro ministers who described conditions for his people as "living seven deep." We were dismayed and concerned.

We invited twenty-five people, Negro and white, to meet at our house and talk over what should be done. Present were ministers, architects, engineers, attorneys, city planners, an owner of Negro property, real estate people, and housewives. The meeting pointed to the need for four elemental changes of immediate urgency in this town, which was not at all the sleepy Negro community we always thought it to be. They were:

1. To eliminate outdoor toilets and improve sanitary conditions generally.
2. To rezone the area. The zoning was entirely commercial, whereas 86 per cent of the buildings were single family homes.
3. To make a comparative rent study and give it wide publicity, showing the great disparity between amounts paid by Negroes and whites for similar accommodations.
4. To conduct a survey, giving the complete housing inventory, the degree of substandardness, environmental deficiencies, etc.

We realized that this was not a job for the twenty-five of us; that we would need many workers plus the approval and moral support of the entire community so as to exert pressure on city officials.

This was the beginning of the Coconut Grove Citizens' Committee for Slum Clearance. The reason we feel our volunteer setup qualifies us to speak here is the fact that from the heterogeneous citizenry in both sides of Coconut Grove we were able to organize a highly effective, interracial, volunteer group which has not only survived the first year of enthusiasm, but has solidified into a permanent working committee. Through the years, we have several times won national recognition.

The following methods have proved effective, some of them in interesting large numbers of people when needed and others in expanding the smaller, permanent, volunteer group that has continued the work through the long pull.

Old-Fashioned Town Meeting

Our first bid for volunteers was to call an old-fashioned town meeting. We mimeographed notices headed "Penny for Your Thoughts," with a bright, shiny penny scotch-taped at the top. These were handed out by Boy and Girl Scouts at the three grocery stores and the bank over the week end. About 300 people attended the meeting; approximately one fourth of them were Negroes. The enthusiasm at this meeting gave evidence that the slum clearance movement was off to a good start.

At this meeting a card was given to each person to sign. On it was a place to indicate on which project he preferred to work. Everyone signed.

The next day, letters went out to those who attended the meeting and many more urging them to write to city officials, asking for Negro police for the Negro area and for action on sanitary conditions. The letters gave the names and addresses of the officials to whom letters should be sent, making it easier for people to comply. Hundreds did. Some sent telegrams. This method was used subsequently, proved very effective, and produced tremendous response. We learned that officials are impressed by a deluge of letters individually written. They are also impressed by large numbers of people attending hearings. As each new project loomed, we got in touch with the three large churches in the white area and were given whole-hearted support and help.

PUBLIC MEDIA

Before our first meeting, a request was made to the *Miami Herald* and the *Miami News* for coverage. Later we went to the owner of the *Herald,* not knowing that what we were asking was against newspaper policy. We requested that one reporter be assigned to all our work, and miraculously it was granted. The support of the newspapers was evident the day after the first meeting, with enthusiastic reports and editorial commendation of our work. We have been told that now our folder in the newspaper morgue is second in size only to that of the racketeers!

Radio and television support was forthcoming, in the form of interviews, panel discussions, and speeches. Often we requested time, but frequently we were invited to appear.

Our Speakers' Bureau also served to spread the word. We spoke before many organizations, often by invitation as well as at our request.

These media are used to assemble large groups to appear at hearings before city officials when our issues are being considered. Also, the publicity attendant upon each big project and accomplishment has brought more and more interested people into the work.

TELEPHONE COMMITTEE

The battery of phoners work faithfully and produce results. Every resident of Coconut Grove who has a telephone is called for our big projects.

BLOCK LEADERS

When it became necessary to convince the city commissioners that Coconut Grove, with almost 100 per cent solidarity, approved the rezoning plan in the Negro area, block leaders obtained signed slips from almost every resident in the Village, street by street, signifying their approval. Block leaders in the Negro area are now formed into a permanent standing committee called the Civic Council. Support for the new building that we built for the Day Nursery is solicited in the Negro area through this group;

it is used to stir up interest in periodic clean-up campaigns; it helps to protect home owners from unscrupulous repair contractors. The work of this council recently has proved very effective in getting Negroes to register and vote. It has successfully consummated many other projects.

INFORMATION AND EDUCATION COMMITTEE

This has been used entirely in the Negro area and has adopted such means as distributing typed notices to each of the thirteen Negro churches to be read at Sunday services and assigning speakers to appear at the churches. This committee spread the word among the people when the Loan Fund was established, informing them that the committee would lend money to help install bathrooms. One of the first jobs of this group was to educate the people in the use of the new bathrooms, in order to minimize plumbing repairs. Notices of meetings are also distributed by this committee.

NEWS SHEET

The news sheet, known as *Ink,* is published only before meetings or when there is a matter of importance on which people should be informed. It also points up where workers are needed and makes appeals of many kinds. As our organization must sustain interest by having project follow closely on project, *Ink* is especially valuable. Volunteers write, mimeograph, and mail out *Ink* to a list of all people who have ever worked with the Coconut Grove Citizens' Committee for Slum Clearance, plus officials and also individuals whose interest we should like to have.

DEFINITIVE POLICY

Because we are an interracial group with Negro and white members on the board and on every committee, we have always been alert to avoid the controversial issues this could entail. A thoroughly understood policy defines our purpose: to raise living standards in the Negro area; in other words, to rehabilitate the area.

Besides the methods we have enumerated under the above headings, there are less tangible factors that contribute largely in extending our staff of volunteers and sustaining their interest. Word-of-mouth is a very important factor in a small town such as Coconut Grove, where everyone knows everyone else.

The complete faith and trust that the Negroes repose in the leaders of the Citizens' Committee account for much of their cooperation and enthusiasm. Their gratitude for improved living conditions also influences their continued willingness to work.

It must be mentioned that success begets success. This organization has acquired the reputation of not taking "no" for an answer and people always like to get on the bandwagon. We are fortunate in having the support of many of Coconut Grove's most prominent citizens. This gives us (let's face it) snob appeal.

Our standing committees now include sanitation, health, service and welfare, juvenile delinquency, summer recreation program in the school, a day nursery, surveillance, adult education, and free legal help. All these are important factors in the rehabilitation of this area. We have cooperated with and worked through many of the social welfare agencies in Miami to our mutual advantage.

Our leaders are not trained in community organization but use common sense and adopt the methods that seem best at the time. Doubtless, we make mistakes along the way, but our rather impressive record of accomplishments seems to indicate that there is value in the methods used.

We passed the rather rigid scrutiny of the Treasury Department, making it possible for donations to our organization to be tax exempt. As chairman and coordinator of the Coconut Grove Citizens' Committee for Slum Clearance ever since the beginning, we are proud to say with impunity that we now stand as a proved, successful group. We hope that our ways and means may, in some measure, point the way to others with similar objectives and ideals.

5
The Deaf

1. Educating People About the Deaf

BYRON B. BURNES

The area of the deaf probably receives less organized assistance from welfare agencies than any other. The chief reason is that the deaf are self-supporting, independent citizens, in little need of assistance of the nature commonly rendered by welfare agencies. Yet, the deaf are in greater need of a special kind of help than any other group, for they are handicapped terrifically by the efforts of individuals and groups who would do them good but, because of their unfamiliarity with the true characteristics of deafness and the deaf, often do more harm than good. Voluntary activity, then, should be designed to effect adjustments in the efforts of the uninformed and the misinformed, to the extent that such efforts would fulfill their purpose of being helpful to the deaf.

The deaf are educated, substantial citizens. They are capable of holding their own in any industry in which the sense of hearing is not an absolute requisite. They own their own homes and drive their own automobiles. They pay taxes and vote. They rejected a recent movement to have an additional income tax exemption granted them because of their handicap. They are different from other people only in communicative skills, and it is for this reason that they have their own social activities, church affairs, and sports events, where they mingle and converse freely with one another in the sign language.

Here is where the misdirected efforts of social workers and others come to bear upon the lives of the deaf. They say the deaf should be taught to speak and to read the lips, in order to communicate with the general public; but the deaf know from long and tedious experience that only a small percentage of their number have the talent necessary to develop these skills to the high degree necessary to make them completely adequate as a means of communication. It frequently happens that parents of a deaf child are advised by welfare agencies or physicians to send the child to a special class in the public schools or to a private school for instruction in speech, and just as frequently it happens that the child is unable to develop speech skills. As a result of his being placed in an environment completely adverse to his interests and abilities, and as a result of his inability to communicate readily with those around him, he acquires a mental and emotional block that warps his personality for the rest of his life.

The deaf themselves, who have been through the mill, recommend to these parents that they send their child to a State school for the deaf, where he will receive an adequate education and training in a substantial trade, and where he will rapidly develop a means of communication, either by speech or by writing or by the sign language. He will be sent on to college if he has the ability for college work. He will grow into a happy citizen.

But parents do not often accept this advice. They prefer to listen to those who do not know the deaf, thinking they are experts because they are so free with advice. They do not realize that in spite of all their hopes and wishes their child will grow into an adult deaf person, rather than a hearing person like themselves. They do not see that they should bend their efforts toward making him a happy and successful deaf person, rather than a feeble imitation of a hearing person.

The greatest handicap suffered by the deaf is not their deafness, but the fact that the general public is not acquainted with them or aware of their capabilities. Too many of the "experts" on the deaf themselves are unacquainted with the deaf. They simply offer theories that the deaf themselves have tried time and time again and found wanting.

Time without number deaf persons have applied for work at which they were especially skilled because of training they have received in their schools, but they have been denied even so much as an interview because they lacked the ability to read lips. Propaganda from experts in oral training had led the employers to believe that a deaf person without lip-reading skill was mentally deficient.

On as many occasions deaf applicants have been turned away because they did not use a hearing aid. Propaganda from manufacturers and salesmen of hearing aids had led employers to believe that if the deaf are of normal mental capacity they can train their sense of hearing through amplification. The deaf—distinguished from the hard of hearing—cannot hear with or without amplification. They cannot be made to hear, or trained to hear.

What kind of welfare activity can be helpful to this class of citizens, who, because of a deficiency in communicative skills are considered "different," or "queer," or "defective"? The answer is organized, carefully planned activity that will acquaint the general public with the true facts about the deaf, aided by dissemination of publicity, talks before business organizations, women's clubs, and employer groups, and by radio and television programs.

Workers in employment offices, welfare agencies, rehabilitation offices, and all such public agencies, few of whom are experts on the deaf, should have access to informative material presenting the facts about the deaf. Courses of lectures on the deaf, by bona fide experts on their problems, should be made available to them. Physicians, ministers, school authorities, and others in touch with parents should be informed of the real needs of the deaf. Uninformed as most of them are now, they merely advise parents of a deaf child to subject him to a course in speech training, which in most cases does not provide the education he needs.

The volunteers should seek the opinions of the successful deaf, and of the organized deaf, who are well able to give expert advice and opinions. The deaf have their own organizations from which factual data may be obtained. The volunteers can help compile and disseminate further data and extensively broaden the channels of public information on the deaf. The National Association of the Deaf, 2495 Shattuck Avenue, Berkeley, California, is a center of authoritative information that is rarely consulted.

Information on the ability of the deaf in all phases of industry, with attestations from employers, should be compiled and made available on an extensive scale. Statistical material should be made available showing the safety record of the deaf as drivers of automobiles, their educational attainments, and their cultural and esthetic achievements. The deaf are able to compile this information but they need help in its distribution and dissemination. Volunteers who can help in this way are helping the deaf to help themselves.

This essay has been written by one who is deaf. It gives the views of the deaf, based on knowledge gained from actual experience as a deaf person among deaf persons, working for and with the deaf. It has been written in hope that it will serve to some extent to induce social welfare workers, voluntary and professional, to consider the opinions and counsel of the deaf themselves, and to work with them and assist them in the particular and unique lines in which they need assistance.

2. A Preschool Oral Training Center

MRS. HARRY R. SORENSEN

It shall be my purpose to illustrate the need and feasibility of creating a center for the oral training of young deaf children ranging in age from two years to legal school age in the San Francisco Bay area. Such a center is needed in many communities throughout the United States, but I shall limit myself to the San Francisco Bay area because of its familiarity to me.

I am in my eighth year of teaching deaf children. The first six years of my teaching career were spent at the Rhode Island School for the Deaf and the Lexington School. The philosophy of education of the deaf at both of these schools is to teach by the oral method of instruction entirely. For the past two years I have been teaching at the California School for the Deaf in Berkeley. Here the educational philosophy is to teach by the combined system of oral training and finger spelling.

Educators have been arguing the pros and cons of these two approaches to the education of the deaf for a good many years; it is not my purpose to continue the argument. Let me say that, at heart, I am an oralist. However, the experience of the past two years has showed me the reasonableness of the other philosophy. It has also pointed out a great need in the State of California to make the most of the educational opportunities offered the deaf child.

The laws under which many private and State schools for the deaf operate provide for oral training to children of preschool years. Such laws have been enacted during the past ten to fifteen years. They are the direct result of scientific research.

It is now an accepted fact that all children babble, deaf or hearing, from the tiny infant's coos to the actual "babbling stage" from a few months onward. The infant babbles just as long as it receives a kinesthetic response from hearing itself and from the action of babbling. A deaf child will normally lessen the amount of babbling at about eighteen months. Psychologists and otologists believe that if the deaf child can achieve a kinesthetic response through touch, rather than hearing, it can be taught to continue babbling. Clear, intelligible speech by a deaf child, therefore, is more easily learned if the child has been encouraged to continue babbling at this early age. The preschool program is specifically designed to provide the opportunity of directing the deaf child's babbling into effective speech patterns. Although this learning process seems only a game to the young deaf child, he soon becomes very much aware of lips and the movements of speech, which in turn help him to develop the skill of lip, or speech, reading early in life.

Where the State or private school does not, or cannot because of the law, provide a preschool program, a very grave speech problem exists. If the average deaf child ceases all constructive babbling ("constructive" in the sense of developing the muscles used in forming the elements of speech) by the time he is two and a half years old, and does not enter school until he has reached the legal age of five and a half, the control of muscles and tongue needed for the learning of the skill of speech has been dormant for more than two years. Thus, not only will it take the child more years on the lower primary and primary levels to relearn this control and the necessary attentiveness for lip reading, but the quality of the speech will undoubtedly be poorer because of the long period when he has not used his voice for a purpose. Furthermore, the naturalness of spontaneity will almost never be recovered.

Intelligence to some degree has a direct bearing on the efficiency with which a deaf child learns the skills of speech and lip reading. There is no guarantee, therefore, that the child offered the benefits of training during the preschool years will be assured either intelligible speech or the art of lip reading. However, I have observed a noticeable degree of difference in the speech of children I have taught who have had the advantage of preschool training, and the speech of the children I have taught these past two years in Berkeley.

The training and experience of the staffs of the three schools where I have taught are definitely comparable. The facilities at all three schools are the best and most modern that science and research have developed. The children are from equally representative American homes. There are those who would claim that the total oral environment, both in school and out, accounts for this better quality of intelligible speech. Although this may be a factor, let us look at the program set up by the State of California at its school in Berkeley.

When the children come to the school at five and a half years, all training through both the lower primary years is by the oral method exclusively. These children see older deaf children using finger spelling as a means of communication during the out-of-school hours. Yet, not being taught the "alphabet-of-the-fingers," they use voice and natural gesture to communicate. Through the three primary years oral instruction is vigorously continued. Yet the speech of my intermediate fourth graders is noticeably less intelligible than the speech of the orally trained deaf children of comparable intelligence and background who have experienced speech training since preschool years. Therefore, it seems most logical for the State to provide speech training centers for the preschool deaf child. Yet it is at this very point that State law interferes, rather than aids, the situation.

California schools for the deaf, as all State schools, are residential schools. It would be financially beyond reason to the taxpayer to have them otherwise. For, as in California, two such schools can adequately care for the needs of all the deaf children within the State who do not choose to attend local, public day classes. These State-supported centers are maintained for the benefit of all, and must constantly be proving their worth to the citizens of the State.

Let us look at the parental views for a moment. A child is born, and much happiness, planning, and hopes are experienced by the parents for their child. Usually when the child is between fifteen months and two years the parents begin to suspect deafness—many much earlier. Being average parents, usually with no knowledge of deafness, they take this child from one doctor to another, hoping to find a cure. Eventually they accept the fact of deafness. Many social welfare organizations, both public and private, but most especially The Alexander Graham Bell Association in Washington, D.C., provide the parents with valuable information concerning the facts of deafness, the psychology of the deaf, and educational opportunities within the particular community. The parents themselves go through a most traumatic adjustment—guilt, rejection, defeat are common attitudes. These attitudes the parent does his utmost to hide, frequently resulting in overprotection of the child. It will be difficult enough to send the child away from home to a residential school when it is five and a half; the thought of doing so during its preschool years is unbearable.

As laws that govern the State schools should and do reflect the will of the people, it is not difficult to understand why the law in most States, as in California, specifically states that no child may enter a residential school until it is five and a half years of age. It is adults who make the law. Yet intelligent adults would conceivably alter a law that is satisfactory to themselves, were they convinced the best welfare of the deaf children of the State was to be improved by changing the law. We must look at the child itself, therefore, to determine if the law is just.

Psychologists have provided much concrete evidence to back up their stand that a young child needs the security of a loving home during its earliest years if emotional stability and maturity is to be achieved. The aim of education is to build well-rounded, well-adjusted citizens. To send the deaf child to a residential school at eighteen months or two years may facilitate the development of speech skills, but this is strongly counterbalanced by the very questionable psychological effects on the child, and the true aim of education.

At first, the obvious solution would appear to be the setting up of day school centers throughout the State. Such centers would, of necessity, be numerous; for a two-year-old child would gain little of value in training after traveling many miles to and from the center each day. Our State is very large. Should such a program be worked out on a geographical basis, literally hundreds of such centers would need to be maintained, at a cost far beyond justification.

The State school at Berkeley maintained a day school, preschool program for five years. Educators at the school recognized the value of the training. Yet, in the final analysis, the program had to be stopped. The school, being supported by the State, was not offering equal opportunity to all, as only those children who lived within reasonable distance could participate. Such discrimination was unjust in the eyes of the law. Much as the educators involved recognized the need for such a program, it was equally clear that continuation of the program would be in direct opposition to the law, and thus to the will of the people by whom the school is maintained.

For a time it was hoped that local city or county governments could meet the need, but, again, the cost proved prohibitive. The cost of such a program must be weighed in relation to the number of children benefited, and in many communities this could mean only one or two children at most. Yet the need remains.

Many of my fellow colleagues feel as I do: that volunteer social welfare could provide some solution in highly populated areas by founding a volunteer oral preschool training center for the deaf. More specifically I should like to consider the founding of such a center in the San Francisco Bay area.

With one of the State schools located in Berkeley, many qualified teachers would be available to give assistance to such a program, for it is they who are, perhaps, the best judges of the real value of such a program. Then, too, each year the school loses a few of its teachers to the demands of the teachers' own families. These women are keenly aware of the true value several hours of their time each week could be in aiding the deaf child. Regularly employed teachers could lead training classes for volunteers lacking formal training, and most especially for the mothers of the deaf children themselves. These, in turn, could train others. The State school could most certainly give actual demonstrations occasionally to clarify the ultimate objectives of a preschool program.

And, again, such cooperation would benefit the school. Parents who are aware of the everyday life of our State schools no longer think with dread of putting their child in an "institution." Such understanding on the parents' part helps the child to adjust more easily to separation when the time comes.

The child benefits in psychological as well as educational ways. Not only is the critical babbling stage continued and encouraged so that the muscles needed for intelligible speech are used and strengthened, but the child is provided the group experience of a normal nursery program. He learns how to get along with his peers, and is constantly given the opportunity to read the lips of many people, not just his own family. When he is ready to enter the formal school situation he is socially prepared, and has the added benefit of a means of communication, with the realization that he can make his wants and thoughts known.

One such center obviously would not meet the needs within the State. Yet, just as the privately maintained John Tracy Clinic in Los Angeles is offering help to many deaf children and their parents, so such a center in the San Francisco Bay area would be a step in the right direction. Other communities, where the number of deaf children would deem it worthy, might be encouraged to follow the example. Administrators at the State school are of the opinion that State funds might be secured to provide a residence to house mothers and their children who live beyond reasonable commuting distance. Such mothers might remain in the area for a three-month period of training, being then equipped to return to their homes and continue the necessary speech training, allowing other mothers from outlying districts a similar opportunity. Not only is the need for such a center acute, but the San Francisco Bay area offers the best location for immediate action because of its abundance of trained personnel able and willing to give voluntary assistance and guidance.

Volunteer welfare *can* aid the education of the deaf, and do much toward helping the parents of a deaf child accept the handicap, recognize their own attitudes, and encourage them to be useful and able, as well as loving, parents. Most important, the avenue of oral communication will be strengthened, allowing the deaf child to secure his place in this, our hearing world.

NOTES

Preschool centers for deaf children and their parents have been established in many cities throughout the United States. The following is a partial list of such centers:

National Society for Crippled Children and Adults, Inc.
  Washington, D.C.
  Indianapolis, Indiana
  Detroit, Michigan
  Columbus, Ohio
  Harrisburg, Pennsylvania
  Columbia, South Carolina
  Dallas, Texas
  Roanoke, Virginia
  Charleston, South Carolina
Public residential schools
  Little Rock, Arkansas
  West Hartford, Connecticut
  Flint, Michigan
  New York, New York
  Pittsburgh, Pennsylvania
Public day classes
  Los Angeles, California
  Detroit, Michigan
  New York, New York
  Denver, Colorado
  Chicago, Illinois
  Milwaukee, Wisconsin
Private and denominational schools
  The John Tracy Clinic, Los Angeles, California
  Atlanta Jr. League Center, Atlanta, Georgia
  University of Kansas Medical Center, Lawrence, Kansas
  Sarah Fuller Foundation, Roxbury, Massachusetts
  Central Institute for the Deaf, St. Louis, Missouri
  DePaul Institute, Pittsburgh, Pennsylvania
  Houston School, Houston, Texas
  Seattle Hearing & Speech Center, Seattle, Washington
  Memphis Speech & Hearing Center, Memphis, Tennessee

6
The Crippled

1. Employing the "Unemployable"

MRS. EARL W. KIBBY

As an employee of a Public Welfare Department for twenty-two years, I feel competent to comment on this subject. At the beginning it seems to me that the definition of a "qualified" volunteer needs clarification. Many willing workers sacrifice much time and effort on all sorts of projects that are manned by no professional staff, or are inadequately manned. Their contribution should not be minimized; but the possibility of the harm of personal inadequacy to those served without trained and competent supervision must not be ignored even in view of the volunteer nature of the service rendered. This caution needs to be increasingly observed in the face of rising costs and the complexity inherent in the cooperation and interaction of an increasing number of agencies. The duplication and overlapping of effort even now apparent defeats the successful operation of the agencies involved, expends energy inefficiently, and has been morally harmful to the recipient of the assistance. On the other hand untold good has been done by carefully conceived, coordinated, and operated volunteer services both by individuals and agencies.

Perhaps one of the most effective volunteer organizations, in my experience, is one that serves in an area of unmet need in our community. For a long time there has been an increasing need for service to the physically (and mentally) handicapped who are considered, generally, permanently unemployable, and are ineligible for rehabilitation services; an area, therefore, where any progress must be assessed more in terms of social adjustment than in terms of financial independence.

Through the doors of any public welfare department pass all sorts of individuals. Until recent years effort at help has been in the areas of elementary needs: food, shelter, clothing, and medical care. The morale and morals factor has been largely beyond the scope of the agency to handle —especially among the mentally inadequate and the physically unemployable. In time perhaps professional psychiatric social workers, family counselors, and other qualified personnel will be added to existing overloaded department staffs. In the meantime the need, if it is to be met, must be met by volunteer workers.

Recently it has been increasingly noted that the psychological problem often contributes greatly to the unemployability of individuals in the above-mentioned categories. So it is that when a volunteer agency was established to meet this specific need it was viewed with not only some skepticism, but also considerable hope for success. After several years of unspectacular service which indicated a continuing concern in the face of financial and other problems—and a continuing success with individuals who participated in the program offered—it became more or less a habit to refer our most difficult cases to it. Of the physically and mentally handicapped, the discouraged, depressed, and the socially maladjusted (the "permanently unemployable"), approximately twelve have been placed in employment of one kind or another over a two-year period.

In the program of which I speak, a group of nonprofessional, untrained volunteers meet with an average of sixteen or more "handicapped" people one or two days a week in a converted three-car garage. They have worked with as few as six persons and as many as twenty-eight. They work closely with, receive, and appreciate the help and guidance of professional agency consultants. They are financed by volunteer contributions and the earned financial contribution of the members themselves.

No pretense is made that the leaders of the group have more than scratched the surface, but it is increasingly obvious that it is a job that almost any dedicated volunteer group can do. In close cooperation with existing agencies it is doing a job that at present can be, and is being, handled in no other way. No financial obligation is undertaken by any public agency, community chest, or individual participant. It is believed that as many as fifty persons could be served for a year for approximately $1,000 or $1,500.

The person who organized the project has been active in the past in social and recreation work, and has an extensive knowledge of craftwork and some business experience. These are all necessary qualifications for the present operation, although they need not be packaged in one individual. Willing volunteers share the responsibility of leadership in the specific department and are drawn from the ranks of housewives, the retired, the professions, and so on. As initiative and ability are developed among the handicapped themselves they move to positions of leadership and, when possible, to regular employment.

The appeal of the program became evident when several of the group were invited to appear on a half-hour TV presentation, in which they became actors and where they unconsciously demonstrated the high morale that is a feature of the group association. The program director for the studio expressed considerable enthusiasm for the project and suggested that a larger viewing audience was certainly indicated.

Referrals are made to the project by the Visiting Nurse Association, the Red Cross, the Cerebral Palsy Association, our welfare department, doctors, and others. Where transportation is needed the Red Cross supplies it.

Individuals who join the group are trained in the type of craftwork best suited to them or contingent on their limitation, physical or mental. A project and quality control committee continually advises on projects and evaluates the salability of articles made. In some cases it has secured wholesale orders from local shops. It is felt that considerable opportunity for expanded production exists in this way. Merchandise made is not always salable but where imagination and ability combine in the making of a project all such products have been sold. Instruction is never static and ranges through many crafts including sewing, ceramics, metal- and woodwork, enameling, weaving, basketry, and so on.

The goal has never been the pretentious one of "rehabilitation," although this seems to have been accomplished in some cases. Social adjustment is the avowed aim—and although this has been impossible in some cases— the success of the "therapy" in general is becoming more and more widely recognized.

The members produce hope, social acceptance, better morale, and other features for themselves in addition to the material items they finish. There is keen anticipation before the annual bazaar sponsored by the Junior Chamber of Commerce Auxiliary. Birthday and holiday observations are appreciated. A Christmas tag project brought in over 500,000 cards from as far away as 1,500 miles. Volunteers from youth organizations sell the finished tags which will one day make the program completely self-supporting— which is what the workers themselves want.

Each year new members are added; some for only a short time. Very few withdraw despite the many limitations of the program. Many move to outside jobs—some for the first time in their lives. The whole program has caught the imagination and enthusiasm of all concerned. The workers themselves have named the program "Opportunities Craftshop."

Here then is the story of the development of a voluntary activity and organization in social welfare. It is built on a firm pyramid of volunteer help with the mortar of professional advice and agency participation throughout the community. The apex of the pyramid is the recognition of the need and the acceptance of the responsibility by one individual. A religious organization volunteers the use of a vacant building; transportation is offered, at first by individuals and later by the Red Cross; volunteer leaders come forward; handicapped persons hear of the offer of help and ask for admittance to the group; referrals are "volunteered" by agencies and doctors; there is the voluntary contribution of funds; individuals volunteer their services as board members; a service group volunteers to run an Annual Sale for the Handicapped; a registered occupational therapist volunteers services; medical and nursing help and advice is offered; youth organizations and individuals volunteer to help with the major tag project; there is volunteer sales help for wholesale contacts—and project counseling; there is a voluntary contribution of tag project materials by over five hundred persons in at least twelve states. And beyond all this are the churches, standard services of organized agencies, counseling services, medical and psychiatric help, to assist in any way possible.

Here is a project with tremendous possibilities—a project that can be successful as a volunteer organization—a project that has proved itself after five years of continuing endeavor and successful effort.

2. A Residence for Crippled Adults

WALTER HALL (pseudonym)

The response by social agencies to the appeals in behalf of the crippled during the past decade has been very generous. Numerous facilities have been established to meet the complex needs of people with orthopedic handicaps. There are at present agencies to cope with the emotional, mental, physical, and social demands of the crippled. By contrast, in spite of many projects, there is a serious lack of an urgently needed facility, namely, a local resident home for the severely crippled young adult.

The proposed project is intended for the young person who is so severely physically involved that he has not successfully responded to the efforts of existing social agencies organized for the solution of many facets of his problems. This crippled young adult is one who has been exposed to various medical programs, with some noticeable improvement, but without achieving an appreciable degree of physical independence. Educationally, he has a diploma to attest to the fact that he has completed four years of high school.

Vocationally, the agencies have not been able to help the crippled adult acquire some economic skill or ability. Socially, this severely handicapped person is completely dependent upon the family's social circle, which he himself unavoidably limits, and in which he usually assumes a position on its periphery. All these factors have an inevitable unfavorable impact on the emotional structure of this adult. All in all he is sentenced to a life of dependency, frustration, and boredom, and at times suicidal tendencies.

In the San Fernando Valley, a rapidly growing community within the city of Los Angeles, there is a considerable number of such young people. Perhaps a composite picture of the experiences of these people may help one acquire insight into their problem so as to weigh the feasibility of the proposed project.

The first year of the discovery of the crippled condition of the child is a very painful one. Since no person is ever prepared to become a parent of a crippled child, there are many visits to various physicians or clinics, for an encouraging diagnosis and prognosis. This is very time-consuming and expensive, and is complicated with various feelings of guilt.

Private agencies have established prenursery schools where the crippled child may attend starting at one and a half and continuing to three years of age. Here there are socialization, various therapies, and parent participation.

At age three the child is eligible for public education in the school for crippled and delicate children. Although educational opportunities through college are available, most of the young people terminate their studies at the end of high school because there are no special facilities beyond this level. Up to this point they are eligible, through community organizations, for various specialized activities—recreational, social, vocational guidance. However, because of the severity of the physical handicap they are limited in the amount they can participate in these programs, and upon graduating from high school, they suddenly find themselves without any regular opportunities for associating with their peers in school.

On reaching adolescence additional problems present themselves. Unresolved sexual drives incite desire for independence with intense feelings of frustration. When the crippled person reaches adulthood the cumulative impact on the family relationship reaches subtle and intense stages of unhappiness. The parents are desperate because there is no existing facility to meet the needs of these physically handicapped adults.

There is therefore a critical need for the extension of some existing private agency to provide a local resident home for these severely crippled young adults. The agency should have had some experience dealing with the problem of the crippled. The importance of its being local is that thus it affords the opportunity for part-time resident care, and also makes possible week-end and holiday visiting by the physically handicapped person. Then, too, the proximity to the home reduces the implication of institutionalization. Since the severity of the handicap makes it most difficult to determine and develop the full potential of the crippled adult, the resident home would afford him more testing and training time.

Personnel Recommended

1. A professional rehabilitation counselor who would be able to observe, test, and procure various industrial projects for the crippled, who would be paid for their work.

2. A shop instructor who would assist in the workshop, functioning as a foreman, and would require that each crippled adult comply with the standards (to the best of his ability) that would ordinarily be required at a business establishment.

3. There should be a program for the improvement of personal appearance and perhaps a part-time counselor should be employed for this purpose.

4. A speech therapist is of major importance because the lack of communication is one of the crippled adults' greatest deficiencies. The inability to express needs and feelings is perhaps the most frustrating to the physically handicapped person; for those who perhaps may never have any speech, some other form of communication should be developed.

5. A physical therapist and occupational therapist who would function under the direction of a physician.

6. A recreation director aware of the social needs of the crippled is a very important asset.

7. Attendants to meet the personal needs of the crippled, who would work in close cooperation with the therapist so as to constantly instill a feeling of independence.

8. There should be a person who would direct the entire operation of the resident home. In addition to operating the home, he would have the important responsibility of interpreting the crippled to the community.

One of the great problems of the crippled adult is the deep sense of being unable to socialize sufficiently with other people. To have the crippled congregate in one room with at most a limited amount of communication, just staring at one another, is very unsatisfactory; therefore, physically normal people should be persuaded to associate with the handicapped adults. Perhaps they may be invited there as junior counselors. This may be a method for interesting and recruiting additional people into the field of the education of the physically handicapped. This may be the proper time to ask why many young crippled adults find themselves in a predicament where it is necessary to provide the type of activity described above, when many of the physically handicapped have been well trained for a productive life; and one may also ask why there is a lack of opportunity for the physically handicapped, when there is a desperate need for trained manpower. An analysis of the reasons for this situation may produce some interesting results.

As stated earlier, many appeals in behalf of the physically handicapped have been answered generously and bountifully. Yet, it is contended, that this perhaps may work to the disadvantage of the crippled, for the following reason. Usually the appeals are made on a strong emotional basis by emphasizing the inability and the helplessness of the crippled. It is an accepted axiom that the more tragic and the more pitiful the recipient of the charity is, the more generous will be the response. It is true that this has resulted in large gifts of money for the crippled, so that many projects could be carried out.

However, let us look into the real effect this has had upon the degree of acceptance of the physically handicapped by the community that has been so generous in its giving. Almost any month there is a drive for persons with some type of physical handicap. Therefore, we are constantly reminding the community how helpless the crippled child is. This can have but one result, namely, that the cripple is one to be pitied but is not eligible for employment. The greater amount the businessman gives because of an emotional appeal, the less likely he is to employ the severely physically handicapped person. It therefore is of prime importance that in the appeals made by social agencies to the community, and particularly to businessmen, the emotional element be reduced or eliminated as much as possible. Appeals should be made to the community to demonstrate the potential of the physically handicapped. It should also be pointed out what research has substantiated, that the crippled afford the employer a source of supply with the least amount of turnover.

The advantages of this type of resident home for the crippled would accrue not only to the crippled adult but also to his family. It would relieve them of great emotional, social, and physical strain. It would release the parents first of all of their fear of what would happen to their child in the event of their being unable to provide or take care of him. It would release them to make contributions to the community themselves by being enabled to indulge in community activity, and indeed, to assume greater economic responsibility in the community. The young crippled adult would be given the security of a greater degree of independence, the feeling of contributing to society, a sense of belonging. He would gain, in essence, the feeling of a God-created man.

The project outlined has a successful precedent in another part of the state. However, there are some important differences. The proposed project only accepts adults from the local area. The advantage of this has already been discussed. The other difference is that those younger than adolescents are accepted in the existing resident home. This has been eliminated in this proposal to ensure that the specific needs of the young adult are not compromised.

The writer has been professionally serving the exceptional child during the past nineteen years, as teacher, counselor, and administrator. The proposed project emerged after consulting with parents and crippled adults, supplemented by professional participation in the crippled program in this geographical area for the past nine years.

3. A Proposed Merger of Groups Serving Handicapped Children

ALFRED H. KATZ

One of the most significant features of the health and welfare scene since World War II has been the rapid growth of organizations of parents of children handicapped or suffering from some specific disease. At least twenty separate national organizations covering a wide range of physical and mental disabilities have been organized, primarily at the initiative of parents, over the past decade. Many of these now prominent national organizations originated as small local groups of parents who banded together to accomplish some specific and limited purpose.

Among the groups are those that help in such comparatively widespread disabling conditions as mental retardation, cerebral palsy, and epilepsy. On the other hand, many of the groups are concerned with rarer and less-known ailments—muscular dystrophy, nephrosis, cystic fibrosis, myasthenia gravis, hemophilia, leukemia, and others. The speed with which new groups are created, their rapid growth, and the rapid changes they undergo, all make it impractical to attempt any comprehensive listing or account of them. No directories, and few guide lines to these groups exist; they have not been widely studied; and to many professionals and agencies they are still a terra incognita.

It is no exaggeration, however, to indicate that most of the groups have made significant contributions in the brief period of their existence. Programs of patient care bringing relief of suffering, and rehabilitation for the handicapped, the crippled, and the disabled, have been created. Fundamental medical research has been directly supported and indirectly stimulated. The attention of the medical profession and ancillary disciplines has been directed to problems hitherto overlooked. The general public has been educated and awakened to the existence of illnesses and handicaps that gravely impair the happiness and adjustment of those afflicted by them. In some cases legislation has been sponsored that has helped to bring about governmental action, especially in the field of fundamental medical research into these problems.

What is especially striking about the self-organized parent groups is that they are citizen movements. Initiated and built by parents, lacking in their early stages the direct assistance and guidance of professionals, the groups represent the application of a creative democratic and voluntaristic initiative that bears witness to the creative potentials of American social institutions. The social achievement of the groups, then, must be assessed as a large one, despite much unevenness in their functioning and many problems in their inner and external relationships.

Special Characteristics

Common to all the parent-organized groups are certain distinctive characteristics which serve to mark them off from other types of voluntary social and health agencies.

1. All have originated through the activities of parents who sought to bring about a better physical, social, psychological, or other adjustment for their children, and to work for greater medical attention to the particular condition or disease.

2. All arose primarily on parent initiative, and reflected the parents' conviction that insufficient assistance was available to them from doctors, hospitals, social agencies, and other existing professional resources.

3. All the groups have developed programs that include direct and indirect service to patients, public and professional education, and the stimulation of research.

4. All the groups are membership bodies and elicit the active participation of parent volunteers. In distinction to most voluntary social welfare and health agencies, the recipients of the services of these groups take part in their management and are represented on their policy-making bodies.

5. All the groups have entered into extensive relations with voluntary and public professional agencies, services, and personnel.

6. Most important of all, all the groups appeal to the general public for support of their activities.

A Proposal to Merge the Groups

Out of these distinguishing characteristics of the self-organized groups arise both the need and the possibility for realizing a proposal that the writer believes would significantly extend voluntary action in social welfare. In brief, the current programs of the self-organized parent groups would be much more effective if the groups could *combine their forces into an over-all health agency that would serve the needs of various kinds of handicapped children, and that would continue to enlist the enthusiastic support, motivation, and participation that the parents are now giving to individual groups.* Such a merging of forces would make for an enormous saving of public funds, of voluntary and professional manpower. It would also reduce one of the chronic and most valid sources of the public's irritation with the voluntary agencies—namely, the incessant multiplicity of financial appeals by innumerable agencies that, justifiably or not, give the public the impression of duplicated efforts and overlapping fields of work.

The proposal made herein has manifold psychological and practical advantages.

In the first place, the self-organized parent groups are citizen movements or "causes" that embody a great dynamism for those who participate in them. Some of the groups have made remarkable progress in a very short time in developing their programs, their organization, their public acceptance, and their level of fund raising. The essential source of this dynamism has been the drive and conviction of the parents. Such drive, conviction, and participation are greater in the parent groups than in many other voluntary agencies that are not based on such direct personal experience and involvement.

From the findings of a detailed study,[1] as well as from association with these groups in a professional capacity, I believe that members of such parent groups share in a distinctive psychology. Parents in the groups identify with one another, both because their children are afflicted by a common problem, and from a sense of common accomplishment to which the existence of the organization itself bears witness. This identification with other parents similarly affected gives the parent groups an aspect of the self-help or mutual aid motivation that has been important in social welfare organization.

Such feelings also provide the basis and possibility for a large merged organization. Identification with other parents in one's own group can be extended to parents in different fields of handicap who, also through their own efforts, have brought about similar organizational accomplishments. Despite the respective problems, interests, and characteristics of the separate groups that have grown up in this field, their likenesses and their common interests are greater than the things that divide them. Their

[1] "An Investigation of Self-Organized Parents Groups in Fields of Physical and Mental Handicap," D.S.W. Dissertation, 1956, New York School of Social Work Library.

long-range mutuality of interest seems to provide an excellent grounding for common effort and organizational amalgamation.

What would such a merged movement accomplish? In the first place, the development of programs, now markedly disparate and often duplicating, could be planned on a coordinated basis. Such services as outpatient clinics, casework and psychological guidance, recreation, camping and special education, vocational training and placement, are similar for all the handicapped conditions under discussion. Through the stimulation of a unified national agency, all these services might therefore be developed on a unified basis in local communities, in the same manner that existing rehabilitation agencies serve disabling conditions embodying a wide spectrum of causation. Such a unified approach would yield great benefits in the care and understanding of these patients by the professional resources of the community. The economies inherent in the approach do not need emphasis.

A unified national and local approach would be similarly beneficial to the public authorities concerned in making arrangements for the various groups of the handicapped in such fields as special education, vocational guidance, training and placement, and research. Nor should one overlook the benefits of such an arrangement to the training of the various medical specialists and the related disciplines active in the care of these crippling conditions—physical and occupational therapists, nurses, psychologists, among others.

The second major accomplishment of a merged agency would be that of bringing about a centralization and unification of fund raising for the groups on both a national and a local level. Such a coordination would alleviate a situation recently described by a prominent professional: "The public is becoming heartily sick of these recurring drives—telethons, mothers' marches, postmen's walks—and all the other products of the fertile brains of fund-raisers and advertising geniuses. Unless the agencies do something about this situation themselves, the public will begin a form of negative action of its own." (P. Reed, quoted in *The New York Times,* March 24, 1954.)

The coordination that the parent groups might bring about would be a provocative example for other voluntary agencies of what can be accomplished along similar lines. Thus, some voluntary health agencies that do not have parent membership, some presently competing organizations in such fields as mental health, juvenile delinquency, and other important social welfare problems, might be led through this example to explore a similar course of action. A movement toward merger, once established, could have wide repercussions in the voluntary agency field.

Is the proposal for merger of parent groups in the field of handicap a practical one?

There are significant precedents, which indicate that organizations with differing areas of interest, but having a similar philosophy and aims, can combine effectively. The unified health agency in Rochester, New York, is one example of such an effective local combination. This agency serves needs in the fields of tuberculosis, cardiac disease, cancer, and other health problems. The local groups previously active in these fields merged their interests and appeals under the roof of a single organization, which now plans programs for all and retains, on a divisional basis, the active volunteer support each group had separately commanded. As might be expected, greater public support has been given to the united agency than accrued previously to the individual causes.

This demonstration of successful local action could be paralleled nationally among the parent groups. The wide acceptance of the principle of federated financing in local communities, and its growing acceptance nationally, provides basis for such a belief. There is reason to believe, moreover, that the proposal would be welcomed by many of the parent groups. Fund raising having become more difficult, the competition for public attention and support keener, the difficulties of supporting a successful program have increased, and many of the smaller groups would welcome affiliation with a large, stable body.

What is needed to effectuate this proposal is a genuinely creative initiative, either on the part of one or more of the parent groups, or of a disinterested public-minded body or group of leaders. The development and circulation among the groups of a prospectus giving details of the proposal, and soliciting comments, would seem to be the necessary first step in a train of actions that accomplish a significant advance in voluntary social welfare organization.

Such a voluntary self-regulation and coordination, brought about on the initiative of and with the consent of the groups themselves, would be a profound demonstration of the validity and strength of America's great principles of voluntary action in social welfare organization and planning. These principles, and their relation to the American way of life, have been well stated by Marts:

> In many directions, the traditional American creed supports—and in turn is supported by—the spirit of *voluntary* philanthropy. This spontaneous uncoerced banding together of free men to further their mutual well-being is close to the heart of the American Way.[2]

[2] Armand C. Marts, "Philanthropy's Role in Civilization," *Harper's,* 1953, p. 196.

7
The Blind

1. A Community Approach to the Problems of Blindness

MILTON A. JAHODA

During the five and one-half years in which a voluntary agency for the blind has been in existence in our community a new and almost revolutionary approach has been developed in order to extend the broadest possible program of services on a voluntary basis to the blind population of the community.

In the course of setting up a program of services to meet the needs of the blind, careful consideration revealed that many of the "primary" services that older agencies often relied upon were not always the most effective means of helping blind people. For example, it was suggested by those more zealous than discerning that a building be erected to serve as a workshop where blind people could learn to make brooms, that a building be secured and used as a social meeting place or "clubhouse" for blind people, and finally that a building be erected for the sole purpose of educating blind children. None of these objectives is necessarily bad. Each of them would represent a *minimum* initial outlay of at least $70,000, and it was highly questionable even at the beginning of the agency's experience that these were the things most urgently needed. The entire budget of the agency was less than $20,000 for the first two years combined.

It was quickly apparent that such expensive ways of trying to help blind people were financially unrealistic, and it was not at all certain that they would be the things that would do the most to promote the welfare of the blind.

Careful analysis of the entire community as well as the blind population resulted in a threefold approach that extended voluntary activity and organization by well-planned, carefully coordinated services that are meaningful to the blind people in this community at all age levels.

The three areas in which the agency for the blind has directed and unified its activity are:

1. Board action
2. "Return to normalcy" policy in direct services to blind people
3. Expanded use of existing community resources

Fortunately, the board of directors of the agency was a true cross section of the community, with representatives from many civic organizations such as the Junior League, Lions Club, and Delta Gamma sorority, as well as representatives from management and labor, from the medical society, and so on. These helped to finance the first demonstration year prior to inclusion in the Community Chest. It is of course axiomatic in voluntary social welfare that the board of directors be a "working board," well informed of the purpose and activities of the agency. Such boards in themselves are effective means of extending voluntary activity and organization in social welfare, but this is not a new concept. What is new is the way the working board of this agency allied itself with the principles and purposes of the agency and went into the community with a sincere desire to develop increased understanding of blind people. As the board members talked to other groups about the problems of blindness, they came to a personal conviction and recognition that blind people are individuals; that many of the problems of blind people are little different from the problems of sighted people; and that more than anything else blind people want an opportunity to live as normal a life as possible and to be treated on an equal basis with sighted people. The pity and sorrow the board members had for the plight of the blind gave way to respect. And as the board learned about blindness and blind people, it was inspired to communicate this different concept to the community. Much of the success of the agency's program of services has been due to the community's greater willingness to accept blind people individually on their own merits rather than to reject them as a group because of fear and ignorance.

The "return to normalcy" policy in direct services to clients may be literally interpreted as a means of helping the blind person become as independent as possible. For many blind people, especially those blind for only a short while, help in learning, or rather relearning, the many and varied activities of daily living that seem so routine to sighted people, was like presenting a beautiful Christmas tree laden with many gifts to a child. To some blind people, this help consisted of only a few things, perhaps showing how to devise a system of keeping shoes and socks in pairs and neckties with the matching suits; to others the service extended to teaching again the intricate process of eating, of buttering bread and cutting meat, and judging the amount and size of the food on the fork. It might include teaching how to differentiate among coins and a workable system of folding bills of the same denomination. It might involve instruction about dialing a telephone, or showing blind women how to apply cosmetics, and to braille canned goods so that when string beans were desired string beans could be located without the risk of opening applesauce or stewed prunes by mistake. The use of timers, and instruction in safety techniques in the kitchen, are emphasized with blind housewives. These are but a few of the direct services designed to help blind people "return to normal," to manage their own lives as independently as possible.

A major service in this "operation independence" is that known as Cane Travel and Physical Orientation. Blind people are taught to get about by themselves with a minimum of fear and a maximum of safety with the use of a new type of long aluminum cane. The significance of blind people's learning to get about independently without sighted assistance can hardly be overestimated. Prior to cane travel training one blind man had as his greatest sense of loss since becoming blind his inability to get by himself to the barbershop without having to use his wife or teen-age daughter as a guide. Travel training made it possible for him to learn to become independent of his family for the first time in years, as he learned to get about the entire community by himself unaided. A blind housewife who had been confined to her home received travel training which resulted in her being placed in remunerative and satisfying employment in the X-ray development room at a local hospital.

Guide dogs are used satisfactorily by many blind people, and have performed exemplary service in helping people understand that blind people can move about in the sighted world, but there are many instances when for one reason or another a guide dog is not possible or practical. Safe, independent foot travel includes skill in boarding buses, entering taxis, handling revolving doors, escalators, steps, crossing streets, and many other situations.

In addition to the public relations activity of the board of directors and the activities of daily living, travel training, and physical orientation services to blind people, this agency for the blind has experimented with and developed a greater use of existing community resources. Agencies serving blind people sometimes evidence a strong paternalistic attitude, which is manifest in a fierce, protective relationship to the blind, and which excludes the possibility of any other source of help. Voluntary agencies for the blind, particularly those long established (and well entrenched) sometimes give the impression that they can be—and are—all things to all blind people. Such agencies are like islands, around which the currents of life swish and whisper, but never reach. The blind people are encouraged to let the agency be their refuge, and never have an opportunity to venture beyond the sheltering lee.

Our agency for the blind was, in the beginning, limited by finances from developing a large and expensive plant that would be all things to all blind people. It had, however, a strong and clearly defined belief that voluntary services to blind people are a community responsibility, implemented to be sure by the agency; but still the trust is the community's. Accordingly, the entire community was evaluated in terms of what needs of blind people could be served by already existing resources. Rather than expending thousands of dollars to build a recreation center, the agency for the blind resolved to work with the recreation specialists in the community to determine if the recreation needs of the blind were so different from those of the sighted as to require new and separate facilities.

It was quickly apparent that blind people are not so unusual in their recreational interests. A little time spent in interpretation of the problems of blindness, and the normalcy and individuality of blind people, quickly brought rich rewards to the blind, and at no additional expense to the community. A blind girl enjoyed the organized activities provided by the City Park Board at a park near her home. A teen-aged boy learned—and taught—a great deal about the give and take fellowship of youth while attending the YMCA camp, and incidentally became a favorite camper with an unbounded enthusiasm for nature study. Several young blind adults wanted to learn to swim, and were helped to join a Red Cross-sponsored class at the YWCA. One older woman had stopped attending the women's activities in her church since becoming blind, and here too the agency was able to pave the way for her to be included again in some of the activities she had previously enjoyed.

The significance of utilizing existing community resources is twofold. Obviously it is less expensive for a community to support a YMCA camp alone, than it would be to support both a Y camp and a camp for blind children. Whenever the needs of blind people can be met by facilities designed for seeing people, it is expensive as well as meaningless to duplicate.

Possibly less obvious, but equally important, the second point in using existing resources is that it literally is putting the blind person back into the community of which he is a part. It helps him to live a more normal life, to express his own interests and individuality, to participate in and contribute more to his community, to become as self-reliant as possible within the confines of blindness. The most dramatic example of this point comes from the field of education. At the time the agency for the blind was organized, the education laws in this State provided for the education of blind children only at an institutional school for the blind located at the State capital. All blind children in the State were educated together, learning about one another but very little about the sighted community where they would ultimately live and be expected to make an adjustment.

The agency was instrumental in having legislation passed that made it possible for local schools to receive State financial aid in educating blind children in their own community. Not only is the financial saving significant: blind children who have the opportunity to attend school with sighted children and to live with their own families in their own communities are going to be much more capable of holding their own as participating, self-reliant members of society. At the time the agency for the blind was organized it was apparent that blind children suffered as a result of having no education facility in the community, and an initial suggestion had been to erect a school for the blind in the city. Through the policy of using existing community resources, blind children and sighted children at last are being educated in the same schools, with the community recognition that its trust to children includes *all* children.

The experiences of this voluntary service for the blind in developing and using an informed and articulate board of directors as the bedrock base of the community education phase of its work, in combination with a battery of direct services to blind people geared to recognizing the individual needs and helping the blind person learn the necessary skills to become as independent and self-sustaining as possible, plus the creative and selective use of other resources already established in the community, has resulted in extending voluntary activity and organization in social welfare work for the blind. These techniques briefly described above, which have worked very successfully in one highly specialized area of endeavor, seem to be equally applicable in other areas of rehabilitation of handicapped persons. Some of the specific services might differ according to the needs of the individuals being served, but the general policies would remain the same.

2. A Complex of Volunteer Services for the Blind

MRS. CARRIE TURNER

I

People with a visual handicap are not the only ones who do not see the obvious. "The Blind" to many are a race set apart to be viewed with curiosity, or, what is worse, to be the objects of fruitless sentimentality. We know that much of this attitude is the result of the lack of sufficient knowledge and direction. When these are supplied by a constant, well-planned program, much of the energy used in useless or harmful action is diverted to productive service.

The Cleveland Society for the Blind, a private agency organized in 1906, offers casework services, recreation and group services, home industries, teaching services, retail sales, and concession stand employment. In the early years the staff consisted of volunteers working under a professional director. Although the professional staff has increased, there are now more than three hundred volunteers actively engaged by it. Some of these are working in special phases of the Society's program, and others are asked to do special tasks, all of which are important in providing services to clients. Some of the results are:

1. The staff can give a more effective and complete service.

2. The staff are stimulated constantly by new ideas from volunteers who help keep them alert and responsive to community problems.

3. Volunteers are important in interpreting to the community a true understanding of the problems and needs of the agency and of blind persons.

4. The trained volunteer usually derives a great satisfaction from his work even when it is difficult and time-consuming, because he realizes that it is essential and makes the lives of others richer and full.

Generally, volunteers are either concerned with administrative matters or with direct services to people.

There are many opportunities for volunteer service at the Society. The choice of service depends on the abilities, skills, and interests of the individual volunteer. These opportunities include the following:

Group Activities:
  Group leadership, program planning, good food preparation, transportation
Special Interest Groups:
  Crafts: ceramics, hand crafts, household repairs
  Hiking, swimming, bowling, dancing, music appreciation, public speaking
Friendly Visiting
Reading to Students
Store Sales
Preparation of Materials for Industrial Sewing Department
Tax Stamp Collecting and Sorting
Psychological Testing
Home Industry Teachers and Courier Service
Speakers at Agency Tours
Assistance at Dances and Other Social Affairs
Packing Christmas Baskets
Clerical Assistance
Guides for Special Events—Theatres, Opera, etc.
Summer Camp Transportation
Emergency Transportation

Administrative volunteers. The Trustee Board is a volunteer group primarily concerned with administration of the Society. As a policy-making body it has general responsibility for directing the work of the agency. Its work is through an executive committee of five officers and several others. This group is served by various committees, both general and special. In addition, some board members are direct service volunteers.

Service volunteers. Those who have direct contact with the people who seek service from the agency are called "service volunteers." They also assist staff members. This group may be divided into two types: (1) members of affiliated committees established in the permanent organization; and (2) individual volunteers to do special work. Each affiliated committee is autonomous and has its own officers and bylaws. The chairmen of all committees, while serving in office, are members of the board of trustees.

Predicated on the philosophy that the value lies in the service given rather than the number of hours, voluntary efforts are more effective. This and the emphasis on training have been two of the important factors that have raised the quality of the services rendered and the number of persons served.

Below are listed some points we feel are important. They are quoted from the Society's current volunteer kit.

1. Each volunteer should have a regular job approved by the Society. These jobs shall be assigned by the committee chairmen or by the Coordinator of Volunteer Services, in relation always to the circumstances and wishes of each individual volunteer.
2. All volunteers are asked to maintain a record card at the Society with indications of interests, skills, available time, and previous training or volunteer work. This enables the Society to make maximum use of volunteer help available.
3. New volunteers are expected to see and to talk with the Coordinator of Volunteer Services.
4. For almost any phase of volunteering, general knowledge of the Society's program is necessary. This knowledge can be gained by the careful reading of materials supplied by the Society, and also by attending institutes organized by the staff of the Society for that purpose. *It is the Society's responsibility to keep volunteers up to date on its program.*
5. In certain aspects of volunteering such as Friendly Visiting, group leadership, and home teaching, more special training is required.

Experience shows that a volunteer who is properly trained and oriented, provides better service to the client and receives more satisfaction.

The Committee system rotates most of the duties assigned to volunteers so that all who are interested may share in the various phases of the work. Assignments are made by the chairmen whose responsibility it is to see that all assignments are covered. Thus all have a chance when there is need for service. The services are departmentalized, but this does not prevent any volunteer from serving any department at some time when need exists.

II

It is evident that all time spent by the Society in training workers is a good investment. Interest and native ability, however good these may be, are better when supplemented by specific training geared to the specific needs of the Society. This is true of any multiple-service unit utilizing volunteer workers, as each agency has specific problems, methods and traditions.

This society has developed its volunteer program long enough for its conclusions to be based on reliable data. The evolution into the present standard is the result of much thought and effort by trained minds; and it can be viewed with a perspective because it has been in operation long enough for validity to be established, even while it meets the changing needs of the community.

My own period of service has been nine years as a volunteer and fifteen years as a staff worker, all in this Society. As caseworker I have had to utilize all the services offered, and I have found the volunteer service invaluable. Because of its well-trained volunteers the agency now accomplishes much that it could not undertake with a small professional staff alone. An instance is the following:

Home Industries provide interest, occupation, and some financial benefit for our applicants; but some of the processing must be done by others: cutting of materials; matching of colors; some labeling, packaging, transportation, and marketing and delivery.

I believe that this Society has been one of the pioneers in the extent to which volunteer services have been developed and utilized. Inquiries in the East and in California have led me to believe that this use is "new" in the sense that it seems to be unique, or at least that it is not yet widespread. I therefore submit this description for your consideration.

3. A Parents' Program for Blind Children

MRS. VIRGINIA BANERJEE

With the sharp increase in the number of blind children during the 1940's and early 1950's, due primarily to retrolental fibroplasia, a disease of the retina affecting premature infants, the special needs of the young blind have received increasing attention from many quarters. The impetus for much of the planning to meet these needs has come from voluntary parents' groups.

In our county, an industrial area with a population of nearly half a million, a small group of parents of preschool blind children recognized their need to organize in such a way as to increase community awareness and community solution of their special problems.

Agreeing on the fundamental principle that every child has a right to an opportunity to develop to the limit of his capacity, several parents began meeting together in order that they might coordinate their efforts to secure this opportunity for their blind children. Their initial efforts were directed toward locating other parents of blind children so that the scope of the need would be better defined. They individually discussed their proposed plans with their own physicians and ophthalmologists who put the group in touch with other families with similar problems. Publicity was arranged in the local press, describing the group's plans for developing community resources to serve their children. Plans were directed toward developing opportunities for these children to be reared and educated in the local community in the family setting rather than in an institutional setting which was the traditional method of educating the blind.

Committees of parents diligently "ran down" every lead that might locate a blind child. They telephoned, or wrote letters to, families that had indicated having a child that "had difficulty seeing" to the tax assessors in their surveys. This activity involved much time and effort as it developed that the assessors' lists included practically every child that wore glasses. The children whose visual impairment was so slight that their needs were being met by services for normal children were eliminated. The effort yielded several additional severely visually handicapped children.

These activities brought to the group's attention a total of twenty-five children whose vision was so limited that they would require a special educational program if they were to develop to the limit of their capacity.

Meetings were held in a private home and later in a public hall. A voluntary, not-for-profit corporation was formed. The aims of the organization as outlined in the constitution are:

A. To educate the public and the parent regarding the problems of a blind child.

B. To unite parents and friends of blind children in an organization for the purpose of discussing mutual problems and means of fulfilling our obligations to the blind child.

C. To advise means of establishing and maintaining recreational and educational facilities for the blind child. Also, to impress upon public officials, the Board of Education, the Welfare Department, and the public in general the urgent need for local education facilities for the blind child.

D. To further the welfare of the blind child.

Guided and counseled by such private welfare groups as the local Society for Crippled Children and the Visiting Nurse Association, the organization planned monthly meetings to begin answering some of the many questions that the parents of a blind child are called on to answer.

Ophthalmologists, social workers, pediatricians, and others were brought in to speak to the group. By the very fact of having organized, many parents found relief from the terrible "aloneness" of their situation. Parents of young blind children for the first time in this community were learning the value of voluntary activity to meet their own needs. They were doing something to help themselves and to make their community a better place in which to rear their children.

Deep within most parents was a spark of faith in their child's ability to develop normally in spite of his lack of vision. Through the organization they learned of current research to reinforce their faith. The necessity for some program for the local education of the blind child with the sighted became a fundamental driving force for the organization.

At this point, a committee of parents sought professional guidance and counseling to help them in planning their program. In their community this professional help was secured through the Child Welfare Division of the County Department of Public Welfare, as the county had no private family agency sufficiently staffed to assume such a program. These parents asked not for a solution to their problems by a public agency, but guidance in ways in which they could meet their own needs. The Department of Public Welfare in this community was so oriented as to see this as an opportunity to encourage voluntary activity and organization in social welfare. A caseworker was designated as consultant to the parents' organization. The consultant was charged with the responsibility of providing casework to individual families to help them in seeking solutions to their own difficulties in areas where group activity and therapy was not adequate.

In response to the need for an educational program for blind children, a committee of parents met with the superintendents of the various school districts to request the establishment of an integrated program for the education of the blind with the sighted in the regular classroom setting. The committee prepared folders of mimeographed material describing similar programs operating in other communities, as a means of demonstrating the feasibility of such a school program. This request to school boards in behalf of their children was further reinforced by their willingness to assist in providing teachers for the Braille Resource Rooms that would be required.

Funds were accumulated through other voluntary organizations—fraternal, social, and service groups having philanthropic programs. Card parties, raffles, and so on, were arranged in behalf of the young blind. Funds thus acquired were, are, and will be used to provide university scholarships for public school teachers interested in acquiring the necessary additional skills required to use a Braille Resource Room in a public school setting. Funds have been allotted to provide nursery school fees for blind children of low-income families that would otherwise be denied this important opportunity for learning to live in a sighted society. Special equipment for the Resource Rooms, transportation for special classes, and other "plus" services will be provided for these children through the parents' council.

The parents' group concurrently conducted a program to educate the community in the needs of the young blind. The primary tool they used was that of speaking to various organizations. Through knowledge and understanding of these children's similarities to seeing children as well as their differences comes acceptance of them as an integral part of community life, which increases their chances of developing into self-sufficient, productive adults.

These, then, are the high lights of a voluntary program that has developed in less than two years to fill an unmet need in this community. The program now serves all the known blind children in the county, including those attending the State residential school, which now number forty-seven instead of the original twenty-five. All are served in different ways to meet their individual needs. A few of school age are attending regular local schools and receiving Braille instruction; several are enrolled in sighted nursery schools; some receive intensive casework from the consultant; and some attend a private physical therapy center. All the parents receive a regular newsletter to keep them abreast of the rapidly developing community resources to meet the needs of the young blind.

This is a unique and pioneering example of what voluntary activity can accomplish in extending social welfare. In addition it points to opportunities for the further use of voluntary effort and funds to meet special needs. There are still unmet needs for this group in this community. The most pressing at this time appears to be a resource to serve the blind child who has emotional problems and/or multiple physical handicaps. Homemaker service or a day-care center for the severely developmentally retarded could serve an important purpose by enabling these parents to share the day to day care of a severely handicapped child.

Such additional services can also be provided by voluntary efforts and funds; and development of such resources would be hastened by grants for research, surveys, and professional staff persons to guide and direct volunteer groups, parents' organizations, and the like, so that the ultimate goal of "total service for all children" might be more quickly and efficiently reached.

8

Chronic Illness

1. Apartment Hospitals

MARGARET T. HUTCHINSON

My suggestion of a way to extend voluntary activity and organization in social welfare in the area of chronic illness is the direct result of trying to care adequately for my own mother during the two years of illness that ended in her death. During that time my family and I became acquainted with many other patients and their families. Sharing experiences, we saw common problems emerge.

Earlier experience with the State Welfare Department as Vocational Rehabilitation Counsellor had given me an awareness of various problems, such as those of finding what medical help was needed for the client; of finding where, when, and how that help could be given best; of the client's psychological reaction to that treatment and to his environment; and of the great demand upon doctors and hospitals because of the large numbers needing attention. Then month after month of close contact night and day with the particular set of circumstances involving the well-being of several close relatives and even the very life of the one most near and dear to me gave the very pressing reason for searching study into the problems of the chronically ill.

Suffering from congestive heart failure with high blood pressure, Mother longed to be at home and our family was equally anxious to have her there. Indeed, we dreaded to be away from her any of the time. Yet all of us realized that only in a hospital would a doctor be near enough to give her whatever relief might be needed quickly enough for it to accomplish its purpose. Nursing could be provided at home and such aids as oxygen could be supplied there, but no doctor would be in our home at all times. Seeing her in even one of those grueling heart failures, watching that cold blueness fade into good color in her skin as a doctor gave her prompt care—one such experience was enough to make a hospital, with a doctor on hand all the time, look like a real haven.

But because family ties mean so much to all of us, we were well aware of a wonderful thing which the hospital cannot give: the deep strength associated with a person's home. The general hospital is not a home and cannot compensate for it. We found that the patients and their families were not alone in their recognition of the situation. Doctors, too, realized the lack was serious, but had no real solution.

Another problem shared by many of us was that the general hospital is likely to say "No" to the chronically ill applicant for admission, pleading too many "emergency" calls for their limited space and too small staff. But who can determine which patient is the greater emergency—the patient who has a broken leg or the patient who has a faulty heart? Actually there are likely to be fewer complications and certainly fewer life and death emergencies for the one with a broken leg. How can the hospital justify its action, when, with the word "emergencies," it turns away the patients who are likely to suffer heart failures at any moment and die from not being given adequate care immediately? Again, which is the greater emergency?

At one time a patient in the room next to Mother's was a man who had been inactivated by a partial stroke. A long illness was likely. Of course the chance that he might need a doctor suddenly was uppermost in the thoughts of his wife, who was all the family this patient had. However, their doctor finally prevailed upon the wife to take her husband to a "rest home," stating that the general hospital was so crowded that "those less ill must give up their rooms for more serious cases—emergencies." The patient's wife did not feel that this was a satisfactory solution since the "rest homes" fell far short of being hospitals and yet hospital care was what her husband needed.

With hospitals overcrowded and turning away the chronically ill, with rest homes inadequate for such patients and with our own private homes too far removed from all the special equipment and professional skills needed, how can we make more adequate provision for this group?

Why not provide an apartment hospital, that is, a combination apartment building and hospital, with a hospital staff and equipment necessary for the constant care and also for the emergencies that arise for the chronically ill?

In an apartment hospital the morale of the patients would be high because of the feeling of security that only the presence of one's own family can give. Also, there would be none of the tension that builds up in all the family when it is feared that, in an emergency, the ambulance might not get the patient to the distant hospital quickly enough, even though it travels at eighty miles an hour. (The mother of a friend of ours died in an ambulance on her way to a hospital following a heart attack.)

The apartments in the apartment hospital would be reserved for families in which there was chronic illness and for the families of at least some of the doctors and nurses on the staff. Families who would welcome such a plan would be the ones who, while realizing the value of professional skill and wanting it readily available, would be glad to have the opportunity themselves to give their sick the routine care that is a very heavy burden to hospitals, taking care of the physical environment, preparing their meals and sharing meals with them. This decentralization of responsibility would do much to make a more bearable situation for patients and relatives and a more manageable one for the staff, who would then be more free to concentrate on the professional problems.

Relatives would have in their work for the patients an outlet for their concern for loved ones, who, in turn, would respond very naturally to the more personal attention. Private duty nurses would still be needed in many situations for part or all of the time, but in some cases relatives could carry on acceptably under the direction of general duty nurses. A family in need of such a helper as a maid, cook, or housekeeper might better find someone directly and independently rather than call upon an apartment employee. However, there could be a reserve of apartment employees and volunteers also, who would be available for regular, part time, or emergency duty.

Services of doctors could be planned to meet the needs of individuals and fees set accordingly so that those requiring more attention could have it and pay for it. For the emergencies especially the big advantage would be that there would always be a doctor available. Someone may ask what could be done if several emergencies occurred at the same time. This happens often in general hospitals and the situation could be met as well in the apartment hospital as in the general hospital. One such emergency arose late one night when Mother's private duty nurse suddenly became seriously ill. Immediately she was taken to the emergency room and another private duty nurse, one whose own patient was across the hall, assumed responsibility for Mother, dividing her time between her own patient and Mother. She and Mother's nurse had often helped each other with the care of their patients so that she was familiar with the routine.

The great advantage in having a doctor always in the building cannot be overemphasized, even though he may be called upon sometimes to handle more than one emergency simultaneously. A doctor "on location" all the time is familiar with the particular problems of each patient. He knows what treatment is most likely to work for each patient, as well as what treatment should *not* be used, so that when an emergency arises he can cope with it quickly. This is, of course, an advantage that comes from having a patient hospitalized. Since general hospitals find themselves too crowded to take care of all those who come to them for care, this suggestion of establishing apartment hospitals seems to be a practical way to furnish such care for more of our sick.

With hospitalization costs as high as they are, the question may be raised whether the costs of apartment hospitals might be reasonable enough for many people to be able to use them. From those of us who have had the experience of paying doctor bills and hospital bills without finding really adequate care, from the thousands of us who have searched might well come the challenge: Why not explore the possibilities thoroughly? Furthermore, whatever the costs in dollars, if such a solution brought either better care or more adequate care for more of our chronically sick (and it might achieve both of these ends), then it would be worth any effort.

Certainly we could expect many individuals and groups to give intelligent and generous cooperation in planning and financing apartment hospitals. It would come from the sick and from the well, from the patients and from their friends and relatives, from doctors and nurses, from builders, from architects, from the people of the great heart and vision that characterize vast numbers of us. We should realize that some of the chronically ill themselves are in the professional groups just named and could provide impetus and continuing support to such a project. The doctor who has had to quit practicing because of a heart ailment would find deep satisfaction in helping to plan an ideal setting for the chronically ill and his part in such planning would be invaluable because of his double role.

A fraternal organization might be a logical group to show the way in providing an apartment hospital because such a project would be directly in line with caring for the wider needs of its members. Also, a fraternal organization could quickly set up a pilot program making the widest possible use of volunteers at many points in the planning and execution of such a project.

Perhaps in presenting this suggestion of a way to extend voluntary activity and organization in social welfare in the area of chronic illness we should state clearly our underlying belief that the best social work ultimately should make organized social work unnecessary. It should help to put in motion solutions so sound that seemingly impossible situations become manageable for individuals and small primary groups. Thus individuals, the family, and the small community can and should be helped to meet the strains of chronic illness adequately so that they may not be overwhelmed by it. To reach that goal many, many of us would gladly volunteer our help.

The apartment hospital plan offers a way of giving better care to our chronically sick than is now available because it would strengthen the spirit of the sick and of their families, too. The good pattern of family life could continue in spite of illness. This is a way that is attractive to those who are financially able to meet the expense involved as well as to those who now need help from welfare organizations. Also, by making it possible for families to give part of the care to their sick in homes of their own, the financial cost to both the family and the community welfare funds might be lowered.

2. The Visiting Homemakers

TONG SAM

Homemaker service sponsored by private, voluntary efforts has yet to enter wholeheartedly into one of the most neglected areas of social welfare. In the last two decades the government has extended a broad basis of financial coverage through unemployment and disability compensations, social security benefits, and more liberal veterans' compensations. Private, voluntary welfare has continued its traditional role of providing casework service to troubled and distressed individuals and families with a great refining of its skills.

A homemaker service reaches the communities in several ways. It aids aged or ill persons who need home maintenance for a few hours a day. It gives employment to women who are eager to work. It lets patients be cared for at home at less expense, freeing hospital beds for more acute cases.

Visiting Homemakers can be utilized by the whole community. For the family with limited financial means it would mean that skilled help is available to perform household chores during emergencies. For the old, blind, crippled, or chronically ill person, it presents an opportunity to have someone come in to clean the room or apartment. Fees can be scaled according to income.

In small communities, especially in rural areas in America, there is usually no recognized and well-known agency where a trained homemaker can be hired. In most large metropolitan areas homemakers can be found, but usually not trained or geared to the income of the low-income groups or those receiving public assistance.

Initially, a committee of civic and welfare leaders can be formed to study the need of Visiting Homemakers in the community. After studying the feasibility of such a project, the group can form various committees to initiate publicity, research, and policy for such a project. Of prime importance is the selection of a board of directors that must lay down the fundamental policy of the agency and formulate the fiscal and personnel procedures. Funds usually must come from private donations, philanthropic foundations, and the United Crusade Councils.

A well-coordinated Visiting Homemaker Service is best administered by a full-time paid director and a salaried or volunteer office staff, plus one or more Home Visitors, who should be trained social workers. A technical advisory committee of physicians, psychiatrists, occupational therapists, home economists, and nurses should be available for consultation. Often these experts are willing to serve on such a committee gratis.

Visiting Homemakers are usually recruited from the general population, but a large number of older women on public assistance rolls are usually eager to learn to be trained homemakers. Women of minority races are often extremely interested in being a Visiting Homemaker.

The training regime for neophyte Visiting Homemakers must be well planned and realistic. The faculty should come from the local school system, or the nearby university extension. The knowledge to be covered should include home management, home nursing, cooking, hygiene, and psychology. Emphasis is placed on the importance of understanding family relationships and the impact of illness in a family. She is taught the importance of the confidential nature of her work, and the danger in giving medical or nursing advice. Graduation from the prescribed course should include actual practice in cooking, light housework, caring of children, and care of the sickroom. A trained Visiting Homemaker in the course of development should be imbued with a feeling of dignity and self-respect in her attitude toward her work. Her personality should reflect tolerance and understanding of people.

A continuous in-service training program should be installed to give supplemental training to the Visiting Homemakers. Lectures by recognized experts in various fields assist in improving morale and self-confidence in the staff. A lecture and demonstration by a qualified Occupational Therapist would enable the staff to help incapacitated or elderly people to constructively occupy their time in an interesting and often economically profitable way.

When a request for service is received, a Home Visitor visits the family or patient to arrange working hours, and to acquire an impression of the personalities in the family and the relationships involved. Then a Homemaker is selected to fill the particular needs of the household. Consultation with the advisory committee members is utilized whenever necessary. Agencies referring cases are kept informed of the Homemaker's progress.

Visiting Homemakers should be under the supervision of the Home Visitor, who would be aware of the problems in the household, and could present constructive advice and suggestions to specific inquiries. The director would benefit by holding monthly general staff meetings to report on new developments within the agency and to invite ideas and comments from the staff on specific aspects of the agency's operation.

Visiting Homemakers available to schools, professions, agencies, and churches would be a godsend in alleviating the situation in families with acute or chronic illnesses. As the aged population increases in number and proportion in the future, there would be a greater use for Visiting Homemakers for the aging and chronic illness cases.

In Summit, New Jersey, the SAGE Visiting Homemaker Service was initiated in October 1954. The sponsoring organization was the Summit Association for Gerontological Endeavor, Inc. Initially, they planned their service for the aged and the chronically ill person. Subsequently, the service was opened to the whole community. The Homemaker, usually an older woman, undergoes sixteen hours of special training through the Rutgers University Extension Division before she is given job placement. The experiment was not only successful for those served, but the idea worked so well that the Homemakers themselves have shown an improvement of morale and increased self-confidence.

About the year 1945 the New York City Department of Public Welfare inaugurated a Homemaker Center and Homemaker Training Institute. A special attempt was made to have older women on public assistance to enroll in the training course. A large number of colored women took the prescribed training course, which was a combination of lectures and demonstrations given by various experts in the professions. The personalities of the candidates were carefully screened, and later they were placed under the supervision of the Department's social workers. Today, after ten years of existence, the Homemaker Service is considered an indispensable division of the city's welfare service. Its large staff of homemakers spend thousands of hours yearly in alleviating the worries and anxieties of individuals and families caused by acute and chronic illnesses. With a staff of nearly a hundred people, the Homemaker Service of New York City has become the world's largest homemaker service.

In the years ahead, private welfare work in America can perform an invaluable task by organizing Visiting Homemaker services throughout the country. In many urban areas of our nation studies have been made of the feasibility of such a service. Many private and public agencies have lists of homemakers, but often those available are far from adequate. Untrained homemakers with defective personalities and meager housekeeping skills can play havoc with the morale and well-being of the families they serve.

The challenge of setting up Visiting Homemakers under voluntary welfare should, therefore, be met with vigor and enthusiasm.

3. Mutual Aid in Myasthenia

ANNE HAWKINS COTTON

This paper reports on a method of extending social welfare work among the chronically ill by enlisting the volunteer efforts of the patients themselves. Personal experience in the Oregon chapter of the Myasthenia Gravis Foundation, Inc., is described by one of the patients brought into volunteer activity. Values of the method are admitted to be less in increasing the volume of social welfare work performed than in socializing [1] seclusive or timid patients. Weaknesses of the method are (*a*) the unreliability of patients in carrying out extended projects, and (*b*) the possible danger to patients of overexertion. Tentative conclusions are offered, for testing, about the criteria to keep in mind in attempting to use the method with other types of chronically ill patients.

BACKGROUND

In 1952, the Myasthenia Gravis Foundation, Inc., was established in New York as a nonprofit corporation of the familiar fund-raising type, modeled after the multiple sclerosis and muscular dystrophy organizations. Its purposes were and are "to raise funds to further research and to disseminate information concerning this strange disease which may incapacitate, cripple and sometimes kill." In its first two years it raised about $30,000 for research, distributing this promptly to projects chosen through a board of medical school neurologists. It obtained general publicity—intended to increase fund-raising contacts by encouraging friends and relatives of myasthenics to write to the Foundation—by press releases, short enough to be widely used by newspapers as fillers, announcing the experimental introduction of each new drug brought into the clinical testing stage, and by a human-interest magazine article (*Cosmopolitan,* January 1953) about the beautiful ex-actress, mother of a beautiful girl myasthenic, who was

---

[1] In the technical, not the political, sense of the word! "Socialize (1) to render social; esp. to train for social environment. . . ." Webster's New Collegiate Dictionary, 1956 ed.

the principal founder. It obtained ethical professional publicity among doctors by a conference of leading neurologists on the subject, the papers they presented being printed as the entire November 1954 issue of one medical journal and summarized as the lead article in the July 1955 issue of another (*Current Medical Digest*). It obtained much potential, and some actual, publicity among both professional and specially interested lay groups by the making of a new 16-mm. sound film on the diagnosis of myasthenia gravis, financed by the manufacturers of the standard drug used in diagnosis and treatment. It also prepared leaflets, of varying excellence, suitable for use either as conversation pieces in fund-raising contacts or as information material distributed through such outlets as county health offices and pamphlet racks in public libraries.

By the end of 1955 the initial impetus was, however, perceptibly slowing down. The cream of the personal-contact funds prospects had been skimmed, the novelty glamour publicity had been exploited once for all, the professional medical publicity had been thoroughly done and could not be redone until new facts should supersede the old, and the research projects intended to discover such facts were proceeding methodically (and from the lay point of view disappointingly). Steady plugging continued to be required.

From the beginning, the foundation had encouraged decentralization by chartering local, more or less nominal, chapters. The method of organizing these seems to have been that the overworked founders sorted the fan mail after the *Cosmopolitan* article by geographical groups, picked the most promising letter from each region, and wrote that person enclosing the other names and addresses from the region and saying, "You are now temporary secretary of your chapter; go to it." It was not quite as haphazard as this, of course. Chapters were centered in cities where there were medical schools with cooperating faculty neurologists, and usually with experimental clinics. Chapters were coordinated by correspondence with the foundation headquarters plus a now-and-then newsletter. They were in regular though sometimes casual touch with their medical school adviser, and the medical advisers coordinated their own activities through membership in a national medical advisory board. Thus the organization consists of two chains—one professional, one lay—connected at each link and again connected at national headquarters. Medical social workers connected with the medical school outpatient clinics may play a part in all this but it is an unobtrusive one.

The first successful chapters, New York (1952) and Los Angeles (1953), were founded by relatives of patients. The successful Northwest chapter (1954), which then by fission became the Washington and the Oregon chapters, was founded or at least led by patients. Mother love as a driving force was replaced (partly) by self-preservation. Direct fund raising was handicapped, since it is easier to say "Give for them" than "Give for us." But something else was facilitated.

In spring of 1956 I received a letter inviting me to attend a meeting to organize an Oregon chapter of the Myasthenia Gravis Foundation. I am a myasthenic. I went. My husband could not go with me, so I went alone. What those four sentences mean is that the attraction of that meeting was a stimulus that enabled me to overcome severe objective and subjective obstacles. I seemed to myself to be performing an athletic feat.

On arrival I walked into a living room full of strangers. I tried to hide my social timidity by a mechanical social remark about the prettiness of the room. The hostess (Mrs. Evans McLean, chapter chairman, a myasthenic) said, "Oh, don't call attention to it! I didn't get around to washing the windows. . . ." Four of us interrupted her with sudden surprised barks of laughter. She laughed too. We were the myasthenics present; it was not the giggling of nervous tension, it was a laugh of recognition. (Myasthenics characteristically feel guilty not about having done those things they ought not to have done, but about having left undone those things that they ought to have done; particularly those things that they know other people seem to find easy. Window washing is an almost classic example; any repetitive muscle action, especially one involving neck and shoulder muscles, is hard for myasthenics.)

The meeting lasted two hours (a tremendous time for myasthenics to sit on straight chairs). All that it accomplished in organizing or planning was that Mrs. McLean did get the charter application form explained and everybody signed it. That could have been done in five minutes. The rest of the time was mainly spent in the most incoherent, and most valuable, general conversation imaginable. The nonmyasthenics (of eleven present, five were patients and the rest relatives) must have been increasingly confused. The myasthenics were increasingly unconfused. This is important. Any attempt to steer that meeting would have done harm.

I remember that near the beginning, while still uncomfortable and trying to make conversation, I asked formally if anyone else there had tried the new drug betasyamine which my doctor was trying on me; and I held up the bottle. A voice said critically "Liquid?" and the same four of us were overtaken by the same surprised laughter of mutual recognition. The joke this time was that a liquid medicine is rather impractical for myasthenics, who must take medication at irregular intervals many times a day; to take a swig from a bottle in church or on the street is likely to be misunderstood by strangers! Not particularly apropos of liquid medicines, there is a valid association here with Alcoholics Anonymous: in several of the autobiographies in the AA "big book" the alcoholic reports, as a turning point, an emotional reaction, "Why, these are people who *know!*" That's what it was. These people *knew*. That's why our conversation was so incoherent—because we were finding our statements perfectly understood halfway through the sentence, so we didn't make the muscular effort to finish the sentence.

None of us had ever seen another myasthenic. I can't know how it felt to the others. But I remember how two of them looked. One was a woman who at the beginning had a blank affected-looking smirk on her face—the same odd look you sometimes see on a woman who has had her face lifted—and at the end, though tired, had come to life. The other was an eighteen-year-old boy, who without apology occupied the only armchair; he caught my eye when I arrived because I thought he must be there by mistake, for his cramped rigid position looked more like cerebral palsy than myasthenia gravis. His father kept doing all the talking for him, intercepting my remarks and answering my questions, and aggressively telling me at great length the dramatic story of onset and diagnosis in the boy's case. (The one thing none of us myasthenics bothered to tell or ask; we all asked each other, "When were you diagnosed? And how long were you undiagnosed?"—which established a sort of seniority of experience and of undiagnosed suffering—and went on to the next thing.) And the first light in that boy's eyes was when I gave him a startled side-glance at a moment when my doing so amounted to saying, "Why, your father's telling it wrong!" At the end of the meeting he did not look like the same boy.

RESULTS TO DATE

As William James said, the test of a mystical experience is its fruits for life.

The effect on the boy: he undertook a correspondence with an out-of-town myasthenic who could not come. I have seen one letter—cheerful, outgoing, full of information about what the chapter was doing and about his studies. He undertook this of his own accord and kept it up under his own steam.

The effect on Mrs. McLean: she organized a public meeting with a showing of the film, sending advance announcements to the press; 55 people came, the newspaper items brought letters and phone calls putting her in touch with nearly 20 previously unknown Oregon myasthenics. She wrote or talked to all these. The rest of her record to date becomes a record of group effort led by her: negotiating an arrangement with a Portland pharmacy to give chapter members a large discount on their essential drugs; inducing a small but important Portland women's club (twenty to twenty-five members, consisting solely of past presidents of other clubs) to undertake as a project the buying of a print of the film so that it may be circulated through the numerous but scattered towns of the northwestern states (to be shown to hospital employees, American Legion and VFW committees for the disabled, etc.); instituting weekly meetings to make ornamental covers for Christmas tree bases, for which a chapter contact has a guaranteed market, as a money-raising project.

The effect on me: I have done very little; looking at the example of Mrs. McLean I am ashamed. All I can claim is three or four visits to a woman myasthenic, among those who wrote to Mrs. McLean, who turned out to live quite near me. She too makes me ashamed, for she accomplishes much more than I, but for years she had been dependent on others for all her shopping, since she was not strong enough to walk to the grocery a quarter of a mile away and was afraid to drive even that distance, on a quiet street, "for fear that if a child runs out in the street I wouldn't be able to move fast enough to get the brake pedal down in time." By observing me drive, and by hearing me report on my driver's license test (both the time I was turned down and the time I passed), and particularly, I think, by hearing me describe how during the successful driving test I slowed down to five m.p.h. where small children were playing and how the examiner seemed if anything pleased, she reached a decision to reapply for her own driver's license and to plan on trying again every month till she passes.

And the effect on her in turn: she has communicated with a Salt Lake City myasthenic that a relative told her about, to put this other in touch with the Salt Lake City chapter, explaining, "This girl's doctor obviously knows nothing about myasthenia gravis; she wouldn't believe it if I told her, because she trusts him, but the Salt Lake chapter can see that he gets educated!"

There it is, to date. Small. Submicroscopic! But not a trifle. Not to the human beings involved.

CRITICISM

The great weakness is that we patients are unreliable. Only short-term projects can be attempted, and even those require to be open-ended, capable of being dropped at any time without the waste of the work up to that point. Even so, an increasing amount of the load of the Oregon chapter organization is, I suspect, being carried by a certain Mrs. Green, of whom I only know that Mrs. McLean says she is "wonderful" and that she is the mother of a patient. Mother love reappears as a driving force!

A second weakness is that the best patients are the ones most likely to work themselves into a relapse. Mrs. Skipworth, founder of the parent Northwest Chapter in 1954, has overworked herself into one.

OTHER EXAMPLES OF THE METHOD

Alcoholics Anonymous has been mentioned, but not as being an example of the same method—which of course it is. Mutual emotional support by the patients there reaches its highest level.

Another example is or was a club organized by a Mrs. Garrigues in Santa Barbara in the 1940's. Superficially an "Over 40" club that held daily tea-dances for aged pensioners, its real objective was to get hemiplegics back on their feet by force of others who had done the same.[2]

A possible example is or was the Society of Tubercular Ex-patients active in San Francisco in the 1920's. If it was decentralized enough so that every member had to make responsible decisions and exercise initiative, it was an example; if not, it was not.

CONCLUSIONS

In my limited and subjective experience, the essentials of the method appear to be:

1. Mutual support by the patients themselves—but not left entirely to themselves; strongly motivated laymen are an advantage, sharing the actual work and actual leadership; medical and social work professionals are essential in the background.

2. Decentralized, very small groups—the chronically ill can do but little, nor do that little long, but they must get their chance to do that in the most independent and responsible way.

3. Homogeneous groups, because the experience of mutual recognition is so vital emotionally—the sensation Lillian Roth describes as, "We looked at them, and knew them for our own."

4. Some group purpose in addition to the mutual support; and this group purpose must be unselfish (for example, raising funds for research into prevention of new cases, not only into cure), organically connected with what the group has in common, and small enough so that the patients can experience successes.

[2] More information can be obtained from her son, C. H. Garrigues, 1373 17th Avenue, San Francisco, Calif.

9
Health Education
and Medical Care

1. Educating Against Separatism in the Health Professions

JOHN L. CAMPBELL

It is my thesis that it may become increasingly difficult to extend voluntary activity and organization in social welfare unless we drastically amend some of our methods of educating people in the health professions. Let us quickly survey the education of several of the health professions that will later be involved in medical care, rehabilitation, and care of the chronically ill.

Physicians, nurses, social workers, physical therapists, vocational counselors, and others in similar fields, go to school for twelve years together and have interests and identifications that are somewhat alike. They communicate with one another to some degree. At college, some choose the biological and physical sciences; others choose the social sciences. Here the split begins. By college graduation, it is already difficult for the biology or physics majors to take much interest in communicating with the sociology, psychology, or education people.

Special knowledge is required for the practice of each profession, and each discipline now develops its own special preoccupations, vocabulary, and methods of working. As each discipline learns more and more about its special interest area, it has more difficulty in understanding the roles and contributions of the other professions. The professional finds it difficult to take time from his own studies to enjoy broadening outside experiences. Later each profession further refines and develops its own specialties within specialties so that the area of skill and interest becomes even narrower.

If we now introduce a patient with complex medical, social, and economic problems into this present setting, we discover that he must be seen by a great number of these specialists. Frequently the problems of the patient become so divided but challenging to the participants that the patient becomes depersonalized. He becomes a technical problem, an object for scientific study, and his personal wishes and needs may be overlooked. The patient finds himself caught up in a huge machine set up for his care, but by this time he can easily "fall between the wheels."

Perhaps no one is sure who is to assume responsibility for the total plan for the patient. The doctor may not know that a vocational counselor can make a contribution to the total care of his patient. The other professionals may not be able to operate together in working out attainable goals for the patient because they lack knowledge concerning existing facilities. In addition, it is a lamentable fact that there are rivalries as to which profession or specialty should captain the team.

As a result of overspecialization, complexity of procedures, and "machine-like" handling of patients, we obtain a low yield for the tremendous cost involved. The cost of this type of medical care is growing so large that we begin to look for some type of government subsidy to pay the bill.

Government is interested in helping to find a solution to this problem. Unfortunately government administration of a program tends to discourage private and voluntary welfare activity. The mechanics of government assistance tends to be cumbersome and impractical if one wishes to avoid further complexity. To date, there has been too little emphasis on educating professional people to think about reorganization and doing a better job within existing facilities.

Extending voluntary activity and organization is one way to reverse the tide. It is a more effective way to handle the complex problems of the ill, whether it be physical or mental handicap or illness, because it will provide a closer personal relationship between the helpers and the helped. Patients' needs are emphasized and more easily discovered in the smaller, close-knit group. A private organization can remain flexible enough to try out new methods and act on new knowledge.

We know that a human being responds favorably to the community recognition that his problems are also the problems of his neighbors, his church, his school, or his family. A cure can be almost complete in the hospital, but the effectiveness of the cure can only be measured by what later happens in the patient's community. Voluntary social welfare can deal with these problems effectively because these organizations consist of members of the community. The extension of voluntary activity is a democratic way of attacking this problem.

The integration of the ill and handicapped into the normal life of the community must concern those interested in voluntary social welfare so that we will not need to create special communities for these people at government expense as has been done in some European countries.

It is my firm conviction that a revision in some of the educational processes of the professions involved in the total care of complex health problems can extend voluntary activity and organization in social welfare. I believe that this will be accomplished by revising curricula so that students in the health professions in the hospital and clinic can unite with each other and with the voluntary groups and agencies in the community around the problems of patients for whom they share responsibility. This would give the student in each profession an early respect for, and grasp of, the role of the voluntary and public agencies in the community. The assumption and sharing of the responsibility for the total needs of patients with appropriate community agencies and under careful supervision is a key concept in this educational plan.

Let us say we wish to acquaint a student with the community services and facilities for blind patients. If we give a medical student the medical responsibility for a recently blinded patient so that he is responsible for doing what he can to speed the process of rehabilitation, under good supervision, his interest in the services of a private or voluntary agency becomes very keen. He will also become interested in what a social worker or visiting nurse can contribute to the total care of his patient. He learns this well because he is emotionally involved with the patient, his family, the community, and the other professions helping him.

The extension of voluntary activity and organization in social welfare occurs continually in this type of learning activity. It is extended by better communication and better definition of agency and professional function. In interprofessional patient-centered conferences, the community worker may learn more about the function of the health professions and often views with new respect and enthusiasm his role in the total scheme. This extension also occurs by helping to avoid waste and duplication of effort.

For the future, we hope that voluntary activity will be extended when these graduates move into the community as potential leaders who can function in an intelligent, interested, and well-informed way. They may become agency executives, board members, competent staff members, and so on.

This revision of the educational process must provide the opportunity for students and faculty in the health professions to study and work together in the seminar, conference, and clinic. This provides for a renewed interest in each other's skills and contributions. Similar values and a common philosophy may be rediscovered, breeding new respect for the other fellow and securing confidence in one's individual role.

An important factor in this change in the educational process is that each student in the health professions must be given an extended period of time in which to follow his patient through various crises, exacerbations, and remissions. He must see the patient regularly over a long period of time to be able to become involved and better understand the total picture. It becomes a very complicated process when educational planners begin to change the curricula of the schools of medicine, nursing, social work, physical therapy, vocational counseling, etc.

This approach to revising curricula in the health professions has been somewhat easier in the Cleveland community because the Medical School of Western Reserve University has recently undergone a revolutionary change in its curriculum and is experimenting with the education of undergraduate medical students. The following characteristics are important parts of the change in the medical school and they are being incorporated experimentally into the schools of nursing and social work:

1. In the medical school, the teaching of the basic sciences is done in a co-related manner by subject committees rather than as independent courses by separate departments.
2. A "preceptorial" method of teaching has been adopted. In this system, each student has an opportunity to closely relate to a member of the faculty who acts as his teacher and mentor for an extended period of time.
3. The teaching of clinical science is done by early involvement of the student in patient care in which he is given personal responsibility for the patient under supervision of his preceptor.
4. A Continuity Clinic has been established. This Clinic is a facility in which junior and senior student physicians, student nurses, and student social workers care for their patients in a comprehensive way throughout a sixteen-month period. The goal of this experience is to create a climate in which each student can be exposed to values, attitudes, and approaches to problems that will affect his sense of professional responsibility in practice. By design, the student is exposed to the frustrating and complex problems of the chronically ill and handicapped patient, in part for the purpose of acquainting him with the role each of the health professions plays in the comprehensive care of his patient.

   The student is not expected to become a specialist in rehabilitation of the chronically ill or handicapped patient, but it is hoped that he will develop fundamental concepts, techniques, and ways of working with other people in his setting and in his community, large or small, that will carry over into medical practice either in general medicine or in the specialties.

To accomplish the aims of the medical school, a group of experienced teachers in the fields of medicine, nursing, social service, physical therapy, and vocational counseling were brought together through funds provided by the National Foundation for Infantile Paralysis. This grant was obtained with the understanding that this staff would have the larger responsibility of promoting experimental programs in their own departments or schools that would enable students in the associated professions to learn to work together in the same clinic facilities and in the community with the agencies involved in the patient's care.

It is the responsibility of this teaching group, of which the writer is a member, to acquaint all the health professions with their responsibility of cooperating with voluntary agencies. The community is our laboratory and its cooperation and response have been enthusiastic. We hope that the graduating health worker's fruitful experience in a community in which voluntary social welfare is well organized will encourage him to exert effort to organize and point out the needs of such services in his new community, be it large or small.

In Cleveland, we have been experimenting with this method. To date, the results have been very gratifying, but we still have much to accomplish. We have found that this educational plan, which brings students together at the end of their professional training, can do much to better communications, raise the level of professional and technical skill, and instill a corresponding philosophy and set of values in the professionals who will be our community leaders of tomorrow. Each profession has the opportunity to rediscover that we depend upon the skills of others. We hope that each professional person will be less preoccupied with his own craft skills, and secure in the knowledge that his skill is defined and accepted by others so that he may act as a catalyst rather than as an inhibiting agent in his job in his community.

2. How Social Workers Might Assist Medical Workers

ROBERT PLANK

THE TASK BEFORE MEDICAL RESEARCH

The innumerable dangers to life and health that plague mankind can be roughly divided into two groups: those caused by external agents—chiefly micro-organisms, poisons, and injuries—and those that cannot, or not as yet, be attributed to an external agent and that must be presumed to result principally from factors within the organism itself.

Traditionally, through the centuries the first group has been the dreaded enemy. It is against them that medicine has won its most glorious victories. The situation with regard to the second group is unfortunately quite different. After the triumphs of surgery and sanitation and the virtual elimination of infectious disease in countries such as the United States, the diseases of the second group have gained even greater and more sinister importance. The overwhelming majority of deaths among adults is now attributable to two groups of diseases in this general category: the cardio-vascular-renal group and cancer. Other chronic degenerative diseases, such as schizophrenia, the arthritic group, idiopathic epilepsy, and others, do not particularly shorten life but most certainly impair its usefulness and enjoyment.

All these ailments have these factors in common: Their physiological mechanisms are more or less well understood but their fundamental causes are not. Their course can to some extent be checked, but this control is woefully inadequate. To buy time at the price of misery is the best that can be hoped in many cases. Any success of medical research in developing control of these ailments would extend the life span and remove a heavy load of fear and unhappiness. Obviously, the elimination of these diseases would not mean immortality but would merely allow the natural process of aging to take its toll—but then, aging itself is somewhat in the same category: because it is true of aging also that its physiology is reasonably well understood but that its fundamental causes are obscure and controls inadequate.

It is, furthermore, evident that the best chance for achieving control lies in extending knowledge of etiology. This, then, is the principal task of medical research in the foreseeable future.

The Importance of Medicine in the March of Progress

The progress of the human race from its primitive state to civilization has involved its emancipation from several subjugating forces: First, the inimical elements. They are done with. (I hope my ignoring certain factors numerically no longer important will not be misunderstood as callousness toward their victims. Still, we cannot overlook that the total number of persons who die from floods, wild animals, lightning, tornadoes, earthquakes, and so on, is but an infinitesimal fraction of those who die from the major diseases.) Secondly, the lack of resources to sustain life and health. This job is also virtually complete. Some deficiencies in distribution notwithstanding, we do not suffer from scarcity of material goods. The question has arisen whether we do not suffer from their superabundance.

Progress in science and technology can today only serve one of the following purposes: to increase knowledge for the sake of knowledge, which is honorable but little else; to increase our comforts—nice but not essential; to improve our weapons; finally, to lengthen life and reduce physical suffering—the task of medicine.

Social work has fought bravely and successfully in the battle against poverty and the evils it has entailed. A certain sense of frustration and futility that attentive observers have noticed in social work since the end of the Depression is perhaps due to the fact that social work has not yet been able to take up another challenge of equal greatness on any equally grand scale.

Casting about for new worlds to conquer, the alert eye alights on mankind's new frontier, medicine. In fact, social work has increasingly steered in this direction: directly as medical social work, indirectly in its interest in problems of personal adjustment. The time is ripe for a more definite commitment, both on the side of social work, which needs an objective of overriding importance, and on the side of medicine (all branches, not just psychiatry), which needs social work as it has needed physics to give it the microscope and chemistry to rewrite the pharmacopoeia.

The Personality Factor in Illness

When the search for an external pathogenic agent fails, other causes must be looked for, and it must be presumed that they are in some as yet obscure way connected with the entire complex of physical, psychological, social, and economic behavior patterns that in their totality are the human personality. An unidentified substance in human tears for instance has been suggested as a possible anti-cancer agent. Apart from its intriguing philosophical implications, such a suggestion, even if verified, would be of little value unless some knowledge were gained as to the type of personality productive of tears. Dietary habits conducive to the accumulation of cholesterol have been thought responsible for atherosclerosis—a hypothesis supported by the observation that in southern Italy, with preponderance of carbohydrate diet, atherosclerosis is relatively rare, but confounded by the finding that among Eskimos, with the opposite dietary bias, it is even rarer.

What is necessary is a comprehensive study of all conceivable personality factors in their relation to the incidence of illness. In its classical and most fundamental form, such a study would take the shape of contrasting very comprehensive personality inventories of large groups of individuals that suffer from a certain illness with similar groups that do not. There is no limit to the variations of this elemental scheme that scientific ingenuity may devise.

That such studies (in huge quantity, of the most splendid quality!) are needed, is shown by this consideration: Even where an external pathogenic agent is identifiable, it cannot be the sole cause of the illness; an internal factor combines with it. This has been conceptualized in such constructs as immunity, resistance, and susceptibility. These have in turn often been reduced to factors of heredity, previous exposure, and observable environmental influences. Even so, a large residue remains obscure. For instance, it is not clear why, with the tubercle bacillus virtually ubiquitous, some individuals succumb to it and others do not. The answer must be sought in "X" factors—which may be connected with any other identifiable personality factors. This being true for the group of diseases for which an external agent can be found, it is even more true where this is not the case. Questions such as which persons will develop arteriosclerosis at an early age, and which will develop it later if ever, can best be approached by studying all other possible variables in which these persons differ.

The Potential Contribution of Social Work

Personality is such a many-sided concept that there is no royal road to its study. All disciplines devoted to the study of man have their specific approach. The psychologist, sociologist, anthropologist, the physician of course, and various others, each has a unique contribution to make. So has the social worker.

As social work matured, it developed methods and skills that in their combination distinguish it from other professions. Outstanding among these are: the technique of diversified interviewing, ranging from the very directed that follows an outline or schedule to the completely permissive and nondirective that allows the client to unburden his mind; the systematic use of collateral sources of information, through the imaginative utilization of such resources as each case offers or formalized through home visits and social service exchanges; finally, and most significantly, the principle of always evaluating information within the context of not only the individual's personality but also of his place in his set of social, family, and economic interrelations. Where the physician is apt to see the person as an extension of the body, and where the psychologist studies responses to standardized stimuli in a laboratory situation, the social worker is trained to focus on the totality of the picture that he pieces together. He constantly keeps these questions before his mind: What sort of man is this? What makes him behave as he does? How does he live? What is his role as son, husband, father, worker, fellow man? Where does he stand in the give and take between people?

A personality study conducted with the help of a social worker is superior to one that is done without a social worker by its greater verisimilitude and by an added dimension.

EXPERIENCES IN TEAMWORK

This contribution of social work is actual rather than potential. It has been made.

In the United States Veterans' Administration, for instance, where I have had the privilege of working for the past decade, teamwork is the rule not only in certain treatment situations but in some diagnostic work as well: Where the law requires the Veterans' Administration to determine not only the nature of a condition but also the degree of disability, and where sufficient clarity is not obtained in an examination in the office, a social service survey may be requested to gain a picture of the veteran's adjustment. In the most progressive hospitals and clinics throughout the country, the social worker, in addition to handling the social results of illness and the patient's misgivings about his situation, helps also by sketching a picture of the patient's personality as a backdrop against which the doctors' findings become more meaningful. Some valuable studies resulting from interdisciplinary research on the relationship between personality factors and specific ailments have been produced.

THE NEED FOR A CONCERTED RESEARCH EFFORT

It is here proposed on the basis of all these considerations to establish a large, nationwide interdisciplinary research effort in order to explore the relationship between personality and social factors and illness, emphasizing the ailments that now and in the foreseeable future play the major role, as outlined above.

Though of course under medical direction, this effort should give full free play to the other disciplines that can contribute to it, specifically social work. It should be thought of as a long-range program, limited by nothing but the final success that would make it superfluous. It should be broad; it should be vigorous.

There are three principal possibilities of organizing such a program: A federal agency could be established which, given a large sum of money, would proceed to set up research centers staffed by teams that would make exhaustive studies of groups; work would be uniform, centrally directed, and systematic. Or a federal agency could work through grants to independent research centers, which would be tied in with supervision to guarantee high standards and uniform performance. Or, finally, an infinite variety of research units large and small, under different sponsorship, could undertake the actual job, with a central agency acting as clearinghouse and giving guidance.

Our preference is for the latter system. We feel that the best chance of success lies with a setup that combines a minimum of direction with a maximum of coordination. Those two elements must be balanced.

To take an example that has recently stirred the popular imagination: If smoking contributes to lung cancer, which factors protect many heavy smokers from developing the disease? Since, on the other hand, lung cancer also develops without smoking, may it not be that heavy smoking is not a cause of lung cancer but that both stem from a common cause (perhaps tension leading to peculiar breathing)? What differences are there between ways in which different persons smoke?

Most studies designed to explore such questions thoroughly can only be based on observation of small groups. If a number of such studies can be accumulated—if a dozen studies of ten cases each can be added to make a study of 120 cases—their value can be immeasurably enhanced. This is only possible if the methods used are comparable, all details clearly stated, and the reliability of the investigators assured. Coordination is necessary to achieve this; also, to stimulate training programs, to channel financial support, and to disseminate information.

If, however, such coordination would become central control, the individual initiative, the willingness to take risks and to choose a new path, would be dealt a heavy blow. We would get more of the usual, and perhaps a better type of the usual, but we would lose the unusual. We cannot afford this in a program that deals with problems of such significance as this.

THE START OF THE PROGRAM

To initiate a job of this size is actually surprisingly simple. It is possible to start both at the "grass roots" and at the top. The elements are here; they merely need to be integrated and expanded. Finances are no particular problem, for the experience of the "health drives" has shown that the American people respond eagerly and generously when a health need is placed before them by persons they know and trust. Neither a new national clearinghouse nor local agencies engaging in research would lack support.

Social workers would have to be given opportunities for additional training and incentives to turn to this new task. Volunteers can do much, and it would be of especial significance to mobilize large numbers of volunteers as subjects of investigation. Herein lies also a hope of making life more meaningful again for individuals who suffer from disabling and destructive illness and who can turn their misfortune to the benefit of others; who in some cases can literally give invaluable testimony with their dying breath.

It is in the nature of any such enterprise that its final outcome cannot be foreseen. If it could, the effort would not be needed. There is reason to hope, though, that this program would contribute significantly to the fight against man's worst enemy; that it would help to extend life and its fullness.

3. Reorganizing a Large Hospital Volunteer Program

MRS. ALAN WIENER

Hospitals confronted with the need for expanding the scope of volunteer job opportunities face the usual problems—inadequate leadership, hospital politics, divided loyalties—and whatever the cause, the result has been a crucial shortage of manpower.

At Albert Einstein Medical Center these problems plus a merger of hospitals confronted the hospital administration with the need for a plan to ensure a large stable staff of volunteers. We had found after ten years' experience in working with volunteers in hospitals that certain features were essential to the success of such a volunteer program, namely

1. Evaluation of staff attitudes regarding use of volunteers
2. Study of departmental volunteer needs
3. Job analysis
4. Screening and referral of interested citizens by trained personnel, orientation, supervision and training, recognition and awards, development of volunteer service to administer such a program

Accordingly we set out on a study to discover the real volunteer needs of the Albert Einstein Medical Center.

The Albert Einstein Medical Center was created in February 1952 by the consolidation of Jewish Hospital, Mt. Sinai, and Northern Liberties and Community Health Center. The new institution had a capacity of 900 beds and served 89,000 clinic patients a year. It operated a medical and nursing education program and had facilities for medical research. The three original hospitals from which the Albert Einstein Medical Center was formed became the North, South, and Eastern Divisions of the New Center. However, in February 1955 the Eastern Division, the smallest, was closed because it was in very poor physical condition.

To some extent all three hospitals used volunteers before the merger. However, the way in which they were organized and the ways in which they were used were quite different from the methods used today. Recognizing that, the medical director of the Center felt the need for a study of the volunteer programs at these three centers and asked the Council on Volunteers of the Health and Welfare Council to make such a study.

For several reasons the creation of a unified volunteer program in this Center presented a unique problem. One reason was that the three units of the Center were located in widely different geographic sections of the city. There was a problem of friction among the hospital staffs, because each wanted to maintain its own identity. Northern Division was the hospital that was the oldest and the wealthiest. Throughout the years, the successors followed the footsteps of the earliest beginners so that the hospital ultimately became a closed corporation. For example, at the time of the merger there were third- and fourth-generation families still running the hospital. The Southern Division was started early in the twentieth century, and was supported by a different type of community from Northern Division. Socially, it was considered more advantageous for doctors to be connected with Northern Division, the one that was wealthy and filled with tradition. Eastern Division was developed by a group of doctors who had found a need for a hospital in that community. Thus, these three hospitals not only had difficulty relating to each other, but each related differently to its volunteer program.

First, to help study the problem we organized a lay committee. This committee, known as the Study Committee, was composed of six representatives from the three divisions; that is, the women's auxiliary of each division elected two members to serve on the Study Committee. The main purpose of the committee was to interpret to the board the results of the study. However, the members of the committee were given specific duties so that they might feel that they were a definite and integral part of the study process. This was a study *with* the people and the institution rather than *about* them; the agency that was receiving the treatment was included in the study and diagnosis. There was also a more subtle aim in including the auxiliary women as part of the study program. If they were made a part of the program planning, they would probably be more likely to consider a planned approach to the study of the problem in setting up a volunteer department. If not, they might consider the setting up of an organized volunteer program a threat to their own program and status in the hospital.

In the beginning, until the study plan was organized, we met with the Study Committee for four meetings. In the first meeting, we presented our outline for the proposed study. The committee accepted the outline with some changes.

The questions that the study intended to answer for the Albert Einstein Medical Center were:

1. What is the extent and the effectiveness of the use of volunteers at the present time?
2. What are the possibilities for expansion of the volunteer program?
3. What type of administrative organization would produce the most effective use of volunteers?

It was proposed that to find answers to these questions, we should hold conferences with the heads of thirty-eight departments to determine needs, to evaluate the services being rendered by the volunteers, and to open new fields for volunteer services. Members of the Center staff were most cooperative and interested in developing a well-organized program for volunteers. The questions presented to the department heads were as follows:

1. Have you used volunteers in the past? If so, how many?
2. Could you find other ways of using volunteers? If so, in what types of jobs, how many, and what time and days will they be needed?

In addition, we studied the records of the existing volunteer program. However, although many volunteers had rendered hours of outstanding service to the three divisions of the Albert Einstein Medical Center, the records describing their services were vague and fragmentary.

The specific responsibility of the Study Committee was to measure to some degree the effectiveness of the volunteer organization at Albert Einstein Medical Center in the past. Each representative took responsibility for a random sampling of the active volunteers. A questionnaire was sent to every fourth person in the file. In all, 124 volunteers who were active in the three divisions were questioned. This questionnaire obtained the experience of the various volunteers by covering the following topics: preparedness, supervision, recognition, and personal satisfaction.

From each aspect of the study came various conclusions. Information obtained from a study of the existing records follows:

1. There was no organized Department of Volunteers in any one of the divisions.

2. North Division gave some part-time direction to volunteers through a member of the nursing staff. This division worked with such organizations as American Red Cross, National Council of Jewish Women, Council on Volunteers, and other service groups. At that time there were 217 volunteers working in ten departments of the Northern Division.

3. Southern Division had relied heavily upon its Women's Auxiliary and residents of the immediate hospital area to support its volunteer program. While there was no over-all direction in the program, except the auxiliary

officer of the day, there were 49 persons serving five departments on a weekly basis.

4. A similar situation had existed in East Division, where 32 volunteers coming largely from two Auxiliaries were serving in two departments.

In all the divisions there were two different kinds of volunteers: (1) service volunteers and (2) auxiliary volunteers. A service volunteer is a person serving a minimum number of hours a week on a regular basis, and assigned to a specific hospital department as part of personnel. An auxiliary volunteer is one who may render occasional service to the hospital by giving financial support to a project or serving in an activity not attached to a hospital department such as sewing aide, canteen attendant, and so on.

The study of the active volunteers revealed these pertinent facts:

1. Although all three divisions of the Medical Center had shown an interest in the use of volunteers, there was no total plan for recruiting, training, and supervising volunteers in any one of the three divisions.

2. North Division had progressed farther than South or East in their volunteer program. This may have been due to its seniority and/or to its use of a part-time director.

3. Some attempt had been made in all three divisions to orient the volunteers with "on the job" training. In addition a number of volunteers received Gray Lady or Nurse's Aid training from the American Red Cross.

4. Even with the obviously uncoordinated and small volunteer programs being carried on in the divisions, a large number of the volunteers who had been used received a satisfying experience and felt that they were appreciated.

From the interviews with the various department heads, we discovered that there were approximately 300 volunteers working at the time of the study. An additional 700 to 800 volunteers were needed to supplement the active workers in newly developed jobs. It was felt that failure to use volunteers was largely due to the fact that supervisors had not considered the subject seriously, or else did not know how to go about getting adequate volunteer service or how to use such service to its fullest extent. The information gathered through the study was thoroughly analyzed by the lay committee. The conclusions were then presented to the medical director for use with his board and hospital staff. It was felt that the following recommendations should serve as a framework for building a sound volunteer program to become an integral part of operations at Albert Einstein Medical Center.

1. The establishment of volunteer services with an administrative director. The size of the Center and the large number of job opportuni-

ties for volunteers also indicated the need for a full- or part-time coordinator in each unit.

2. The director should be charged with the following duties: job analysis, training, and supervision; general orientation; improving recruitment techniques; coordinating the volunteer activities of groups; maintaining of ethical and high standards of performance on the part of individual volunteers; and developing a system of recognitions and awards plus opportunity for advancement.

3. Ensuring adequate status for the Director of Volunteers through administrative action in placing that department on an equal level with all other hospital departments.

4. Establishing good working relations between professional staff and volunteers through direct interpretation by Center administrator.

Since the study was made and recommendations acted upon there has been sustained improvement in the volunteer program. There has been a quantitative and qualitative improvement in the volunteer personnel serving the Center; actually there are now between 600 and 700 active service volunteers. There has been a decided improvement in the acceptance of volunteers by hospital staff. The most invaluable reward that has accrued has been the ability of a well-informed citizenry to interpret the function and service of Albert Einstein to the community at large.

The above-mentioned principles have guided the development of volunteer departments in fifteen hospitals in the Philadelphia area, including Philadelphia General Hospital, St. Christopher's Hospital, University of Pennsylvania, and others. In all of these hospitals we have seen the same metamorphosis take place, namely, the change from the haphazard, hit or miss method of using citizen interest to the well-organized professional use of the layman.

It is as a result of our experience with the successful development of volunteer programs in hospitals that I recommend this process of study analysis and implementation of sound principles of volunteer work to other institutions facing the problem of a manpower shortage.

4. Training Hospital Volunteers

MARY JEAN SHAMLIAN

Basic medical research today, as at no other time in world history, stands challenged for the answers to man's problems of pain. Its laboratories are endowed, supported, and encouraged by the interest of the public. That same public volunteers its services through a thousand and one organizations. Convinced of a need, volunteer groups step forward to conduct surveys, stage collection drives, and even to distribute educational material house to house.

When a research staff works through a hospital, many agencies may assist through volunteer services. Clinics are supplied with receptionists, nurses' aides, and clerical personnel. Patients are furnished transportation through one or more volunteer motor pools. Children's wards are staffed with recreation aides; volunteer toymakers supply toys. The ways in which organized voluntary services benefit basic medical research are many. So many, in fact, that in some instances hospitals have set up coordinating councils in order that the offered services complement each other rather than overlap. Such a munificence of voluntary service exists, in fact, that it is probable no medical research staff today functions entirely without the support and cooperation of some voluntary group.

In order to best effect the use of group volunteers, however, more highly trained and responsible leadership is necessary. Although the average hospital staff or clinical research facility can use group volunteers in many capacities, the integration of these lay people into a medical background becomes a problem that can be surmounted only by volunteer training.

For many volunteer aides the fascination of medicine is soon found to be submerged in dull, stultifying routine. No matter what strong impulse has led the volunteer to offer service, if that service does not seem important to the project as a whole, that volunteer is going to function at less than best effort or eventually give it up entirely. How differently the volunteer who types clinic cards one morning each week would feel about her job if she could follow the information on that card through the channels of research it may take, to become, finally, a statistical part of world health information, vital to all mankind. To her, they are such a small contribution to basic medical research that she just doesn't show up one morning.

Ask a floor nurse at the University of California Hospital, a training hospital for doctors and nurses and a research center, how she feels about volunteers. She will start out by saying, "It's not that I don't appreciate them . . ." Then she adds, "Sometimes they do a lot for the patient, undoubtedly they contribute a good deal to his welfare when they write letters, do manicures, read aloud, and so on. All this helps maintain morale, of course." Then she makes her point. "Well, they don't understand hospital routine, for one thing, and you can't count on them. They just aren't reliable. When they try to help with actual aide work, you just get them trained and they are gone. Even though they are helpful, we nurses would rather double up on our duties when we are short-handed than depend on volunteers."

The nurse was speaking of volunteer aides working through organizations, and she is not alone in her attitude. Yet there is an answer. The volunteer is part of an organization, works under the chairmanship of some member of that organization, and only insofar as his parent group is responsible to the research center can he be expected to be responsible.

Civic and fraternal organizations, labor unions and employee associations, schools and colleges all offer volunteers to basic medical research. But integrating these groups into the severity of clinical procedure and laboratory routine is impossible as the situation now exists in a majority of cases.

There can be no area of public welfare more vital than basic medical research, yet this is an area at once as demanding as it is rewarding. But the majority of those who come as volunteers, offering sincere hearts and willing hands, are lost in the shuffle and drift away. They are lost through lack of understanding, and they drift away because their effort does not seem important. No amount of recognition and service credits from his organization can make the job he does valuable if the volunteer doesn't really see himself as a part of all medicine everywhere, his little effort one of a vast total for man's common good.

Although no football team begins a game without a pep-talk from its coach to build up team spirit, ordinary folk with a hundred and one outside responsibilities are turned loose daily in our medical centers as volunteer aides, without any comprehensive idea of what they are doing and why. Somehow it is assumed that the volunteer does not really need to know much about the project since he very likely could not understand anyway.

Yet no one capable of assisting in a medical facility is incapable of understanding the objectives he is helping to further. As volunteers are lost to service through lack of training and group responsibility, a very real loss in human effort occurs. This is reflected in a dollars and cents loss also, for these same volunteers who give their time also support the medical center directly through financial contributions, as they participate in drives, nationwide appeals for funds, and local collections for the benefit of medical research. The spirit of helpfulness that first allied the volunteer to the cause of welfare must be re-evaluated, and steps taken to broaden his orientation to medical research, to give him necessary training, and to utilize the service he offers.

The City of Hope Medical Center at Duarte, California, just outside Los Angeles, receives support from tuberculosis, heart, and cancer foundations. It was built largely through the financial support of labor unions, and maintains a four-hundred-bed hospital and research facilities for the study of these three divisions of medical welfare. This big, busy medical center has proved that ordinary lay people can understand complex medical facts and procedures when there is a need for this understanding.

Although the City of Hope has the usual volunteer groups serving in many capacities, everyone associated with these service organizations has become fully acquainted with the aims and objectives of the center through a training program. A tour of the facilities, including laboratories, outpatient clinics, and hospital wings, precedes the volunteer's assignment. He is given literature on the center and its history and goals for the future. The volunteer group's chairman is thoroughly indoctrinated with the ideology of the program before he begins training volunteers. In this way, no individual volunteer gives one hour of work without being aware of the importance of that hour to the whole of human welfare. The direct line of communication between the group chairman and the hospital's representative in charge of volunteer service is responsible for this increased sense of human values, and for more effective service.

Most unusual is the way in which one group of volunteers, bound together by only one tie, contribute to medical research through studies of leukemia in children. The City of Hope's leukemia wing, built through the voluntary donations of many organizations, functions with volunteer aides almost unique in medicine. These aides are parents, a dozen or more who come in daily to spend as much time as they can with their children. They act as nurses' aides, recreation aides, babysitters. They are there because their very presence adds immeasurably to the normalcy of an abnormal situation for the child.

The one thing these parent volunteers have in common is that they are all waiting. They are waiting for the day that the little child they watch over will die, or waiting for one more day that it may live. Years do not count here, even months are doubtful. Each day is sufficient unto itself.

Christmas trees decorate a bedside table in July; for this child, Christmas must be now. The wonderful thing is that although these parents wait, they do not vainly wait.

They are banded together in a plan of parent participation, as it is called, in which they actually do participate in the child's welfare and lessen the difficulties of the child's adjustment to a new and sometimes frightening situation. A coldly scientific fact made these volunteers a part of the medical center—the fact that these children, with whom studies are progressing that will mean a new lease on life for all children everywhere, are better off in every way when parents keep close to them and assist in their daily routine.

The parent volunteers learn methods of care that are invaluable when they are alone responsible for the child's treatment, during those periods of time when improvement or remission allows the child to be cared for at home temporarily. They learn to keep records of medication and clinical data that are important to the doctors in keeping in touch with the little patients during their stays at home. The parents learn to exchange sympathy for empathy, to widen their horizons from a desperate love for their child to loving care of all children. Those patients whose parents could not come into the hospital often because of work or other children at home are included in the service of these parent volunteers, and benefit thereby.

Yet, was this a plan that couldn't work? Everyone associated with the hospital at the time the leukemia wing was being built doubted that it would work out. How could you bring a lot of emotionally involved parents into a hospital and maintain nursing disciplines and stable patients?

The first children came, and soon after, parents began to spend many days at the hospital. We saw strollers in the hall; a mother would bring a "picnic" and two or three little patients would enjoy the fun. Story hour was especially good with a real mother there, and medical treatment took less of an emotional toll when a mother explained that it would make Johnny better.

Experts in hospital routine and administration had said it couldn't work. It had been tried in the East, worked out all right according to reports, but how about all those emotionally upset parents, people faced with the almost inevitable loss of their child in the near future, what about all those people taking up doctors' time, interfering with nurses, being frightened of clinical procedures which were essential to the patient . . . ?

The answer lay in training, in group forums in which the parent began to see his child as the representative of many children. In medical treatment, in new methods lay his child's only hope. Research was staving off death day by day, but days gained might grow into weeks. Even when there was no hope extended, the parent learned about the child's treatment, and the terror of the mystery of leukemia was lessened. Here, then, ordinary people learned to function within the strict regimen of medicine, and to bring homely skills and unselfish service right into the hospital.

Because of this extreme example of a group of people learning to function in a new environment, to channel the emotional drive of family love into work for the good of all, the author believes that volunteers from every community can serve more effectively in medical centers near them, if only they are given the opportunity to learn enough about the project and methods at hand to function effectively.

From the Samaritan who stopped by the roadside to present-day volunteer service groups, the motive has been the same, helping a fellow being. The need to be of service, to participate in human welfare, is present in everyone. But today we find that as medical research grows, so too do the areas of knowledge that preface effective helpful service. Let us not turn away anyone who comes to offer his service, but rather let us see that the volunteer is equipped with fundamental knowledge, the understanding of his part in the work he is doing. Only in this way will he become a valuable volunteer and be a responsible part of basic medical research.

The premise of this discussion is that volunteer aides must be able to identify themselves with their part in basic medical research to be effective.

In extending voluntary activity in public welfare, in particular basic medical research, we must first give the group chairman all possible training, through actual classes in clinical procedure where necessary, with the aim of extending his understanding of the job to be done so that he can see that his individual volunteers also become, not only trained for better service, but a part of that service. This better understanding will call forth a more intelligent approach to service and a more personal identification with the project as a whole.

The volunteer may wear an arm band that shows him to be a bona fide volunteer aide, he may receive a certificate of merit from his own organization, but only when he fully realizes the value of every hour of his own service, will he begin to function wholly in basic medical research.

5. Community Health Education Through a Museum

WINFIELD G. DOYLE

Health today occupies a position of growing importance in the lives of all Americans. This emphasis starts with local governments in city and county health departments and works up at the national level to the executive Department of Health, Education, and Welfare, to the international level in the United Nations World Health Organization.

With respect to private agencies, the nation is honeycombed with local chapters of diabetes, tuberculosis, heart, infantile paralysis, cancer, and a host of other associations, all of which conduct research or educational programs. The success of their appeals for funds through television, radio, mother marchers, seals, and other devices is familiar to everyone. In addition, there are the annual Community Chest or United Fund drives for financing local health and welfare agencies—drives that this year (1956) exceeded their quotas in many cities, such as Cleveland and Detroit.

We see, then, evidences on all sides of an enormous individual and community interest in health matters. And for good reason. Nothing is more important to a person than his "state of complete physical, mental, and social well-being," to quote the World Health Organization's definition of health.

Yet the nation was shocked at the revelations of the President's 1956 Conference on Fitness of American Youth. Although American children are the best clothed, the best fed, and the best doctored in the world, they are far below par in physical strength and flexibility. Of the nearly four and one-half million men called to military service in the last six years, 41 per cent were rejected for medical reasons. Automobiles, television, spectator sports, and other sedentary activities are responsible for the trend toward a nation of softies, according to many authorities, and yet our people show a great interest in, and lend generous support to, health matters. Why this apparent paradox?

The answer probably lies in the apathy—it is not a total indifference—

to many preventive measures. Lack of muscle tone, which causes so many children to fail in meeting minimum standards of physical fitness, is a general term—less tangible and less dramatic than a child whose muscles are paralyzed by polio. Our people appear to be more interested in curing a disease once it has occurred than in preventing it in the first place, and it is to the credit of our several private health agencies and medical societies that they are gradually educating us to the benefits of periodic chest X rays, diabetes detection methods, planned immunization programs, fluoridated water supplies, and other preventive procedures.

The question of what can be done to create a greater awareness of the benefits of good general health is being answered in some communities by the health museum. In some instances, these are separate and independent organizations as in Cleveland and Dallas. In others, they are planned as an operating unit of a hospital, as at the Lankenau Hospital in Philadelphia. In still others, health is treated as a separate or additional subject in an existing museum, as at the Boston Science Museum and the Chicago Museum of Science and Industry. Whichever of these approaches the individual community adopts, the health museum is living testimony to the worth of the visual approach to health teaching.

"Now I See Why . . ."

Join us in the Cleveland Health Museum's Science Theater. We are a fifth-grade class from one of Cleveland's suburban schools, and we have come here to study about nutrition. We have just taken our seats, and our museum instructor is about to introduce the transparent woman standing before us. Our instructor asks us to watch carefully for various organs of the body as they light up, and to listen to what is said about them. Juno, as the transparent woman is called, tells us in her own voice the story of where these organs are located and what they do in the body.

After a quarter of an hour, we leave the Science Theater and go to the Lecture Hall for a film. Our instructor, in introducing the film, refers to some of the remarks Juno just made and tells us that for the next few minutes, during the film and afterwards when we look at some exhibits together, we will be concerned with the part food plays in our daily lives.

The lights go off and the film starts running. We like it from the start because it is a cartoon in color. The main character is a man named "Careless Charlie" who feeds his family only corn bread and dried beans. The members of the family aren't very healthy, and they don't have the pep and energy to keep their house clean and their yard tidy. But soon "Careless Charlie" learns how to grow fruits and vegetables on his farm, and he also has pigs, chickens, and other livestock which supply him with meat, cheese, milk, and eggs. In the end, the family eats well-balanced meals every day; the house is clean; the farm is neat and tidy; and instead of being "Careless Charlie" he is now "Careful Charlie." Following the film, several of us have questions, and finally the instructor asks if we won't wait a couple of minutes for further answers until we get upstairs to the Nutrition Room.

As we sit on our camp stools with all the nutrition exhibits around us, our instructor talks to us first about a preserved human digestive tract that is mounted on the wall behind a plastic bubble. She describes the esophagus, stomach, and intestines, and even though we had heard Juno talk about the appendix, some of us didn't understand exactly where it is located until it was pointed out to us. After we reviewed how the food we ate is digested, we talked about the different kinds of food our bodies need, and saw from the exhibits that we need a balanced diet instead of just one or two kinds of food.

We have been here now about an hour and a quarter, and we are anxious to see other exhibits in the museum. Our instructor dismisses us for quiet browsing, and some of us rush over to the special telephone that records our voice. Others crowd around for a demonstration of our heartbeat. That little microphone is certainly sensitive! It can pick up the heartbeat just the way a doctor's stethoscope does, and you can hear it over the built-in loudspeaker.

We're pretty well scattered now, looking for buttons to push, handles to turn, flaps to lift. No hands-off signs here! What other museum has an exhibit about heredity that works like a pinball machine? (Our instructor told us that exhibit was made out of two pinball machines confiscated by the police department.) Or lets you crawl into an iron lung that really works?

Oh, oh! There goes the announcement on the public address system that we're ready to leave. And here we haven't seen everything yet. Oh well, we'll just have to come back soon with our parents when we can spend more time. Goodbye. Thanks for joining our class.

A Multi-Faceted Program

Such a typical school visit represents an important phase of the Cleveland Health Museum's program, but to be sure not the only one. Space does not permit a complete discussion of its other activities, nor is this necessary. Just mentioning a few of them is sufficient to show the great variety of exhibits and of community participation that a health museum has in bringing health information to its public.

During World War II, a series of exhibits was installed to show how rationed foods could best be combined with unrationed staples to give interesting and balanced diets. When the 1950 census was published, many of the vital statistics it contained were translated into exhibit form as a study in population; it was titled "We the People." Medical rehabilitation was highlighted within the past three years by building into one of the large museum rooms a kitchen, a bathroom, and a bedroom, all equipped for the convenience of the wheelchair patient and others with physical handicaps. A current exhibit deals with alcoholism as a medical problem, and within the next year the rest of the exhibit on human genetics will be completed, one part of which is designed to deal with the question of genetic changes caused by radiations, just as the exhibit with the pinball mechanism mentioned above deals with dominance and recessiveness.

Community health projects take a major portion of the staff time and energies. The museum is represented on the Health Council, the Adult Education Committee, the Mayor's Air Pollution Committee, the Family Health Association, the Health Education Committee, and the Cleveland Center on Alcoholism. It cooperates with the public schools, the area councils, the hospitals, the medical school, the Cleveland Academy of Medicine, the Cleveland Dental Society, the Nutrition Association, and many others in regular or special projects and programs.

In addition it conducts many programs of its own. The doors are open seven days a week for anyone who wants to visit. For three years it put on a weekly television program jointly with the Academy of Medicine titled "Prescription for Living," sponsored by the Standard Oil Company of Ohio. It had a vacation program for children this past summer which included a story hour, science crafts, junior biologists, and a course for Girl Scouts working toward their public health badge. It is currently cosponsoring with the Junior League a monthly Saturday morning puppet show in which the Everbright Family is waging a constant battle against Dingy, the villain, to keep healthy.

A HEALTH MUSEUM IN EVERY CITY

The worth of a health museum is attested by the growing number we find in the United States, either as separate institutions or parts of others. Our national museum in Washington will soon make health one of its exhibit departments when the new Hall of Health is opened at the Smithsonian Institution. A new health museum is in the building stage in a suburban community near Detroit. Several other cities are in the process of organizing their own health museums, but it would be premature to announce their locations at this time.

Every community will and should have its own way of starting and supporting its health museum. Without dwelling on the details, some of the organizational principles and administrative policies followed in Cleveland may be helpful.

The Cleveland Health Museum is a private, self-supporting, nonprofit institution with its own board of trustees. It is entirely independent of city tax support, and even of Community Chest funds, and is not affiliated with any other museum, any hospital, any medical society, or other organization. Its big initial push came when the late Mrs. Elisabeth Severance Prentiss donated her home as the first museum building, and after her death left about a third of her estate as an endowment. The small handful of founders received support and encouragement in those earliest years from several hundred interested medical, dental, and lay members, and this number has increased steadily until today the Cleveland Health Museum boasts over three thousand members. The Museum's first budget was $25,000. Today it is six times that figure, with approximately one third of the income provided by the since-augmented endowment, one third provided by memberships, and the remaining third from miscellaneous sources such as workshop earnings, contributions from trustees and friends, and foundation grants.

What Cleveland has done other cities can do, too. There is no pat formula for getting a health museum started. Some communities might find that a tax-supported museum is the answer, while others might have a small group of civic leaders and one or more financial "angels," as in Cleveland, to organize and finance the venture. Local voluntary agencies such as the Blue Cross, the Heart Society, and the Nutrition Association can often be induced to pay for the building and installation of exhibits, and business and industry will sometimes contribute funds for exhibits in their area of special interest, such as a telephone company on the ears and hearing or an electric illuminating company on the eyes and sight. Even public agencies such as the health department and the schools will lend encouragement and support with few strings attached if such support can be justified through public service rendered. Let us not forget, either, our stanch friends in the medical and allied professions: physicians, dentists, nurses can not only form the core of a solid and loyal membership, but in some instances have been known to sponsor a health museum in its infancy and beyond.

One of the difficulties with a health museum, as with all museums, is establishing a criterion for determining how effective a job is being done. It is to be hoped that through the program conducted within its own walls; through its publications, radio and television programs, and other means of communication; through its participation in community health programs, it would ultimately contribute to improving individual health practices and attitudes. However, these influences cannot be measured directly.

We do know, however, that the same schools use our services in Cleveland year after year to supplement their school health education work, and the number of new schools increases each year. We know that our membership is not remaining static, but increasing, and although this speaks well for the efficiency of our membership secretary it also indicates that the public is sympathetic enough to our program to support us. We know that a sixfold increase in the budget has enabled us to expand our services to many times those of sixteen years ago. If these are legitimate criteria for evaluation, then we are succeeding.

The health museum, then, can not only capitalize on an already intense public interest in health but can also heighten that interest in the community it serves. The health museum can be the one constant force—a community "conscience," if you will—in keeping health matters in the public eye, as compared to the various "drives" which focus attention on only one aspect of health for a short time during the year. Any amount of planning, hard work, and financing that may be required to get one started will pay rich dividends in helping people learn and practice good health habits.

10
Migrant Workers

1. A Migrant Ministry in the Southwest

WILLIAM H. KOCH, JR.

The social problems of agricultural migrant workers present to American communities and their welfare institutions what may still be considered a frontier to be conquered. While there have been many efforts in behalf of this occupational group over the past thirty years, and a quickening of concern in recent times, many thousands of migrant families today still lack even the most elementary health, education, welfare, recreation, and religious services.

It is recognized that a mobile force of workers is necessary to the agricultural economy. Manpower is sought afar each season so that local crops may be picked for the markets of the nation. Yet many states and their communities penalize the migrant worker for his mobile status. Residence laws often disqualify migrants for health and welfare services. Migrant children are often excluded from the schools. Migrant workers have no union to speak for them and, disenfranchised by their mobility, they cannot speak for themselves. As political nonentities, their needs can safely be ignored by administrative and legislative bodies.

As they move from one small community to another in the rural areas of the states they serve, migrants face other disadvantages. The communities themselves often have none of the voluntary services in health, welfare, recreation, and informal education, that might meet needs where residence laws prevent governmental assistance. And the double-edged handicap of economic status and cultural difference combines against migrant families, creating barriers between them and the community, so that they are left to face their problems by themselves. In "good work" times, migrant families often are continually handicapped by lack of normal community services that might help them better their lot. In times of seasonal work shortage, migrant families often face dire and critical hardship, with nowhere to turn for even the rudimentary needs of life.

The Role of a Voluntary Agency

In these not uncommon circumstances, there is clearly a need for the extension of voluntary services to migrant workers. Whereas governmental agencies occasionally initiate new services, social welfare history gives evidence that the pioneering role goes to the voluntary agency that is limited neither by statutory purpose nor legally restricted funds. In assuming responsibility for migratory workers, a voluntary agency may well serve in an area of need where no other agency serves. It may develop services of many kinds, it may coordinate existing services, or it may use already established services, finding ways to extend them to an unserved group. Further, the voluntary agency may find itself providing services that ordinarily might be considered the "public" responsibility, such as the establishment of health services or relief activities.

Although all such services are ends in themselves, it is important that the voluntary agency use its experience and the concern it generates in the communities where it operates as a means of bringing about public interest and eventually the establishment of both voluntary and governmental programs that will include the migrant worker. The dual functions of social service and social action are not separate parts of the program. Jane Addams first expressed it, and the welfare professions have given continuing currency to the principle, that just as the symptoms of the social problem must be treated, so too must the cause be sought and cured.

How a State-Level Voluntary Agency Might Extend Service

Let us suppose that a State-level voluntary agency dedicated to serving migrants is enabled to employ staff and initiate a program to extend services to migrant workers in the State. Just how would its board of directors proceed to plan and carry out such a program?

Assuming that a fundamental statement of purpose has been enunciated that accepts the foregoing role of a voluntary agency, and that planning takes place within a framework of facts, agency planners must then fashion "operating principles," guideposts to action, that cast the agency and its staff in their operating roles. Such principles may well include the following.

1. Treatment of symptoms and causes together takes place at all levels of operation.
2. The communities in which migrants work and live have primary responsibility for taking direct action in their behalf; without the ac-

tive concern of the local community, no permanent good can result from voluntary welfare services.

3. The community and its members must be educated concerning the facts of migrant life and problems.

4. The community must be stimulated to want to act, and then helped to develop specific services to meet needs.

5. Every project, whether so intended or not, is a demonstration of the feasibility of serving migrants. Local groups developing services "show the way" to other groups, communities, and the nation.

6. Efforts in behalf of migrants should be coordinated at all levels so that sound planning will assure good results.

7. Cooperation should be sought among all groups related to the problems of migrants: farmers, businessmen, teachers, social workers, and others, since the best efforts of all are needed to solve so huge a problem.

If the operating role of the voluntary migrant agency were to be described in one word, perhaps the term "enabler" would be the most appropriate. Through the functions indicated above, the agency and its staff make it possible for communities and their groups to do the job that must be done if voluntary services are to be extended to the migrant population.

Using the foregoing principles as a guide, specific areas of program might then be considered. Program activities can be seen to fall into four categories, effective at State and local levels. The activities falling into any one category may also fall into one or more of the others; the categories are not mutually exclusive.

Community development or organization is a category of early priority. Its activities aim to help the community find ways to organize and provide services to meet needs of migrants in the locality. The process would include informing the community about existing problems, stimulating concern, helping the community organize committees and service groups, locating local resources, and determining the nature of specific programs and services.

Staff of the voluntary agency would have to discover ways to reach community groups. Staff might work through established structures such as church groups, PTA's, women's clubs, and community councils. Or, perhaps, a special committee might be formed, with representatives of various concerned groups.

A certain amount of "seed scattering" is required. The staff worker may have to develop contacts with key individuals in the community. He may procure, through contacts, a speaking engagement before the Kiwanis Club or the Merchants' Association. If the agency has developed any reputation at all, staff may be called in consultation on a seasonal welfare emergency involving migrant workers. Or staff may work through State organizations, appearing at conferences or institutes, and making it known that invitations to present the program to community groups would be welcomed.

In helping a community organize for migrant work, the voluntary agency must use all of its professional insights and skills. It would never do, for example, for staff to descend upon a community with a prepackaged program. It is far wiser to let program ideas develop among community members, then provide assistance to them in planning and carrying out an idea.

Staff, by intelligent application of skills, *enables* the community to solve for itself the problems it faces. And staff does not withdraw when the immediate goal of establishment of program is accomplished. Rather, the agency continues to help the community solve new and more advanced problems it begins to see as it gains experience.

Provision of services is the next category. The nature of specific services will differ according to the community's view of the needs and its resources to meet them. The voluntary agency's job is to help the community find its way in developing the services chosen.

The community may decide to establish a "migrant relief center." It may want to work out a practical method of centralizing and coordinating welfare giving. Its clubwomen and physicians may want to work together to establish a well-baby clinic for migrants. Its school teachers may want to organize literacy classes or recreation for adults and teenagers. The churches may feel that bringing religious services and Bible schools to the labor camps is important. Volunteers may act as "friendly visitors" finding, as doors open in friendship, family problems that existing community service might be able to solve. And if the problems discovered cannot be met with current resources, the community is at least made aware that problems exist.

The role of staff varies with the activities chosen. The extent of leadership given to a community group will depend upon how much help its members desire and upon how competent they may be in rendering the particular service chosen. The pattern will probably take the form of early attention and help in beginning stages of program. Yet staff is wise to train community members to take over various leadership responsibilities, withdrawing gradually from active leadership as they become competent. However, staff will probably never withdraw completely from some kind of secondary leadership or consultative role.

The question of whether or not volunteers are competent to bring certain social services arises. The aim of the program is to find the most competent volunteer possible. Where there is no competence, as in the practice of medicine or casework, the volunteer does not attempt to practice, but relates the needy migrant to the qualified practitioner in the community. And the very act of referral is an important service in itself.

Further, "the program" is not any *one* of the activities mentioned; it is *all* of them, generically described as "extending the community's concern." Certainly, any member of the community is a competent practitioner within this definition.

As to whether the total program of activities would be carried out more effectively by trained staff, the answer is that no voluntary agency could support enough staff workers to meet the needs of the tremendous numbers of migrants in the States. The voluntary agency can best extend its services by multiplying its efforts and its staff through taking an enabling role of secondary leadership.

Public education is the third category. Based on fact finding and appropriate interpretation, this program area operates on all levels to inform, arouse, and stimulate to action the general public. All available media should be used and appropriate materials developed for the "publics" to be reached. It is important to base all materials solidly on fact and it is also wise to avoid imposing blame for conditions on one group or another. A sound theme for public education is: "It's the problem of all of us, and we're in it together."

Cooperative action is the final category, and the term is chosen carefully to negate the suspicions aroused by the term "social action." Carrying the thought "we're all in this together" into action, this program area recognizes that no one agency can solve the problems of migrants alone. It calls upon all agencies, groups, and organizations concerned, governmental, voluntary, civic, professional, and religious, at all levels, to work together to find ways to help the migrant worker help himself.

At the local level, the voluntary migrant agency consults with, informs, stimulates, and cooperates with other agencies and organizations. It does the same at the State level. And on the national level, the voluntary agency should be aware of federal agency and national organization movements in behalf of migrants.

Depending on its own choice, the voluntary agency may or may not be active in seeking legislative change. It is probably more desirable that it stimulate other groups who might do so more appropriately. However, the voluntary agency may join with others in developing a movement to seek social change.

Through its program of cooperative action, the voluntary agency may well extend not only its own services to migrants, but also those of other agencies, public and voluntary.

A Case History

It may be revealed at this juncture that the plan described here is not hypothetical. Rather, it is an accurate description of the planning and program of the Migrant Ministry of a southwestern State over the past two years. The agency is church-related and the writer has been executive director during the carrying out of the program described.

The ultimate effectiveness of the program cannot, of course, be evaluated at this time. Yet, in terms of extending services to migrants within the State, an encouraging report can be made.

Less than three years ago, the agency served fewer than 500 migrants in a limited geographical area, with a seasonal staff of only two partially trained workers. Today, 5,000 migrants are being served in three major agricultural counties by 14 seasonal and full-time staff and more than 200 volunteers from eleven communities, large and small. A program of varied services is being provided for migrant men, women, teenagers and children, including religious education, health, home management, literacy, recreation, and related activities. A demonstration child-care center, the only one of its kind in the Southwest, has now operated through two seasons, serving 100 or more different preschool children. As a result of this project, two communities are planning establishment of similar centers in their own localities.

A teen-canteen has been conducted in a county housing authority camp, serving 60 boys and girls each week during the harvest time. This year, an isolated farm community, with agency assistance, established a maternal and child health clinic for farm workers.

Through development of community concern and referral of migrants in need, other voluntary agencies have been induced to extend their services to this group. Countless conferences, institutes, and other educational programs have been conducted by the agency at local, regional, and State levels with civic, fraternal, religious, business, and professional groups.

Finally, the Migrant Ministry, through its total program, has brought about top-level State concern for the problems of migrants through successful urging of the appointment of the first Governor's Committee on Seasonal Farm Labor, a body into which representatives of all concerned groups have been brought for study and long-range planning.

Conclusion

The essence of the proposed plan for extending voluntary and other services to migrant workers, as has been demonstrated, may be found in the verb: "to enable." By making it possible for many individuals, many groups, and many resources to become involved in the solution of a great socio-economic problem to which they are intimately related, we adhere to the fundamental democratic principles of social organization we believe in. As the voluntary agency and its staff become "multiplier factors" in this area of concern, perhaps we may even look to the day when the true goal of all social welfare can be accomplished and we will find ourselves "out of business."

2. Building a Migrants' Community

STEPHEN THIERMAN

The motion picture version of John Steinbeck's novel, *The Grapes of Wrath,* portrays the migration of sharecroppers from the Dust Bowl to the mirage of a free and happy life in California. I saw the picture in Philadelphia in 1940 while I was still a college student. Its story of the harsh life of the Joad family, typical migrant workers of the thirties, roused my first concern for the needs of migrant workers. It was not until eight years later that I had an opportunity to shift this concern from the mind to the world outside.

I had moved to California, the promised land to which the Joads had emigrated, and was working with the American Friends Service Committee in San Francisco. In March 1948 headlines in the San Francisco *Chronicle* thundered: "50,000 Migrant Farm Workers Are Unemployed," "Migrant Workers Out of Funds," "Farm Unemployment to Last All Summer."

Several of us on the Friends Service Committee staff were dispatched to the San Joaquin Valley to determine whether migrant needs warranted a concerted appeal to the public for help. We discovered there were adequate local public and private resources to meet the emergency and that the Friends should serve only as a self-starter to set the relief machinery going. Nevertheless, as a consequence of this visit my interest in the migrant was revived. Since then I have familiarized myself with the geography of California's Central Valley, not only physical but human. I have talked with people in a dozen California agricultural counties, stretching 800 miles from Shasta in the north to Imperial in the south. I have spoken with migrants, growers, church leaders, educators, home agents, agricultural employment officers, concerned laymen. From these conversations I have reached some firm conclusions about the needs of California migrant workers and the kind of private, voluntary effort that could be extended in their behalf.

The California migrant worker falls into two predominant groups. There is, first, the unalloyed nomadic migrant. He and his family have no fixed base but continuously follow the crops. He numbers 60,000 and constitutes about 20 per cent of the migrant labor force in California. Second is the larger and increasing number of the settled or settling migrant. He is trying to establish a residence in a shack town, sometimes called a fringe area. He travels alternately short and long distances to work but eventually returns "home." He represents about 125,000 persons or 40 per cent of the migrant workers in the State. The balance are contract nationals drawn from Mexico, Japan, and the Philippines.

Whether nomadic or settled, the migrant breadwinner has an average employment for only 32 weeks in a year. Even this is intermittent employment, averaging about two weeks with each employer. The worker's vocational skills are limited, and his sense of insecurity and lack of experience often prevent his attempting new types of work even when they are available to him. He does not save—indeed how can he on such a marginal income?—and is therefore ready prey for the salesman who holds out the lure of "easy terms."

Where the migrant has settled in shack towns the population may range from 25 to 2,500 persons. Some of these towns are almost entirely Negro, some largely Mexican American, some entirely Anglo, but many completely mixed. The inhabitants of these settlements have in common a great suspicion toward government officials, toward any outsider, and indeed toward one another. Each man is for himself. The leadership expected from older, better-established citizens in normal communities is lacking, and if anyone tends to assume leadership he is quickly discredited by his neighbors. This makes the job of helping migrants one of extreme delicacy and of extreme slowness. In many of the settlements there are no street lights, no plumbing, often not even water. Those without means of transportation pay as much as twenty-five cents for a 15-gallon can of water, to be hauled to their door. These communities, as might be expected, have a heavy welfare caseload; there are large families, juvenile delinquency runs high, and in certain school districts 100 per cent of the children from these areas receive free school lunches from December until March.

Of the two major groups of migrants, I believe the fringe area or shack town migrant in California is more in need of help and can benefit more from voluntary activity and organization. In contrast to the settled migrant, the nomadic migrant already receives aid from the Migrant Ministry of the National Council of Churches. Church staffs provide organized recreation, secure health services, and give religious instruction to migrants in encampments up and down the Central Valley. Catholic priests are frequent spokesmen for the nomadic group, yet neither Protestants nor Catholics have concerned themselves with the needs of the settled migrant. Not only does the shack town migrant need help, but he is in the best position to benefit from it. He has established residence, however marginal, has demonstrated a certain degree of personal responsibility, and has become eligible for State and county welfare services.

Having once decided that the fringe area migrant offers the best hope of fruitful organized effort, what should be the long-range aims of work with these underprivileged, untutored people? The migrant worker who desires to shift to industry should be given help to train himself and to relocate. The migrant who wishes to remain in agriculture must have an opportunity to supplement his income during the lean months. Any project devoted to the needs of the settled migrant ought to introduce a stream of proposals for income maintenance. These could include handcrafts, home industries, seasonal manufacturing, and State and county public works timed to seasonal unemployment.

Better housing is imperative. Ways should be found to forestall the growth of blighted areas and at the same time provide house and home ownership within the means of the worker. Housing authorities, planning commissions, private real estate interests, and the federal office of the Housing and Home Finance Agency can help here. Public health programs and adult education are needed. The shack town wants running water, oiled roads, and street lights. The possibility should be explored of interesting growers in developing an improved system of labor–management relations.

Granted these goals, what can be done practically to achieve them? Many a fine idea for helping the migrant worker has been swamped in the stormy voyage from the mind to the rugged shores of life. The answer, I believe, lies in voluntary activity and organization on the part of three groups: the migrant, the citizen, and the grower.

The migrant is plagued by a sense of insecurity and defeatism, both of which carry over to cooperative effort at community improvement. Before the migrant will venture forth into community activity, he must have the encouragement of modest success. He must learn to walk before he can run. To initiate anything new, some stimulus from the outside will be required. The method I propose begins with friendly visitation by a welfare worker from a suitable agency to residents of the shack town.

In order to meet people and find potential leadership, the worker will have to go from house to house and street to street and gradually build up relationships on a purely personal basis. One baffling aspect that all these communities have in common is the absence of any central meeting place or focus of activity. Most areas have a store, a bar, or a club where people congregate to talk, but not the California shack town. At the bar people throw down a drink and leave in a hurry. The many pentecostal churches divide the inhabitants into little jealous congregations. The worker must be willing to listen, to appear absolutely nonpartisan, to build confidence by nonaggressiveness, to offer suggestions tentatively, and to hope that such suggestions will emerge as the group's own thinking. However worthwhile his preconceived goals, the worker will have to begin where residents feel the greatest need. In one settlement it will be water, in another training for citizenship, and in a third wholesome recreation where young people have no resources of any kind and delinquency is prevalent. "Here we don't get married," said a teenager, "we just change partners." In another town the need may be for training in auto mechanics.

Once the worker sees potential leadership developing, and, what is equally important, consent of other residents to let that leadership represent them, he can introduce plans for community improvement: housing, street paving, off-season industry, or cooperative credit.

Evidence that there is great potential in this method of voluntary activity with the migrant is afforded by a small pilot experiment of the American Friends Service Committee in Teviston, California, one of sixty-three migrant shack towns in Tulare County. Teviston is a tract of 183 acres, sold by a speculator mostly to Negroes during World War II. Eighty families reside there, most of whom work in agriculture. The greatest need has been water. Home owners have to pack water from a distance of 2½ miles. The Friends Service Committee furnished the services of a staff member to this community to test the possibilities in voluntary organization of the residents. Since the need for water was very urgent, the development of a water district became the staff member's entering wedge to help this group tackle a common objective and to learn how to merge their differences for the sake of community welfare.

The orderly steps of procedure for setting up a Community Services Water District are simple to those familiar with the American form of government and the typical middle-class community. The procedure at Teviston was not simple. First, suspicion had to be overcome. Questions arose as to motivation of the Friends worker. Gradually trust and confidence grew, mostly through patient noninterference during the incredibly long-winded and laboriously slow weekly discussions. Suggestions were presented only at the crucial points where an impasse was reached, or the techniques of further procedure were beyond the knowledge of the group. (It took twelve meetings before even the better educated began to understand the procedure involved.) When the officers for the Improvement Association were elected old resentments flared up, but these difficulties were mild compared to the conflict created when bonds and taxes were mentioned in connection with financing the water system. Endless time was spent by the staff worker explaining the wisdom of bonds and tax financing. The project was delayed two months over the issue of whether or not to employ a lawyer to help draw up the petition. "Why should we pay $800 for a lawyer? What do we have a Board of Supervisors for?" were typical questions. It was a moving experience to see these Negro people, weary from long hours of work in the fields, gathering in the little bare wooden church, with its battered piano and uncomfortable benches, to discover their rights as citizens and to experience for the first time the privileges and duties of democracy. At long last the petition was drawn up, presented to the Board of Supervisors by the tall, lanky, very dark deacon, and approved.

Space has been given to describing this pilot experience because it is typical of the voluntary activity that could and should be extended to about 500 migrant shack towns. Such simple engineering feats as the introduction of water offer great opportunity for major social engineering achievements.

Voluntary activity on the part of two other groups is needed to maintain the momentum of reform once under way. I refer to concerned citizens and to the growers. The citizen can make his major contribution through volunteering time and energy to committee service. Committee work is the heartbeat of voluntary activity and organization. Because it is so close to us, so familiar, we can easily overlook it. A good committee pools community strengths and gives them wider circulation and utility. It freshens stale problems, renews staff inspiration, and links staff, community, and the recipient of help into a single body. This sense of common cause is important both for migrants who feel isolated and rejected by neighboring large towns, and for the so-called responsible citizens who have largely ignored the migrants' existence. These citizens must be led to feel a greater concern for the workers upon whom a large percentage of agricultural wealth depends and who participate very little in the prosperity. Committee organization is the way to do it.

Effort is also needed to interest the growers in voluntary help for the migrants that can be advantageous to both grower and laborer, and will offer the security that each group desires. The grower requires a stable and reliable labor force. Even with increasing mechanization in the production of sugar, cotton, and other crops, California agriculture will remain dependent on an abundant seasonal labor supply. Unfortunately, many growers have accepted a stereotype of the migrant as worthless and hopeless. This stereotype tends to prevent the employer from embracing solutions that would eventually work to his own benefit. Given evidence of successful self-help on the part of the settling migrant in the fringe area and of support from citizens, I believe growers might be interested in establishing a management–migrant labor council. Just as many industrial corporations have seen the wisdom of pooling their resources to provide financial aid for higher education, so growers might be willing, through the medium of such a council, to solicit funds and distribute aid to welfare agencies working with the migrant. A council of this kind could assist welfare agencies in selecting and introducing new seasonal home industries and in developing marketing outlets. It could explore ways and means to permit the people with low incomes to avoid becoming the prey of loan sharks, pressure salesmen, and excessive rates of interest. Negroes, Mexican Americans, and even white migrants of low incomes find it next to impossible to procure loans from banking and building and loan institutions. Such a council could cooperate in initiating private low-cost housing. Members of the council could finally serve as liaison to citizen committees.

To extend voluntary activity to the settled and settling migrant will require the combined efforts of a friendly and patient staff, enlightened employers, and responsible citizens. We can be confident, however, that like the crops he harvests, the migrant himself has hidden resources that will respond to skill, care, and concern.

3. Six Steps in Aid
of Migrant Workers

MRS. HARRY TALBOTT

Here is a grass-roots method of extending voluntary activity and organization in behalf of migrant workers which can be used by the concerned person who must begin without experience, money, or much time in a locality where little or nothing is being done for these disadvantaged people. It can be used equally well by the large organization that must depend heavily on working through concerned persons. It begins with the individual and culminates in a county migrant council composed of clubs, churches, interested people, industry representatives, and professional workers with migrants. This plan was followed in our county, and represents my personal experience. We now have a vigorous Council which is making marked progress in extending to migrant workers the protective benefits of community life in the fields of religion, health, and education. The Council coordinates activities in their behalf, develops programs such as a Free Child Care Center to meet their needs, and cooperates with State and federal agencies working in this field.

BUILDING A STORE OF ACCURATE INFORMATION

If you are going to "win friends and influence people" for your cause, you must merit their respect by knowing your subject with accuracy. It is presupposed that the concerned person has firsthand contact with migrant workers, and that the concern arises from direct observation, constituting in itself a valuable basis for broader and more specific knowledge. Local information is got by telephoning or writing county officials in the proper field. For example, the State Employment Service County office can furnish the data on recruiting practices, housing, number of workers in an average season, length of stay, and so on. To find available welfare services, the County Welfare Department should be questioned. The County

Department of Public Health has the facts on health services available.[1]
Information is vital, but it is inadvisable to linger at this point; it is important to move into action.

ADVISABILITY OF IMMEDIATE ACTION

Action on your part is an evidence of sincerity in the eyes of those, now
unknown to you, who are going to become your future helpers. A blueprint isn't necessary, and your information, experience, and opportunity increase as you go along. In my own case, my husband and I, as fruit growers and employers of migratory workers, undertook to demonstrate in our
own business what the average small farmer can accomplish on his own
ranch and within the limits imposed by restricted finances. We provided
the best housing we could afford, doing the work ourselves, which cov-

---

[1] There are also sources of information covering the problems of migrants on
a national basis, some of which tell of efforts to help them in other sections.
A very comprehensive study is contained in the *Report of the President's Commission on Migratory Labor* which can be ordered for seventy-five cents from
the Superintendent of Documents, U.S. Government Printing Office, Washington, D.C. Most concise and usable is the well-illustrated booklet, *Colorado Tale,*
which is free on request to Colorado citizens, and fifty cents to others. It can
be had from the National Child Labor Committee, 419 Fourth Avenue, New
York 16, N.Y., which made the investigation at the request of Governor Walter
Johnson in 1950. *Our Robbery of American Migrants* costs fifteen cents from
the Council for Social Action, Congregational Christian Churches, 289 Fourth
Avenue, New York, N.Y. *Free* materials may be had by writing for the following:

Selected Articles on Migrant Labor
  The American Child National Child Labor Committee
  419 Fourth Ave.
  New York, N.Y.
Selected Agricultural Labor Bulletins
  National Council on Agricultural Life and Labor
  1751 N St. N.W., Washington, D.C.
Migratory Farm Workers in 1949
  Louis J. Ducoff, U.S. Department of Agriculture
  Washington, D.C.

For the story of what the churches are doing, write
  Dean S. Collins, Western Regional Director
  Migrant Ministry, Div. of Home Missions
  National Council of Churches
  3330 West Adams Blvd.
  Los Angeles 18, Calif.

ered the minimum requirements of privacy, shade, and protection from weather, insects, and mice. Sanitary precautions were observed in the care of the showers and the handling of food served in our at-cost dining room. Machinery and other equipment were put in a safe operating condition before each harvest; buildings were cleaned, and freshly washed mattress covers put on the beds. The dining room was stocked with table games, magazines, and a radio. We carefully thought out our own hiring practices to establish those that were fair to both employee and employer, including the carrying of insurance to cover injury. Letters for procuring help carried full information on wages, accommodations, date of harvest, and possible length of the employment period.

At first many growers laughed at our extra efforts. At a club meeting, a friend explained that I was absent because I was cleaning the bunkhouses for harvest. One woman replied, "Oh, I never bother to do that! If our workers like things clean, they will scrub things up themselves. If they are dirty, they won't mind." It was not many years before it was noticed that we had a better class of worker, returning regularly, working more efficiently than average, and giving almost none of the trouble usually encountered in dealing with migrant workers. In addition, we had plenty of help in seasons when workers were so short that a good deal of fruit fell to the ground. Having seen the financial value of our practices, some followed suit who would not have been moved by any personal interest in the workers. However, we felt discouraged by the magnitude of the problem—pretty much as if we were bailing the ocean dry with a teacup. At this point, a step forward occurred.

ASSOCIATION WITH A NATIONAL ORGANIZATION

In 1948 our peach industry bought a Labor Camp from the government through its administrative body, the Peach Board of Control. At this time, I did not know any groups who were helping migrants; hence the matter of communicating was done by them. It happened that I greeted a stranger after church one June morning, and asked her if she were a new resident or just a visitor. She answered that she expected to be in our town for three months, and then, giving me a rather disconcerting look, said, "May I come up and talk to you tomorrow?" "What could she be selling?" I thought to myself, and replied, "Tomorrow afternoon would be all right, but I am really very busy this time of year." The next day I found she *was* selling—but ideas and not articles. This was my introduction to Mrs. Kay Smith, at that time Supervisor of the Migrant Ministry of the Division of Home Missions, National Council of Churches, for the State of Colorado. Thereupon began a very fruitful relationship in which information, opportunities for wider usefulness, and the stimulating contact with other agencies working for the benefit of migrants was extended to us through this organization.

LOCAL ACTION THROUGH A COMMUNITY-WIDE CHURCH ORGANIZATION

Mrs. Smith had come to pioneer a work in our newly acquired Labor Camp, and asked me to invite representative women from the various churches to meet her there. This was done, and our committee realized the need for a local organization to support this work. To that end, we reorganized the United Churchwomen of Palisade (the local branch of the Council of Churches) for the express purpose of uniting to alleviate the conditions of migratory workers in our vicinity. This was the next natural step to be taken, and proved very successful.

It seems to me that it is far wiser to start local action through a *group* of churches than through a service club, because in dealing with migrants, workers often find them unlovely. It is easy to arouse sympathy for people with crippled limbs, but hard for the public in general to be moved by the crippling of mind and spirit. The compassion for the task is most often found in the church; also, it is invariably the most mature Christian people who are attracted to groups that cross denominational lines to meet a need. It is also these same people who cause service clubs of which they are members to join in the task. It is not necessary that every church accept the invitation to the community-wide group, but the strongest should certainly be represented for the very reason that the Labor Camps are usually privately or grower-owned, and are simply not open to work of any one religious group.

In our town, the re-activated group of United Churchwomen set to work enthusiastically to support the efforts of the two Migrant Ministry workers residing in our camp. The project committee undertook yearly tasks such as cleaning the community building at the camp and the shelters in which the Migrant Ministry workers lived. We asked the Future Farmers of America to join us in a long-range project of planting a tree by each shelter, the Red Cross to supply free swimming lessons to the children while we furnished the transportation and suits, the Recreation Commission to give us worn but usable sports equipment, and so on. The churches, both Protestant and Catholic, took turns, week about, in furnishing cookies and juice to the children participating in the day-long program of the Migrant Ministry, consisting of elementary Christian education, crafts, and recreation. Tasks such as the yearly cleaning of the sandbox, the toy washing, and others, were assigned to the different young people's groups, both secular and religious. The Peach Control Board, which had at first been antagonistic, endorsed the work as they found the people using the camp much better satisfied and more likely to return. The management of the camp became easier, and there were almost no calls to the police. In turn, the churches devoted at least one program a year at different age levels to the work of the Migrant Ministry, and asked for projects they might do.

We tried to interest public agencies in the camp by asking that the County Health Department make a regular inspection of the sanitary facilities there and send us a carbon copy of their report. In the beginning, the camp manager had refused them admittance, but fortified by our interest, they exerted their authority to inspect. Sanitary conditions at the camp improved, and the incidence of fly-borne diseases decreased in surrounding ranch areas also.

News came to us that the Federal government was financing a health project at the larger Fort Lupton Camp. We corresponded with Dr. Roy Cleere, who is the head of our Colorado Department of Public Health. Consequently, Dr. Ruth Howard, Chief of the Bureau of Maternal and Child Health for Colorado, visited here, accompanied by social worker Helen Mason, and made an evaluation of the local situation. Later, Dr. Margaret Beaver, Director of the Mesa County Department of Public Health, telephoned to ask if I knew of an organization that would request the Peach Board of Control to invite Dr. Howard and Helen Mason to discuss a health project at the local Labor Camp. I telephoned each member of the executive board of the United Churchwomen for their approval, and then telephoned Oscar Jaynes, Executive Secretary of the Peach Board, telling him our group urged that he arrange a meeting with the Peach Board and Health Service. The meeting resulted in a clinic in the Labor Camp, staffed by two public health nurses, and assisted when necessary by a social worker.

Our efforts now had attracted some outside attention, and the Girl Scouts of America chose the Palisade Camp for a pilot project. Miss Rebecca Taft visited here, and made arrangements that were carried out by the nearby Grand Junction troop. Its success was such that the Girl Scouts will make it a yearly project, not only here, but in other camps.

ENLISTING A SECULAR COMMUNITY ORGANIZATION

At this time, the work of our United Churchwomen sagged slightly because of an unfortunate provision in the constitution that did not allow officers to succeed themselves, and to the custom of passing the offices from church to church each year. Soon we were short of vitally concerned people who could act in any official capacity. It was also obvious that there were many needs we were not big enough to meet. Spurred by the pressure of the situation, and by the opportunity presented by the local Woman's Club, which needed a project of size, club members who were also members of United Churchwomen suggested that they see what they could do about the local migrant situation.

The club unanimously accepted, and in this way another step was consummated which is vital to any plan to extend voluntary activity in behalf of migratory workers: the enlisting of a secular community organization. Such a group can bring effective social pressure in many areas because of the broad scope of its membership.

As a Woman's Club, we first called a meeting of a few members whom we knew to be deeply concerned. The program director of the Migrant Ministry, Miss Pat Theimer, was also included, as the club work must be planned to extend and strengthen the activities of the United Churchwomen. At this meeting, we assessed the needs of the migrants in the fields of health, welfare, housing, education, and so on, and suggested about six projects we might do. A few nights later, the welfare chairman presented these at a meeting of the Executive Board so that they might choose the ones to present to the entire club. The board then presented their selections to a full session of the group at a specially called meeting. They recommended that we operate a Sewing Center, using our members as amateur instructors in mending and remodeling; that we hold Thrift Shop sales of mended clothing at the camp; and that we use the funds from such sales, together with gifts solicited from other clubs, to finance a Free Child Care Center during peach harvest. Last but not least, in the fall we would organize a Mesa County Migrant Council to correlate activities of all groups working with migrants, and to establish programs to meet special needs. This ambitious program was accepted, committees were appointed for each project involved, and all were carried out successfully in 1955. With a membership of around seventy, the load was not heavy on any particular person.

The committee in charge of the Free Child Center then wrote letters to ninety-five fraternal and club groups in nearby Grand Junction. Since the mailing list provided by the Chamber of Commerce proved to be out of date, it was remarkable that twenty-five groups responded with volunteer workers or gifts of money. Through United Churchwomen of Grand Junction, four volunteers were sent daily for the two weeks the center was in operation. The center closed with all bills paid, and its value well established.

SETTING UP A COUNTY MIGRANT COUNCIL

In late October, the Palisade Woman's Club sent out an invitation to the organizations that had sent volunteers or money to join in forming a

Mesa County Migrant Council. Churches were also included. Dean Collins of the Migrant Ministry served as speaker, and thirty-five organizations and eight interested people, along with representatives from Health, Welfare, and others, responded by attending this first meeting.

Following Robert's Rules for organizing a new group, we elected an acting chairman and secretary. The chairman then appointed a committee of seven to write a constitution, and present it for approval of the group on March 10.

The constitution offered a problem since the membership of the proposed group would contain both Catholic and Protestant churches, agency representatives, interested persons, industry representatives, and clubs of all types, as well as fraternal organizations. The chairman, Mrs. Paul Bardell, and Lew Wallace, Director of Public Welfare for Mesa County, joined with five others in writing a very effective constitution, and deserve the bulk of the credit for producing an instrument broad enough, and still effective. Each club, church, or fraternal organization would be permitted one voting member; interested persons were permitted membership on the same basis; and agency representatives (Health, Migrant Ministry, etc.) were constituted associate or advisory members. The test for membership was merely that the organization or person do something for migrants each year. There were to be two program meetings each year. At the fall one, we would make reports and evaluations, and elect officers; in addition we would hear an outstanding speaker. In the spring, we would present a budget and plans for the season, as well as have the program. In between, activities would be handled by an executive board of five officers and six members.

This constitution, adopted at the March meeting, was signed by thirty-five organizational representatives and five interested persons. A nominating committee was appointed to report at the April program meeting, the March meeting being merely to transact the business necessary to found the council. And thus was accomplished the final step necessary in extending volunteer activity and organization: the creation of a county migrant council.

We have just held our fall meeting after a summer of accomplishment proving the wisdom of the step. Our membership now comprises representatives of forty-five organizations and eight interested persons. Having adopted the Free Child Care Center as our project, we greatly improved its services by securing permission to use the elementary school building. At our request, the Health Department extended its services to include a free night clinic staffed by doctors from our Mesa County Medical Society. The TB Mobile X-Ray Unit was in camp during harvest, and a blood study was made.

Mrs. Lucile Latting, Elementary Supervisor, Colorado Department of

Education, met with our Migrant Council board in June, with the result that we requested Superintendent I. K. Boltz of School District 51 to make a six weeks' school available at Palisade for migrant children July 23 to August 31. This was done, and forty-two children attended. During harvest, the school bus also carried the children attending the Free Child Care Center. At 2:30, when school was out for the older children, the Migrant Ministry workers arrived at the school grounds to conduct a period of recreation and craftwork, thus keeping the children off the ranches and away from the danger of machinery and canals while the parents were working. At 5:30 the bus returned the children to the ranches.

Next year, we have the promise of the Migrant Ministry to extend its work to include the June thinning season, and of Mesa College to provide a free night class in automotive repair under their Distributive Education program. All other services, such as the school and clinic, will be repeated. In addition, we will extend the small beginning made at the S. J. Miller Canning Co. Camp at the other end of the county. The council has already shown its worth as a coordinator of existing activity and an initiator of further needed services. The saying that there is almost no limit to the good you can do if you don't care who gets the credit was amply demonstrated.

11

Child Welfare
and Aid to Mothers

1. Foster Day-Care Service

DAVID ROTH

World War II witnessed a tremendous increase in work opportunities for women. National needs and inducements were so great that millions of married women joined the labor force for the first time. Since this group included increasing numbers of mothers of young children, the need for extensive day-care facilities for children became manifest. Many voluntary and public organizations, aided by federal funds through the Lanham Act, responded to this need, and many new group day-care centers and nurseries were established.

However, the trend of the working mother extended beyond the wartime crisis, and in 1951, two million of the five and a quarter million working mothers had children under six years of age. This upward surge has continued in our expanding economy, and it was soon apparent that in many communities very young children under three needed much more than the limited group day-care arrangements.

Actually, the first program of voluntary family day care was organized as a separate agency in 1925 in Philadelphia. Despite the acknowledged need for such a service in other communities, there was little interest or money to set up family day-care programs as a professional social service. Thus, as late as 1954, there were only twelve independent family day-care programs throughout the country! There were nine other family day-care units, but each was a part of a larger child placement or family agency.

This neglect stemmed from a peculiar confusion in community planning. On one hand, family day care was viewed as exactly like full-time foster care; on the other, it was thought to be totally different. Some people felt it might be an extension of a group day-care program; others believed that day placement of young children indicated serious family problems and required only the ministrations of a family counselor. Many communities simply encouraged parents to make independent placements through neighbors and friends, rationalizing that two working parents or even just a working mother could pay for and supervise day care for the children. However, it has become evident that such makeshift arrangements for the young, impressionable children under three were completely inadequate.

For some years, prior to 1952, the Jewish Child Care Council of New York, a voluntary social planning organization, was noting in its Information Service that increasing requests for family day-care service were being made. For a variety of economic, social, and medical crises in Jewish families, the possible solution seemed to be linked with a professional family day-care service for children. There was no public or private family program anywhere in the largest city and in the largest Jewish community in the United States.

As a first step, the council arranged a conference with the Foster Family Service in Philadelphia. At this meeting the director of the New York Jewish Child Care Council sought to learn the procedures of organizing and operating a successful program. For example, it was important to know how foster day homes were recruited, how close they should be to the child's own home, how much supervision was necessary, what kind of problems the children presented, what the optimum minimum age for acceptance of children was, and so on. Following this, a simple questionnaire was drawn up and sent to a number of group day-care centers to determine the number and kinds of requests for care of children under three that came to the centers' attention. In this way, it was possible to ascertain further the needs of the community and to pinpoint the areas that could best use a foster day-care service. The contact with the group centers also served as a beginning in publicizing such a new service. It was clear immediately that the demand for foster day care was considerable and that it would be necessary to limit this pilot program.

Prepared in this way, the council approached the two largest voluntary Jewish child-caring agencies and the Federation of Jewish Philanthropies, and after further study by a joint committee of board and staff representatives, it was decided to establish a foster family day-care service for a two-year experimental period under a coadministration plan by the two operating agencies. The initial budget was $11,400 per year with the Federation adding a limited grant to the equal contribution of the two agencies. A small board consisting of twelve members of the study committee was set up with a professional advisory subcommittee. Meetings were held monthly and sometimes oftener. Plans were made to serve fifteen children initially.

Much discussion and thinking went into the board's planning of this new project. There was unanimous expression that, despite the permeation of family problems in so many of the situations, this service was more akin to foster home placement experience. Therefore, the "know-how" of the foster home agency with respect to home-finding, foster home studies, supervision of foster homes, and work with the foster child and parents of the foster children was indispensable for successful operation. Nevertheless, to test the feasibility of the program and to follow its independent development, it was recommended that the entire service maintain departmental separateness. Thus, whereas the new Foster Family Day Care Service was to be lodged in one of the two cooperating agencies, it would have its own intake, home-finding, and supervisory responsibility, and also have separate professional and clerical staff, separate publicity, and separate procedures and records.

The philosophical underpinning of this project was that only in those situations where foster day care is beneficial to the child and strengthening to the family unit should a child be accepted. It would provide a professional service to Jewish families in two boroughs who needed to have their children, aged eight months to three years, cared for in an accepting, loving home atmosphere during the working day of approximately 8:00 a.m. to 6:00 p.m. The area served was limited by the board, since there was recognition that only a small number of children could be helped and that the foster homes needed to be close to the parental home because of the twice-daily contact. The eight-month minimum age was set in cognizance that at this age a child may be old enough to take on a new relationship besides the close one to his mother. Practically, after he reaches eight months, he can adjust to the experience of going out in every kind of weather and should be ready for three regular family meals instead of frequent formula feeding. Although a child at three years of age is often ready for the competition and stimulation of a group experience, it was soon apparent that there were youngsters over three who needed the individualized foster family care because of their own problems, the parental situation, and the placement of siblings. Hence, in certain instances, children up to six years of age were eligible for care. This was a difficult decision for the board to make, since it could mean depriving another child under three of a foster day home.

The keystone of the program was the highly experienced social worker who was hired as the sole professional to function as a supervisor and caseworker of the service. This involved the added burdens of publicity work and of setting up the structure and procedures. Though there was clerical and administrative help available, the primary responsibility lay, at times, all too heavily on the social worker. Her work involved regular meetings with the board and considerable contact with community lay and professional groups. She drew up news releases, brochures, posters, and other publicity material with the help of the publicity department of one sponsoring agency and suggestions from the active board. She developed application forms and a manual of procedure.

Above all else, the worker-director was the pivot on which hinged the ramified relationships among child, parent, day-care parent, and agency.

The parent brought a family or personal problem that made part-time placement necessary and that inevitably involved guilt and anxiety around sharing a very young child with another mother and an agency. The natural mother might be in conflict over the more positive influence a day-care mother could have on her child. She might be struggling to make maximum beneficial use for the child of her evenings and week ends with him. More often than not, the mother needed a referral to another family counseling, psychiatric, or medical service. The worker was sensitive to all these facts, protected and supported the mother's prerogatives with her child, and helped her to understand the agency's and foster parent's role. In addition, she worked with each family around a sliding scale weekly fee for this service.

Since the financial motive plays a larger part in a foster day-care application than in the standard foster home application, the worker needs to be especially alert to the foster day-care mother's handling and understanding of a placed child. The day-care mother must be able to share any problems and to use the worker's guidance in this area. Most important, she must accept the continued close parent–child relationship and be able to relinquish the child at the end of every day and to begin anew the next day regardless of the small regressions a youngster may suffer at times when in his own home. She must provide close, relaxed care, which entails outdoor play, wholesome meals, and a regular nap. The worker was able to provide helpful supervision to the foster day-care homes so that many have remained in use for several years.

Any day-care program is child-focused despite the natural concern for the whole family unit. Since this service specializes in the care for the young child, the worker had to bring expert knowledge of the developmental growth process of the child to the job. She had to be aware of the anxiety and confusion a child faces in separating from his mother—even if it were only for part of a day. Then, too, the worker had to ease the child's way, if possible, in relating to two mothers. Furthermore, careful medical and psychological evaluation was often called for in deciding whether a child was ready for or could use family day care. In the case of the verbal two or three year old, direct casework treatment through use of play materials was occasionally necessary. To this must be added the responsibility of preparing and terminating a day-care placement with the child, parent, and foster parent. Unfortunately, too, the worker had to deal with transfers from one day-care home to another when unforeseen difficulties arose.

As a guide to the worker, criteria for acceptance of a child were adopted by the board. A child was considered eligible depending on the individual case if:

1. The mother was employed or seeking employment and day care was essential to the well-being and maintenance of the family, regardless of whether there was a father in the home.
2. There was physical or emotional illness of either parent which made day care the most sound plan.
3. There was no mother in the home and day care made it possible for the child to remain with his father or family.
4. The parent–child relationship was such that partial separation was desirable.

With regard to payment arrangements, the Foster Family Day Care Service set a $45 monthly payment to foster parents. This was expected to include a hot lunch and two snacks for the child, but breakfast and supper were deemed responsibilities of the parent. Experience soon proved that this rate did not attract day-care homes, so that the rate was subsequently raised to $55 per month. Initially, the fee to the parent was set at from $1.50 to $17.50 per week, but with the increased board rate, the minimum was increased to $3 per week and the maximum is now the actual cost of care. This came as a result of constant evaluation of what parents could and should be expected to bear of the cost of this voluntary project. Parent fees have met only about 10 per cent of the budget.

The validity of the service was demonstrated by the 188 inquiries from families for this program in the first year of operation. There were interviews with seventy-three families, and thirty-eight children involving thirty-one families were accepted for placement. However, a sizable number of children were withdrawn. Eighteen children were actually placed, which was more than planned for at the beginning.

At the end of two years, the funds of the two voluntary child-care agencies and the Federation were renewed for another two years, at the slightly increased total sum of $15,000 per year. This amount provided care for an average of from twenty to twenty-five children including a group carried in after-care on a casework basis. Another extension of service by the board involved placement of a limited number of school age brothers and sisters of youngsters in family day care on a part-time basis (after school) to keep them off the street.

In July 1956 the New York Jewish Child Care Council was able to interest a day nursery group to come into the program and to double the existing funds so that an enlarged program serving thirty-five children, at a cost of $30,000 a year, is envisaged. It has also been the goal of the Foster Family Day Care Service to enlist the support of the state legislature to provide some State funds which would stimulate wider community programs of foster day care.

In summary, foster family day care, a young and comparatively uncharted field of child welfare, has been given a start and impetus in New York City through the untiring devotion of a group of lay and professional leaders. Voluntary activity and organization has been extended in a new field of service with private welfare funds. Apart from the direct service to New York children and families, a set of standards and principles has been painstakingly forged that may form a basis for broader community service in New York and elsewhere. If the Foster Family Day Care Service in New York can provide some guideposts for voluntary efforts elsewhere to anticipate and to prevent family breakdown, and to deal with people who usually might not seek help through social agency channels, it will have served a notable function.

2. The PTA Wardrobe

MRS. RAYMOND KITCHEN

Suppose that you are the mother of a family in an average neighborhood, in an average town. When your children outgrow clothes that are still good, if you cannot "hand them down" within your family you look around for someone else who can use them. Suppose that one of your neighbors has children a little smaller than yours. You know her well enough to see that certain of your children's outgrown things might be welcome; therefore, one day you call her over to choose what she can use before you fill the Goodwill bag. And, if you are handier with a needle than she is, or if she must work away from home but you need not, you may mend the garments before she takes them home. She does not feel that she has accepted charity, or you that you have given alms. But if you do not happen to know such a family as this, you will give your children's good outgrown clothes along with worn-out and outmoded things to some impersonal agency.

Let us enlarge this picture; among the thousands of families in an average community there are some who are very poor—and many more whose resources do not meet all their needs. Housing, transportation, food, are bought first. Other necessities, including clothing, come out of what is left. Unless they have relatives or friends who "hand down" clothing to them, these people will often be unable to keep up appearances, sometimes compelled to keep their children out of school for a few days until money for new shoes can be scraped together, or a warm coat found at some rummage sale. That their morale suffers, and that the lives of their children are affected by these experiences, is obvious. All the while in this community garments that would supplement these inadequate wardrobes are hanging in closets until they are out of style, being included in donations for foreign relief, or torn up for rags. And these things would be given gladly to neighbors in need, if the needs were known and the contacts made.

In our town there is a means of making many such contacts and meeting many of such needs. Known as the "PTA Wardrobe," it is a project in child welfare (which is the basic object of that organization). Begun in the depths of the depression by a single PTA member to aid children who came to school clad in pathetic makeshifts, it has operated for more than twenty years on the same principles with which it began, namely: to offer a means of bringing wearable clothing no longer needed to those who do need it; to do this with a minimum of machinery and without embarrassment to anyone; to meet the needs as stated, assuming that the person or agency who sends a family in knows that they need the Wardrobe service.

The local school administration, aware of its obligation to contribute to the well-being of children, has always managed to provide the Wardrobe with a room that serves as a storeroom, workroom, and distribution center. The PTA Council (made up of representatives from school units, now twenty in number) designates a committee to operate the Wardrobe. Local PTA units conduct drives for suitable clothing through the schools and recruit volunteer workers. These workers, all busy mothers, come into the Wardrobe room to sort, mend, press, and do other chores necessary to turn the masses of contributed articles into a conveniently arranged stock of wearable clothes. Some workers take laundry or other work home.

All the work is directed and coordinated by a permanent staff worker, the only paid worker in the Wardrobe. When there were only eight or ten schools in the district the committee appointed by the PTA Council divided among themselves (there were usually two members, sometimes three) the task of supervising the Wardrobe, then operating on a one day a week basis. But when the postwar population boom hit our town, the pressure from having more clothing and more volunteers available, and more needs to be met, became too great for the all-volunteer program. Consequently, about four years ago the Community Chest was asked to pay the salary of a staff worker who would keep the workroom open for two days a week, five hours each day, and direct the work of the volunteers. This left the PTA committee free to concentrate on collecting clothing, recruiting volunteers, and making up their schedules.

People to whom the Wardrobe should be available are invited to come and select what they can use from what is on hand (certain types of garments are always in surplus, of others there is never enough) by those who have the opportunity to know their needs. School and public health nurses send the most people in, and teachers, principals, and counselors refer many. Others are led to the Wardrobe by social agencies. Any citizen in our town can send a family to the Wardrobe, if he feels sure someone he knows needs its service. The volunteer workers are told that they may, and some do so. School people and nurses use mimeographed slips giving the Wardrobe's days and hours and its location, to introduce persons they send. These slips are more convenient than telephone referrals, but are not a requirement.

Suppose you are the mother of a family in an average neighborhood in our town. You belong to the PTA and try to help in some of its activities.

When your child brings home a notice of a clothing drive for the Wardrobe, you gather up the outgrown things that would not fit anyone you know and send them in. And suppose that you are asked to give a couple of hours' work in the Wardrobe during the time allotted to your unit; if you can, you go.

While you are working you may see people come. Mothers with their children. Teenagers alone or with a counselor, visiting nurses to pick up a layette, or garments for someone ill or aged. (Yes, practical adult clothing is collected, too. Helping any member of a family helps the children.) You hear the words of thanks, you see the smile of a little girl over new color added to her life. You know that what you have given in time and material is useful to people who walk on the same streets that you do, whom you might even know, and it makes you feel rewarded, not merely that you have given alms.

During the PTA year 1955–56, there were 244 women working for Wardrobe. Eighteen Girl Scouts and nine Cub Scouts were also given credit as volunteers. There were 6,641 garments given to 466 children and ninety-one adults in our town. Over seventeen thousand articles were collected. In the previous year just under seven thousand were collected, over seven thousand were given out and the number of volunteers was about the same. Statistical variations from year to year have several causes. Within the ascending curve that reflects increased population, fluctuations may be due to the timing of drives for clothing, economic ups and downs (lower-income families feel these dramatically), the amount of publicity given Wardrobe, and so on, but the over-all picture shown by records of twenty years is one of a continuing service in conserving useful things for the benefit of people.

Aside from the staff worker's salary paid by the Chest, the Wardrobe is financially self-sustaining. Clean cotton rags and a few other surplus items are sold to provide money for dry cleaning of nonwashable things and for other expenses. The Wardrobe stock is continually "weeded" of many garments that are not likely to be chosen. All surplus is sent where it might conceivably do good: to American Friends Service or other church-related agencies, the Salvation Army, the Save the Children Federation, or the Goodwill Industries. Last spring over a thousand better-grade surplus garments were given to a clothing project operated by one woman among Spanish-speaking farm laborers' families in a nearby community. Our volunteers are happy to have a part in her good work. When Wardrobe can serve beyond the boundaries of our town they want it to do so.

Volunteers help to keep the simple records of the Wardrobe, which list the number of children and adults in families helped, the school district in which they live, and the person or agency that sent them to Wardrobe, but never the family's name. They can see for themselves that gossip is uncalled for and that a child's schoolmates need not know the source of his clothes if he does not choose to tell. It is significant that mothers who have themselves been helped often reappear among the volunteers. "Silver and gold have I none, but such as I have I give" could well be the Wardrobe's motto. In that spirit volunteers started it, volunteers have guided it, formed its policies and procedures, and keep it going on.

"Our town" in this account is Palo Alto, California, with a population of nearly forty-four thousand, having a unified school administration for both its elementary and secondary schools, and a strong PTA organization. I myself was recruited as a Wardrobe volunteer for the first time about eleven years ago. I was impressed, and my interest continued. I served as Wardrobe chairman for my local PTA unit, and was eventually appointed to the council's Wardrobe Committee where I served for several years. During this time the school population ballooned, and when the Community Chest consented to provide for a paid staff worker in the Wardrobe the position was offered to me, because I was both familiar with Wardrobe and free to spend some additional time there. I accepted and still hold it. It is easy for me to tell the Wardrobe story, having both personal experience, acquaintance with its original founder, Mrs. C. M. Wedde, and access to the records of the past years.

Last spring the Board of Education of the nearby city of San Jose appropriated a room and a sum of money for their PTA council to establish a similar service there. Representatives were sent to Palo Alto to inspect our Wardrobe and I was asked to explain its operation to them. I believe that they will set up a successful program because I believe in the Wardrobe idea.

That this type of service is being done in many places, I know, under many auspices, and with varying degrees of success. According to the reports from various PTA sources, the only ones familiar to me, ours is outstanding in many ways. I feel that our Palo Alto Wardrobe is successful in using volunteers for probably the same reasons that many other volunteer projects may succeed. It is a program practical enough to work, imaginative enough to inspire. It deals with tangible things and individual people. It meets needs which it is easy to feel conscious of, and which might not otherwise be met. It satisfies for the volunteer a need all persons have: to feel important. It has a well-established procedure, and utilizes common skills. It adapts to the time that its volunteers, in this case busy mothers, find most convenient. It has no elite, is not a prestige group. It seeks publicity modestly, on its merits, knowing that there is some local news value in much of what it does, and that many human-interest stories can be told about its service in ways that avoid violating anyone's privacy. People generally feel that its work is worthwhile and it has strong support in the community.

Concerning community support, it must be noted that our Wardrobe on its present scale could not function without the threefold support given it by the Palo Alto school system, the PTA, and Community Chest, yet its beginning was with one woman who saw needs, and set out to use existing means of enlisting others to help meet them. Such a beginning could doubtlessly be made in many another average town.

3. Emergency Housekeeping for Children

THOMAS M. BRIGHAM

The field of child welfare has progressed to the point where there are available various possibilities for placement of children when for any of several reasons it is deemed advisable to remove them from their own homes. However, most authorities in the fields of psychology and social work today feel that the best place for children is the family—their own family. This, then, raises the question most directly, perhaps, stated by Dr. Albert Kahn, Associate Professor at the New York School of Social Work, as quoted by Henry Epstein, Deputy Mayor of New York:[1]

> We concentrate on technical questions in our professional discussions, and we urge more and better foster care facilities in our community-action roles. But do we stop often enough to ask whether the aggregate energy represented by these efforts would keep more families together if expended differently?—I sometimes have the feeling that there are child caring agencies so completely oriented to processing children for placement, and supervising or serving them in placement, that they do not raise the principal question regularly, or fail to raise it well: does this child absolutely have to leave his father and/or mother?

Here is one of the most important questions imaginable, one that should be primary, but one that often in our desperation to erect more agencies and facilities in child welfare we seem to overlook. The question might, perhaps, even more comprehensively be rephrased: Does this child absolutely have to leave his home?

Let us consider some examples of situations that are common in most communities, large or small.

A young family with limited resources and no nearby relatives is in a quandary because the mother must go to the hospital for a few days and after that will need to rest for a week or so. The father, already facing high

[1] City of New York, *Children Need Families*, 1955, p. 15.

196

medical and hospital expenses, seems to have alternatives that will increase the family's financial problems, the children's insecurity, or both: he could take time off from work to care for the children himself, which would mean loss of income; he could hire someone to care for the children, which would mean more expense, and he is not sure he can find anyone competent; he could work out a placement with an agency so that the children are in a temporary-care institution, emergency or foster home, which would mean they would be separated from, not only their mother, but also their father, each other, and their school situation.

Another not uncommon experience occurs when police, probation officers, or child welfare workers are faced with the problem of making a midnight or early morning placement of a family of sleepy, scared children who will be without parents for a few days because of an auto accident, temporary detention of parents, or other emergency. The fact of the parents' not being able to be home for a few days is frightening and disturbing enough to these children but when added to it is the necessity of being taken from their beds to some strange place and perhaps separated from each other, we cannot estimate the damage done to them. In addition, this particular situation is a very difficult one from a purely physical point of view for the worker or officer involved: not only finding a facility at this hour, but dressing the children, conveying them there, taking adequate clothes, and so on, and either making arrangements for or disrupting the schedule of school for those in the family who attend.

A situation somewhat like the first one cited but with even greater depth of emotional strain frequently occurs when the mother's absence is to be prolonged because of commitment to a mental hospital or tuberculosis sanitarium, or is permanent owing to divorce, desertion, or death. In any of these situations the child's world may be abruptly shattered by the event itself and the consequent removal of the child from all that he has left of security, his father, his home, and his brothers and sisters.

Other situations may arise in which great home pressures and difficulties are built up because the mother in the home has to give extensive attention and care to one child, perhaps a post-polio case, or one recuperating from other serious illness or surgery, at the expense of the care of the home and the other children. This can be a tragic problem in a family of limited means and several small children. The tremendous amount of purely physical work necessary to keep abreast of meals, washing, ironing, and housework becomes overwhelming or even impossible in these situations; sometimes if some measure is not taken, the family may be catapulted into a severe crisis by the breakdown of the mother. The "measure," unfortunately, often consists of sending the child needing care to the hospital, a rest or recuperative facility, or of hiring help—any of which involve expense the family cannot stand; and the first two involve separation of the ill child, who most needs the love and care he gets at home, from that love and care.

Within American social welfare practice there already exists a method of coping with cases of the nature of those cited here, a method that has been used by both private and public agencies for two decades or more, but only sporadically and without sustained effort. This method, I believe, is one particularly adaptable to voluntary welfare agencies, and if utilized skillfully, can, I am convinced by the example of a voluntary agency with which I have been associated the last two years, lead to excellent public interpretation and appreciation of services as well as lower the community's welfare budget and prove a successful way to sell the agency's services to the supporting public.

The plan I am suggesting is not original; but, based on my recent agency experience, I am convinced that if it were used by more agencies, in small communities and large, it could greatly further the efforts of voluntary social welfare and because of its appeal as a concrete service it could also lead to more successful fund raising. This plan is simply the greater utilization of homemaker service—the program by which the agency provides a person to go into the home as a mother substitute, to dress the children, get the meals, and take care of the house, generally while the mother is away or incapacitated. The homemaker is not a substitute for the trained social worker; she may work with the caseworker in a supplementary or complementary role. A homemaker service is far less expensive to maintain than institutions or foster homes, and it enables the family to stay together in its own home. Homemaker service may be provided on a sliding scale fee basis where the family pays what it can afford—meaning a range from the full cost to nothing. Homemaker service is easy to interpret and in voluntary fund raising it has a special and legitimate appeal that has been largely missing since voluntary agencies have been doing less work of a direct relief or material assistance nature.

For the last two years I have been a member of the board of directors of a voluntary agency in Fresno, California: The Community Family Service Center, a member of the United Givers Plan (Community Chest). This agency had had a homemaker service that had been allowed to atrophy; it was no longer publicized or actively kept up. A year and a half ago the agency was facing difficulties securing recognition and funds, partly because the concept of family casework-counseling was not well interpreted or understood, and the agency no longer wished to give direct relief as a major part of its program, believing this to be the responsibility of the county welfare department. The agency began reactivating its homemaker program and found it a service that the community could understand, recognize the need for, and support financially. In case after case the agency was able to point to many dollars saved for the community in institutional and foster home care and to individual families. The community fund group approved a larger budget for the agency's total service, at least partly because of the impression made by the homemaker service.

This year in the same community the Child Welfare Services of the County Welfare Department has had a series of conferences with the Community Family Service Center relative to greater use of homemaker service. At present, the indications are that for two reasons, greater economy in terms of actual dollars and cents expended and the far preferable manner of serving the family need by keeping the children in the home, the County Welfare Department will either contract with the Community Family Service Center for homemakers or set up its own homemaker service.

I am convinced a well-utilized homemaker service is a good way to extend voluntary welfare activity because from the examples in my community I believe that this service can accomplish at a relatively small expenditure of money and professional effort what more elaborate, complicated, and costly institutional programs cannot—the retention of the child in the home, where he most needs to be in an emergency. If the emergency is short term, homemaker service minimizes its effects on the child or children; if it is long term, homemaker service provides an interval in which satisfactory long-range plans can be carefully worked out. In addition, homemaker service is relatively easy to interpret to the public and has an appeal that is very effective in fund raising. Although homemaker service has existed for several years, it is not today extensively used by either public or private agencies; for example, New York City Welfare Department has a Homemaker Service that consists of only seven homemakers—a situation the department itself considers woefully inadequate. I believe voluntary welfare agencies need to take leadership in this area that has so much to offer for child welfare, and that many existing agencies for families and/or children could add this service without major program readjustment.

4. A Plan for Helping Retarded Children

J. NORMAN HEARD

In 1955 facilities for training the mentally retarded children of Hidalgo County, Texas, were but little improved over those of medieval times. In a county containing more than a thousand mentally deficient children not one public school class designed for their needs had been established. Children with milder mental handicaps were stumbling about among the inevitable frustrations of classes patterned to capabilities of normal youngsters. Children with severer handicaps stagnated at home, concealed in many cases by misguided parents who feared neighborhood ostracism.

This tragic situation prevailed when my family arrived in Edinburg, the county seat, with our two retarded children. There was one bright ray on the horizon, however, for we were just in time to help organize a local parents' council affiliated with the National Association for Retarded Children. We had belonged to a council in Kingsville, Texas, and we were aware of the tremendous accomplishments made possible by release of parents' pent-up feelings when they are channeled into constructive work for their children.

The new council formulated a long-range plan designed to provide learning facilities for every retarded child in the county. As chairman of the projects committee I was privileged to help develop this plan, which includes public school classes for educable retarded children, private classes for trainable children, a State school in the county for institutional cases, cooking and sewing lessons for older girls, and sheltered workshops for vocational training of youths over school age. The plan has achieved marked success in its first year and can be recommended to organizations with similar objectives.

The council decided that before we could progress with our projects we would need to carry out the following preliminary steps: (1) take a census of retarded children and bring their parents into the council, (2) survey existing organizations and institutions that could assist us, (3) acquaint the public with the true facts regarding retardation, and (4) raise funds to finance the program.

We used a variety of approaches in locating the families of retarded children. Council members discussed the problem with neighbors, friends, and professional people, particularly those who had lived in the community for a long time. These contacts, particularly doctors and ministers, frequently led us to families who shared our problem.

The School Census Office was an important source of information, as its records provided names of many children who were not attending classes.

Other good sources were the County Health Unit and the Child Welfare Office. The Texas Association for Retarded Children provided names of parents in the county who had communicated with them and the State institution provided home addresses of children in their care.

Perhaps the most effective means of reaching parents was through notices in newspapers and television. Announcements regarding the council's objectives gained new members from throughout the area.

In surveying existing facilities in Hidalgo County, our second preliminary step, we found a number of organizations and institutions that were promoting the general welfare. Most of the school districts maintain classes for physically handicapped children. In Pharr the Crippled Children's Association operates a clinic. Near Mission is located Moore Air Force Base. Edinburg is the site of Pan American College. The county has two daily newspapers, three radio stations, and one television station. Each of these has played a significant role in our operations.

The council realized that the support of an informed citizenry was essential for progress toward provision for the county's retarded children. This, our third preliminary step, was a large undertaking, in as much as the subject of mental deficiency had never been forcefully brought to public attention. School board members and even superintendents, lacking knowledge of the problem's scope, doubted the presence of enough retarded children in their districts to warrant special classes.

To present the story of the retarded child the council's vice-president, who had had previous publicity experience, was appointed to work with the press. She has written articles for the papers about newsworthy council activities and has appeared on television to present films dealing with mental deficiency. Other members have appeared on the programs of various school and service organizations. A device that has helped increase understanding of mental retardation is the rotation of meeting places. Each month the council meets in a different community and local members urge school officials and civic leaders to attend.

The fourth preliminary step that confronted the council was the financing of our projects. Knowing that a number of Texas councils had conducted successful Christmas wreath sales, we contracted with a Duluth, Minnesota, wreath company for delivery of 435 wreaths. Each member set his own quota and almost every wreath was sold at substantial profit. We soon learned that almost everyone decorates for Christmas and, even more important, everyone is eager to help handicapped children. We look forward confidently to doubling our profits this year as we plan a coordinated drive throughout the county with carefully selected purchasing, public relations, telephone, and delivery committees.

It was realized at the outset that service clubs and other public spirited organizations provide one of the best potential sources of funds. A file of clippings regarding the activities of these organizations proved invaluable in preparing us to enlist their aid. In several instances these organizations have contributed equipment, transportation, and cash.

In some cases federal, State, and foundation funds are available, particularly in the area of vocational training. The federal government provides matching funds for vocational rehabilitation workshops and we will apply for them as soon as we raise our own share.

Other major fund-raising projects are under consideration for next year. During National Retarded Children's Week we hope to enlist the aid of our county's television station for a "telethon" featuring college talent. Council members will be presented at intervals to describe our program and its need for support. It is hoped, also, that we can bring one of the motion picture stars who shares our problem to the area for benefit performances.

In two of our communities subcouncils have worked out plans to raise funds for local projects. In McAllen they will operate concession stands at Little League baseball games. In Edinburg benefit baseball and basketball games will be played by Pan American College.

The first project the council undertook in 1955 was the promoting of public school classes for educable retarded children. On the staff of Edinburg's Roosevelt School for physically handicapped children was a qualified teacher of the mentally retarded. She could not be spared from her existing class, however, unless a replacement were found. Another seemingly insurmountable problem resulted from the fact that the deadline for State approval of classes for the mentally retarded had already passed. With the consent of school authorities I visited the office of the State special education supervisor and the teacher training colleges in search of a teacher. Although all qualified teachers had already contracted with other schools, the trip was successful in one important respect—the State supervisor agreed to waive the deadline for establishment of units in the event that we found a teacher. Just a week before the beginning of school the Edinburg superintendent learned that a Moore Air Force Base officer's wife was qualified to teach the physically handicapped, thus releasing the Roosevelt School teacher for the retarded children's unit.

This was a heartening development but it barely scratched the surface of the problem. Seven communities with populations ranging from 7,500 to 32,000 still lacked classes for retarded children. No additional qualified teachers lived in the county and a critical shortage prevailed throughout the State.

In several schools outside our area officials paid teachers' expenses for college summer courses that qualified them to teach retarded children. To encourage this practice in our county the council set up scholarships for teachers who agreed to instruct retarded children in our public schools. During the summer of 1956 a teacher received a $300 scholarship. As a result McAllen now has the county's second class for educable retarded children.

In order to make it easier for our teachers to take the required courses we petitioned Pan American College to offer special education work. During the past year the college has offered several of the required courses. This has enabled another teacher to qualify, thereby resulting in an additional unit for Edinburg. Moreover, much interest has been inspired among college students and hopes are high that several will enter special education.

Meanwhile our second objective, providing facilities for trainable children, has not been neglected. During the summer we employed an able kindergarten teacher to direct the program. Her salary of $100 per month came from a nominal tuition fee. For her helpers we turned to the college. Two professors of education, an art instructor, a physical education teacher, and several students volunteered to spend scheduled hours each week working with the children.

In searching for a classroom I learned that no public school facilities were available. Then I remembered that the Edinburg Catholic Parochial School had vacant rooms. The school officials kindly placed classroom, lunchroom, auditorium, and playground facilities at our disposal.

The class, which began with twelve students from five towns, was an immediate success with a program of play and preprimer activities. The parents formed car pools to deliver pupils and volunteer helpers. A man who owned a swimming pool offered its use and a lifeguard volunteered to give swimming lessons. Although none of the children learned to swim they benefited greatly from the hydrotherapy.

In the fall it was decided to move the class to McAllen since most of the pupils lived there. This necessitated finding new quarters. As no classrooms were available we broadened our search to include any suitable building with a fenced yard. The Girl Scout "hut" contained the necessary facilities and was placed at our disposal. Our teacher had returned to her kindergarten and, in searching for a replacement, we turned once again to Moore

Air Force Base. The public relations officer published an article about the council's program in the Base paper and described the council's problem at an Officers' Wives meeting. This resulted in obtaining a teacher who had worked with retarded children in another State.

The third category of youngsters whom we were determined to help consisted of cases requiring institutionalization. The State School for the Mentally Retarded is located three hundred miles from Hidalgo County. Many of our parents are reluctant to be separated from their children by such a distance. Another drawback is extreme overcrowding at the institution, which results in long waiting lists.

The State School Superintendent spoke at one of our meetings and agreed with us about the desirability of establishing a branch in Hidalgo County. A committee was appointed to invite State legislators and other officials to meet with the council to discuss the problem. A petition was drawn up for presentation to the State Commission on Hospitals and Special Schools listing the advantages of our area as a site. This was signed by all council members and many public spirited citizens. As a result Hidalgo County will receive real consideration when a branch is established.

The fourth class of retarded persons needing help consists of youths past school age. Sheltered workshops that train teenagers to perform routine tasks enable them, in many cases, to become partially self-supporting. Our council has definite plans in that direction.

Our model in this instance is the Marbridge Ranch, which was established near Austin by a parent to provide vocational training for his son and other retarded youths. The eighty-acre tract contains a dormitory with rooms for twenty boys, a recreation hall, workshops, barns and other agricultural buildings. The boys are taught agriculture and animal husbandry, ceramics, upholstering, and other crafts designed to enable them to find and hold jobs. The staff at the ranch consists of a director, a house mother, a farmer, a cook, and a handicrafts teacher. Expenses amounting to $2,000 per month are met through sale of products, a subsidy by the State rehabilitation office, and monthly tuition of $125. (Youths whose parents cannot afford the tuition are sponsored by service organizations.)

Our council's plans differ in some respects. To reduce initial expenditures we probably will begin with a day school and add dormitories as funds become available. We expect to accept boys of twelve, because many are dropped from school at that age. It is hoped that our tuitions will be lower owing to larger revenues resulting from the diversified crop program that our climate affords. We also expect financial aid from service clubs and philanthropic foundations.

Our council's program for teen-aged girls is already under way. As few retarded girls seek employment outside the home, morning classes were organized in cooking and sewing. The girls are taught by a Pan American College home economics teacher with the aid of members of the council. All are volunteering their services. The class uses kitchen facilities of the Edinburg Federal Housing Project. Supplies and utensils are provided by service clubs. The girls are now carrying over what they have learned into their homes. Finding a place of usefulness gives them much satisfaction.

While pursuing our objectives for children the council has not neglected a second major need—parent therapy. Last July we held a workshop for parents, led by a professor of special education from an upstate college. Our monthly meetings also provide opportunities for parents to ask for advice with their problems. Frequently other parents who have faced similar situations suggest solutions. These informal sessions have helped in reducing embarrassment and reticence on the part of new members.

In reviewing our first year of activities we can point to several accomplishments. The council's efforts were instrumental in establishing three public school classes for educable retarded children and were entirely responsible for organizing classes for trainable children and for older girls. These steps, satisfying as they seem, serve only to point up the tremendous need that remains. We believe, however, that our plans are sound and, with God's help, we will persevere until all mentally retarded youngsters in our area receive the type of training that best suits their needs.

5. The Sponsorship Plan in a Home for Unwed Mothers

MRS. MARGARET B. SWEITZER

This paper will deal directly with my own experiences as they relate to volunteer activities. It covers a period of four years during which time I was employed as a psychiatric caseworker by the Florence Crittenton Home of Trenton, New Jersey. Its viewpoint is largely that of the professional worker; its orientation is mainly based on recognition of the psychological factors involved in the needs of the group of persons served by the Home—the unwed mothers.

The Florence Crittenton Home in Trenton not only offers institutional care for the unwed mother, but also includes hospital care, which is provided by a hospital unit consisting of labor room, delivery room, nursery, and four-bed ward, plus other essential equipment. The girls who become residents do so on a voluntary basis, and one of the responsibilities assumed by the Home is protection of the identity of each resident. This limits admission to the Home to the staff, residents and their authorized visitors, and other authorized persons.

Growing knowledge about the unmarried mother, her personality development, needs, and motivations, indicates that each girl who becomes pregnant while unmarried is fundamentally an emotionally disturbed person in need of much help and understanding. This help must be made available to her during her usually all too short (therapeutically) stay in the Home. Every effort is made to help each girl, not only by physical and medical care, but also by helping her gain new understanding and by awakening and directing desires for a more mature way of living.

The ultimate responsibility for the operation of the Home rests with the board of directors, twenty-five in number. The actual running of the Home is done by the administrative and professional staff. The board, unusually active and interested, deals with finances, physical setup, general over-all supervision, and, in fair degree, contacts with community, both on the fund-raising level and on a broader base.

The staff operates freely in its defined areas of functioning and the relations pattern between board and staff are good.

How does volunteer help fit into this picture? Four years of experience in the Home, plus several more in child welfare and clinic work, provide an interesting and sometimes awkward and disturbing picture in relation to agency and volunteers. There are many motives that lead people to volunteer to "do good," and not all of these motives can result in helpful action. There are always friends of board members who apply to help, free, in just "any way I can." There are other people who offer specific skills and talents.

In my experience, except in rare instances these offers, though well meant, when accepted have given little satisfaction either to donor or recipient. There are too many uncontrollable factors. Volunteer and recipient each have many needs to be met. All too often there develops the attitude that the volunteer is a "necessary evil."

Screening presents a delicate problem that we did not always have the skill to handle. Interpretation very often fell on barren soil because the listener felt no real lack of comprehension of the situation. She was being helpful, and nothing could be simpler than to give great thanks and accept the offer of her help. Here, as is inevitable, neither staff nor volunteer was fooled by a make-work policy, as such invented tasks fell of their own weak structure.

For instance, there was the woman who sewed. And in truth she did sew beautifully. She volunteered to teach the girls. Her offer was accepted with unexpressed reluctance, because her evident coldness and precision presented warning signals. And the girls immediately sensed the danger—the fundamental rejection. Net result: no interested students to whom to teach sewing. Worse than that, the volunteer was convinced that those "no good girls" were really "no good."

Then there was the energetic minister who was going to reach the girls through group therapy. This he elaborately and skillfully painted as the great good desperately needed by the Home. Somehow, a few sessions later, the girls were either present but openly ridiculing, or very busy elsewhere. After the minister had aroused, needlessly, much anxiety, it became evident upon investigation that his training was far afield from qualifying him for such skilled and technical work as group therapy.

The young woman who volunteered to do typing, an item never adequately covered in our budget, seemed like a real find. But she failed to appear at agreed times, and, unforgiveable, gaily inserted into her outside social conversations various "tidbits" about the girls in the Home.

Actually, there was one very successful volunteer. She was a most charming, warm and friendly person, who accepted people as she found them.

And the girls responded to her genuine interest and enthusiastically came each week to her group singing sessions.

The balance, as can quickly be seen, was largely on the negative side. The volunteer, though well meaning, was unable to see or meet the most pressing need of these fundamentally rejected girls, that of accepting them as they are and giving them the right to be themselves. On some occasions actual harm resulted from well-meaning efforts.

These experiences, plus similar ones over the years, led the staff to a position where the gradually evolved screening and interpretation routine established to protect the Home became so successful that it warded off all individual volunteers. This at least allowed positive work to continue within the Home.

At the same time that this was occurring, there was developing a growing awareness of the interest of people in Home activities and the potential body of energy for use in service. Any well-functioning agency knows that it needs the community, individually and collectively. The always present need to interpret and explain the agency function and the relation between agency and community became more clearly defined.

Interestingly enough, all the while that the above experiences were happening, there was slowly and steadily growing a different way of handling volunteer interest. This is what I call the Sponsorship Plan, though it had been developing gradually over a period of years before it was labeled anything. Some small elaboration is necessary to clarify the plan as it operates in the Home.

The Home consists of individual bedrooms to house fourteen girls, plus rooms for director and assistant director. There are the usual living room, dining room, and kitchen, plus large laundry, recreation room, and office. These are in addition to the rooms of the hospital unit.

Many years ago a circle of women nearby, wanting to help and knowing the need for infant clothing, agreed to supply some and has been doing so ever since. As the years went by other groups, often Parent Teacher Associations, became interested and took on responsibility to meet some continuing need in the Home.

This provided the basis or seeds for what is now firmly established as the Sponsorship Plan. Under this plan, a service group in the community can, as a project, assume responsibility for any one room or group of rooms in the Home. This entails providing all the needs of that particular room. If the project is a bedroom, the group agrees to give linens, furniture, curtains, rugs, paint when necessary, and as much or as little more as the group decides. If the project is a specialized room, such as the nursery, it may include new plastic baby beds, respirator, or any number of always needed equipment or paint.

As the plan has evolved, many PTA groups and other service groups now sponsor a large percentage of the rooms in the Home. It is clear that this is a great benefit to the Home, operating as it does on always limited funds. In this manner have been provided such items as trays for nursery beds, curtains for ward beds, attractive and appealing furnishings for the bedrooms, maintenance of the grounds, plus so many items that a listing would be impossible within the limits of this paper.

An even greater gain, in a less material way, is the opportunity offered to us to interpret our function and our girls to new groups. For example, a local women's auxiliary, hearing of the Home and experiencing a growing member interest, telephoned the director. There ensued a general discussion of the situation, and our Sponsorship Plan was outlined briefly. A date was set for the group members to visit for a coffee hour and discussion plus a tour of the Home.

After the group arrived and was enjoying cookies and coffee, we presented, in general terms, the setup as far as the Home is concerned, its history, sources of income, procedures, and so on. We also described in simple and general terms some of the psychological factors involved in the problem of unmarried motherhood. Questions were immediately forthcoming and took many forms, not only about the physical and mechanical details, but also about the girls and their problems. In our experience this has always resulted in the beginning of a real understanding that forms a firm base for later growth.

After the discussion the group was shown the Home and the various available sponsorships outlined. The decisions both as to whether or not to sponsor, and if so, what project to sponsor, are entirely up to the group. They take their ideas home for further discussion and decision; later, through the director, specific arrangements are made for their sponsorship. They have, as a group, taken back into the community the information with which to give further interpretation where it can spread and grow. And their decision to sponsor adds one more strength to our solid Home foundation.

This procedure allows us to meet our responsibility to the girls at the highest level and their protection is guaranteed. No individual is made to feel unhappy, unwanted, or unappreciated. The resulting impact, a group one instead of individual, is channeled into constructive ways.

In actual practice the Sponsorship Plan has been a particularly successful way to use volunteer help. The tangible evidence of united efforts can be seen in every room of the Home. And the intangible benefits are manifold.

Similar arrangements have been made in other agencies with adaptations to suit individual circumstances. For instance, a local child guidance center received continuing financial pledges of help from the Junior League, which first allocated its funds to equipment but later to other pressing needs. A child-placing agency has had successful volunteer help from groups who sponsor the providing of clothing for the various age groups of children helped by the agency.

Because of the particular nature of the Home, the Sponsorship Plan can be applied on a very large base. It meets a very real need by providing nonbudget items for the Home, thus freeing allocated funds for more technical use. At the same time it offers to any and all groups the opportunity to support a real "cause" and to see the tangible results of their efforts. And all the while the sponsoring members are learning, increasing their grasp of and understanding about a vital part of their community.

It seems that some such plan could apply, with minor adjustments, to many agencies, both private and public. Interpretation at the initial stage is essential, and this must include tying the individual energies of the volunteers to a united goal. There might even be developed new groups who could pool their talents and energies in some outside activity to acquire the means to promote sponsorship. This, though initially time-consuming at the selling stage, can result in more extensive benefits than can frequently result from individual effort no matter how earnest and sincere. And it offers an excellent screening device that is impersonal, yet effective. For the volunteer who "really" wants to help, it gives a solid, valid need into which she can put her energies and gain satisfaction. In time she comes to feel she belongs to her project. The volunteer, once an "unnecessary evil," becomes a deeply appreciated and respected helper.

6. Helping Mothers to Gain Self-Sufficiency

FRED H. STEININGER

Public assistance should not be a way of life, if it can be prevented. This statement is made by many persons, public welfare administrators, taxpayers, and often, more importantly, by recipients of public assistance themselves. Individuals who are able and willing to work should have the opportunity to do so. This, too, is a frequently made statement.

In our county, the board of the County Department of Public Welfare has professed the philosophy that public assistance recipients should be given every opportunity to be self-sustaining through employment. The staff of the department is encouraged to help individuals who come to the department for assistance and service to develop their own capacities in order that they may live more adequately and creatively. The applicants and recipients of assistance are to be helped to become self-sustaining citizens, personally, socially, and economically.

This philosophy of the County Welfare Board is much more easily professed than carried out in practice. The community in which this County Welfare Department is located is made up, in terms of employment, of heavy industry. Steel, oil, and cement are the principal manufactured products. More than 75 per cent of all employees of the community are engaged in the manufacturing of these heavy industrial products. The industries seek young men with brawn as employees. The physically and mentally handicapped, the aged, and women are not hired and are offered no encouragement in seeking employment in these industries. The County Welfare Department in this community does not administer a general assistance program. The three categories of the Social Security Act, old age assistance, blind assistance, and aid to dependent children, are its major programs. It also administers a child welfare program.

To the limitation of employment opportunities for the aged, the handicapped, and women are added some other factors that make it difficult for the staff of the County Welfare Department to carry out the sound principle that applicants and recipients of public assistance should be helped to become self-sustaining. The State in which this County Welfare Department is located has a legal maximum on the amount of assistance that a person or family may receive. The legal maximum for a person or family does not meet their minimum needs according to a standard budget that is compatible with decency and health. (With employment or other resources they can acquire sufficient income to meet minimum needs.)

For example, the legal maximum allowance for a mother and her first child in terms of aid to dependent children assistance is $64 a month. For each additional child the maximum is $23 a month. In this highly urbanized, industrialized area a mother and one child would need at least $100 a month to meet her family's elemental needs of food, clothing, shelter, and personal incidentals. This does not take into consideration medical and dental needs. The legal maximum allowance for an aged person is $60 a month. It has been found that $75 a month is the minimum needed for an aged person to have a minimum standard of living compatible with decency and health.

An additional complicating factor in terms of employment possibilities for the women who make up the aid to dependent children caseload is the characteristic makeup of the group. They are women who generally married young, many without completing their education and usually without any work experience before their marriage. The majority of them are migrants from the South and/or members of the Negro race.

How to do something about implementing the County Welfare Board's philosophy of "helping applicants and recipients of public assistance to become self-sustaining, to obtain employment," in spite of the obstacles mentioned above, was the task facing our County Welfare Director.

The referral of many recipients to the local public and private employment agencies was not fruitful. From the point of view of employment they were considered "low on the totem pole of employability." They lacked the skills and characteristics needed to work in steel mills and oil refineries. Some were able to obtain part-time or full-time jobs as "domestics." However, to do a good job and obtain an adequate wage as a domestic required that the person have real skills in household management. Not many of the recipient group had the necessary skills. In terms of such employment as sales personnel they also lacked the necessary qualifications.

With a caseload of recipients who were considered marginal or poor candidates for employment, a labor market consisting mainly of heavy industrial jobs and not suitable for employment of women and aged, and a Welfare Board policy that public assistance recipients should be helped toward economic independence, the County Welfare Director and his staff faced a difficult situation. What should be done?

Our County Welfare Director initiated several projects, such as a training program for "household management," and special campaigns for employment of public assistance recipients. However, the one we wish to discuss here is the development of a training program for practical nurses. This project, we believe, dramatically illustrates the "way to extend voluntary activity and organization in social welfare." It reveals how a multitude of voluntary groups can cooperate in implementing some fundamental principles of social work—"the creation of conditions which help to make a more satisfying way of life possible, the development within individuals and community of capacities to live more adequately and creatively."

In 1954 it was recognized in our county that a severe shortage of professionally trained nurses existed. Consideration was being given to how this problem might be met. One suggestion was the greater use of practical nurses. Practical nurses could be trained in less time than the professionals. With an increased number of practical nurses the routine nursing tasks could be given to them and the professionally trained nurses would be used more freely in areas where their special skills were most needed.

When our County Welfare Director learned of these developments he talked to a local chamber of commerce that had taken a special interest in the development of a training program for practical nurses. He encouraged them in their thinking and pointed out that with the development of such a training program several positives could result. Not only would such a training program help relieve the professional nurse shortage but also it would offer an opportunity for some mothers who were receiving aid to dependent children's assistance from the public welfare department to become self-sustaining and economically independent. He emphasized that the welfare department had on its rolls a number of mothers who wanted to work and who could be employed without jeopardizing the welfare of their children. They needed training to obtain employment and were eager to learn some skill so that they could become economically and socially independent. The welfare department would recommend mother-students from its rolls on a "case by case" basis and the caseworkers would plan, with the mothers, sound child-care programs. There were many relatives, grandmothers, sisters, and others, of these potential mother-students who could be used for providing sound child-care plans while the mothers were in training and later employed.

The County Welfare Director also emphasized that these women on the welfare rolls not only were willing to learn and work but also *had* to work because of the limitations on assistance granted to their families by law. Such a training program would help in several ways: relieve the professional nurse shortage, give some public assistance recipient mothers an opportunity to be self-sustaining, and relieve the community taxpayers of some public assistance costs.

The County Welfare Director pointed out that public assistance laws would not allow funds for payment of tuition and other expenses for the training of these mothers on the aid to dependent children assistance program. However, he did not see this as a deterrent. He saw this obstacle as a real opportunity for private citizens and voluntary groups to cooperate with a public social agency in the rehabilitation of some public assistance families. He said that he would seek scholarship funds from the community to pay for the training of selected mothers who were receiving aid to dependent children assistance.

In the fall of 1954, the practical nurses training program was established in a local extension division of one of our state universities. This program was worked out in cooperation with the local private hospitals. The length of the course is twelve months. The first four months are spent in classroom instruction at the university and the remaining eight months at one of the four private hospitals in the area. The students receive some financial remuneration during the eight months' training in the hospital. After completing the full course the students are eligible to take the State Board of Licensing examination.

A few months before the first training course was to begin the County Welfare Director announced through newspapers, speeches, and letters to civic and social organizations the need for funds to send potential candidates (from the public assistance rolls) to the school. The cost of tuition and other necessary expenses was $220 per student.

During 1954–55, eight women from the aid to dependent children assistance rolls completed their training for practical nursing. Six of the mothers are now completely self-supporting and no longer are in need of public assistance. Two have had their assistance reduced and are partially self-supporting. In the 1955–56 class which is now coming to a close, nine more women from the public assistance rolls are enrolled. Scholarship funds for the 1954–55 class were obtained for these women from Altrusa Club, Junior Chamber of Commerce, National Association of College Women, several sororities, and a number of other civic and social organizations. Scholarship funds for the public assistance recipients in the 1955–56 class were obtained from the Jayshees, National Council of Jewish Women, Childhood Education Association, Business and Professional Women's Club, and a number of other groups and persons.

Some groups were able to contribute only five dollars toward a scholarship; others were able to contribute the full tuition for a student. Some groups took a special interest in "their student" and attended the student's graduation exercise.

This venture has been, and is continuing to be, a real demonstration of voluntary welfare cooperation with public welfare to achieve a soundly professed goal of "helping people help themselves."

This project has led this County Welfare Department into establishing a "County Welfare Department Rehabilitation Fund." The moneys for this fund are all donated voluntarily by persons and groups. This is a separate fund established solely for the purpose of providing for the rehabilitation of public assistance recipients—for vocational training of recipients so that they may become employed and fully or partially self-supporting. The fund is now being used not only to provide scholarships for public assistance recipients to obtain training in practical nursing but also for training in fields such as beauty culture, sewing, stenography, and others.

This Rehabilitation Fund in a County Welfare Department, supported completely by voluntary activity, appears to be a sound venture in the rehabilitation of public assistance recipients. It is truly a dynamic illustration of cooperation between public and private social welfare. The achievement of the establishment of such a fund in this county (modest as the fund is at the present time) is even more praiseworthy because of the scarcity of formally organized private social welfare organizations. This county does not have the numerous strong private social work agencies that are prevalent in counties of comparable population and social characteristics. In terms of its population which is now reaching a half-million it is a relatively newly populated area. Its largest city was founded in 1906. The public welfare agency has always been the major social work body of the county.

The idea of having voluntary groups support a fund for the vocational rehabilitation of persons who find it necessary to receive public assistance, especially women receiving aid to dependent children's assistance, is unlimited in its possibilities. There are many programs for the rehabilitation of the physically handicapped such as the blind, the amputee, and others. Very little consideration has been given to the vocational training of the many women who prefer not to receive public assistance, who are physically and mentally able and willing to work, and who can be employed without sacrificing the well-being of their children.

In many counties of the United States the public welfare agency is the agency carrying the major burden of providing assistance and service to people in need and who have problems of social adjustment. The opportunities for voluntary participation in helping the public welfare agency in these communities rehabilitate (particularly in terms of vocational training) is unlimited. In all communities there are shortages of certain types of skills. It may be practical nurses, seamstresses, stenographers, or domestic help. The potentials for meeting these shortages are on the rolls of public assistance agencies. With an investment in the persons on public assistance rolls by "voluntary activity and organizations in social welfare" much could be accomplished. A "Rehabilitation Fund" in many counties of the United States supported solely by private contributions will strengthen the relations between public and private social welfare. It will add to the morale of both groups. It will offer a multitude of opportunities for more persons to make a sound investment in people and will provide a greater appreciation for both private and public social welfare.

The "Rehabilitation Fund" for public assistance recipients need not necessarily be placed within a county welfare department. It could be a private incorporated group whose project would be to provide vocational training funds for public assistance recipients. Whether the funds are held by the county welfare department or private incorporated group is not essential. The main idea is that something be done to help the persons on public assistance obtain employment and to give them an opportunity to be economically and socially independent.

With reference to the training and employment of mothers who receive public assistance, under this plan it is assumed that only mothers who can be trained and employed without jeopardizing the family life of their children will be selected. They will be trained for jobs where there are shortages and where the nature of the employment will not interfere in the mothers' basic responsibility of providing nurture and guidance to their children. There are a number of employment opportunities in fields such as beauty culture, practical nursing, and stenography, where the hours can be regulated so that the mothers will have time for their children and their own household responsibilities.

12
The Aging

1. Organizing a Community
for Helping the Aging

MRS. FRANK M. BARRY

The thesis to be presented here is predicated on the assumption that welfare services should be based upon the needs of people and that welfare organizations should be sufficiently flexible to move into new patterns of service in order to meet changing needs.

The focus is on community planning and the way one community has extended services for its aging population. Certain generalizations will be drawn that may be useful in other settings.

It is difficult to find the right way to extend activities organizations in social welfare. This is not because there are no welfare problems; these are legion. It is not because ideas are lacking, nor services that can be expanded or developed. Nor is it primarily because of lack of financial and personnel resources. The difficulties arise out of our strengths—our strong belief in self-determination. We do not want, nor should we have, a blueprint. For we are a people that believe in the rights of people, that respect each other's institutions, that value the individual and his independence. Yet we are a people that want to help others, particularly those less fortunate than ourselves. Hence we may think that because our ways and our institutional patterns are good for us we should tell others what to do, thus negating our own beliefs.

It is dangerous to say this is *the* way or even to imply that one's way is best. But we have found that there are guideposts that direct the way. These we have learned from religious and political philosophy, from studies of sociology, anthropology, and human behavior, and from the application of this knowledge through professional service.

We see many guideposts to follow when we plan a way to extend voluntary activity and organization in social welfare. What are some of these?

We start where people are, with the needs as they exist and are felt, with the strengths and potentialities that are present, with an honest appraisal of facts and feelings, and yet with a goal of health, happiness, se-

curity, and freedom. We think not only of the problems but of all the resources there are to meet them. We think about how individuals and groups
and communities can use their strengths, individually and collectively, to
meet their own problems. And we think how we can help, as professionals,
so that problems are solved in a manner that creates independence, not dependency. We realize that to do the job takes understanding, knowledge,
and skill. Just as the doctor must diagnose the patient and treat his disease
specifically but in the light of all knowledge about that disease and that
patient, so must we diagnose the social problem and base our treatment
upon our knowledge of the problem and the people it affects, approaching
the problem specifically in light of general knowledge.

Enough of this brief glimpse of theory. One finds oneself in a job as
director of a department on older persons. The needs are many and varied.
They are not waiting to be sought out; they are encroaching like weeds.
The voice on the telephone asks how he can live on a $65 per month pen-
sion check; he can't find a room, he is not well, he is lonely, he can't get
a job. The social agency worker asks why there are no more nursing home
beds in this city, whether anyone is doing anything about compulsory retirement, why is the matron in the philanthropic home so punitive, why
doesn't the Board of Education have classes for oldsters, why is there no
recreation center, what is being done about homemaker service and home
medical care. And at every party someone is sure to tell about his parent
or grandparent, aunt, uncle, or friend.

Communities all over the country are alerted to the needs of their older
residents. And the communities and those charged specifically with helping solve the problems of older people are faced with the task of analyzing
these needs and finding the best ways to meet them.

It is our belief that in any large-sized community there should be some
acceptable organization that is authorized to do coordination and planning
in the field of the aging. This is logically within the scope of the welfare
planning council if it is representative of health, welfare, and civic organizations and has the confidence of the community. Such an organization
should not confuse its function with that of the direct service agency. In
simple terms, the planning council sees that needed services are provided
by the appropriate existing direct service agency or by one newly formed
for the purpose.

In planning services for the aging it is particularly important that there
be broad representation because of the varied and interrelated needs of
older persons of all walks of life. We therefore consider those who represent the older persons themselves and their major groupings, the organizations serving their needs, potential resources for service, and those with
general community knowledge and leadership position. Finally we would

encourage a flexible structure that is dynamic—that allows for an imaginative, creative, and differentiated approach.

So far our suggestions appear intangible. Theory is useless unless effective in practice. To suggest application of this theory we shall briefly describe several activities that our Committee on Older Persons has initiated or promoted.

Our committee is composed of about eighty members representing various organizations and interests. It operates through a number of subcommittees, some of which are jointly appointed by other committees and councils. An executive committee directs the work of the large committee and coordinates the activities of the subcommittees. The staff worker, serving as secretary to the committee and director of the department, conceives of the job as one of community organization.

The activities described here are selected with a view to variety in type and approach and to illustrate the applicability of certain selected principles. Space prohibits a comprehensive, analytical description.

The Golden Age Center

Several years ago the committee decided that a recreation center for older persons was needed. The golden age clubs, meeting in churches, libraries, and settlement houses, met only part of the need. The director of the public housing authority became highly interested in housing and other needs of older persons and offered the ground floor of a proposed public housing apartment for a golden age recreation center. While the golden age apartment was being designed and constructed the committee set up a new private agency, with its own board of directors, supported by foundation and Community Chest funds. The many details of establishing a new agency were worked out, including administrative and policy matters, equipment and facilities, program, and staff. The center opened in August 1955. The program includes regular daily activities, special events, excursions, cafeteria service, and personal counseling. The director operates a golden age camp and is consultant for the city's many golden age clubs in addition to his center responsibilities.

This new agency provides a needed service. It also is significant as an illustration of public and voluntary cooperation and of the usefulness of a planning committee in mobilizing community support for the establishment of a new agency.

Retirement Housing Conference

The committee recognized the need many older persons have for suitable living arrangements. This problem may affect middle- and upper-income persons as well as the indigent, particularly persons whose homes may be too large, poorly designed, or deteriorated; whose health limits their housekeeping activities; or who are lonely or cannot live happily with relatives.

A housing subcommittee was appointed to examine the problem and see what might be done. The chairman, an attorney, had no known connection with "welfare" but considerable knowledge and interest in housing both in America and in Sweden. On the committee were architects, a builder, a banker, a public relations man, an insurance agent, several persons experienced in work with the aging, a housing official, two retired lay people, and other interested individuals.

It took several months to study needs and to determine focus and objectives. Finally the committee agreed to concentrate on "independent living arrangements," as differentiated from institutional living, and to direct attention to housing needs of middle- and upper-income older persons. After examining various housing plans throughout the country, the committee decided that it must convince private interests of the housing needs of the aging, describe successful developments elsewhere, and show the potential market that this growing segment of the population represents. Furthermore, it believed that religious, fraternal, and labor organizations also needed to be made aware of standards of design, types, and quality of facilities and services.

Therefore, as one of its activities the committee decided to sponsor a "Retirement Housing Conference" aimed particularly at builders, realtors, investors, architects, and bankers. Committee members approached major associations of these groups to cosponsor the conference; all accepted and designated representatives to the planning committee. In addition to these associations, the Chamber of Commerce and the three daily newspapers participated. A local foundation granted money to underwrite the cost. Six experienced out-of-town speakers were selected for the program. The sponsors have been enthusiastic and helpful. As one builder said: "We're businessmen interested in a profit but we're interested in the welfare of people too."

Unfortunately for this story the conference is three weeks hence. But the process and results to date seem significant. We have realized that since housing needs of older persons have to be met, in part, by those who design, build, and finance private housing, these interests need to be represented in planning and will respond when invited. Also there is already evidence of an awakening interest that may lead to tangible housing results.

Although uncompleted, this activity is selected because it illustrates aspects of extension of service consistent with our thesis, namely, the utilization of appropriate community resources to meet need; the existence of need among various economic groups; the fact that needs are not always met through philanthropy or public assistance, vital though such programs be; and the usefulness of a voluntary planning committee in focusing attention on a problem and in mobilizing support.

SENIOR COUNCIL

Over a year ago Mr. X found his way to our office. He is a retired business executive now operating his own small consultant service. He said, "Many of my retired friends are alert and able; they have retired from busy, productive lives to lives of boredom. Isn't there some way that their abilities can be put to good use?" A few members of the Committee on Older Persons met unofficially with Mr. X; ideas grew and finally, through personal contact, a group of about twenty-five prominent business and professional leaders, retired or near retirement, met to discuss the possibility of forming an association. A planning committee was authorized to set up a plan of organization and program objectives. It is an organization for business, professional, and civic (older) leaders established for the purpose of serving the community (and themselves). The objectives are to provide a panel of members available for community service and to do business and personal counseling. The regulations state that there shall be no overlapping with the work of other organizations.

Currently there are over 150 on the roster—former bankers, lawyers, and presidents and vice-presidents of large and small businesses. The council has an office and a modest staff, and has engaged in a variety of activities. For example, it provided a college with a consultant to advise on setting up a fund-raising campaign; it provided personnel to study the county auditor's office; it cosponsored a city-wide conference on aging and its representatives helped plan and conduct the event; some of its members advised a small welfare agency on bookkeeping and inventory procedures; it has recommended for employment several competent older men with specialized skills.

The council has received local and national attention. It still faces organizational problems and is hopeful of more substantial accomplishments. But there is conviction that the purpose is sound and that the council will be successful.

What is the significance of this development? First, of course, is its service to a group of older persons not generally considered to be in need. But in addition it illustrates (*a*) that a welfare planning council can move outside the walls of established agency patterns and help others mobilize their own resources, and (*b*) that welfare needs are felt, although perhaps not expressed as such, by all types of people and that the welfare agency and worker must differentiate the kind of "help" that is needed and will be accepted and used. No golden age club for this group! To receive they must give; "help" consists of calling upon them for service.

These illustrations point up some of the essential principles underlying extension of service, namely (*a*) a broad concept of need, (*b*) programs based upon a careful analysis of need, including community readiness, (*c*) utilization of pertinent community resources, and (*d*) representation of appropriate groups, both the users and providers of service.

We have by no means covered all considerations related to extension of services but have pointed out those that we believe essential. We have used these principles ourselves as guides in a variety of situations calling for many different approaches. Our committee, for example, initiated a friendly visitor program in old age assistance; encouraged Family Service to extend homemaker services to the aged and chronically ill; established casework and groupwork programs in several philanthropic homes; studied persons needing institutional care and persuaded the county to provide additional facilities; prepared a resource pamphlet for use by corporations in preretirement counseling; and encouraged a local university to set up a training institute for personnel in nursing homes.

In summary, we believe that there is no one way, no one pattern, whereby programs are extended. We believe a way can be found but the particular way depends upon the existing situation in the community, on a careful analysis of need and readiness, and on mobilizing the various resources, material and personal, that have a part to play in diagnosing and meeting the problem. Then the result is likely to be good, the program vital and suitable. We believe this to be a valid approach based upon our American philosophy, upon social science theory, and upon successful practice.

2. Guardians of the Aged

CHARLES W. McCANN

America has grown older during the past half-century. In the fifty years from 1900 to 1950 the total population doubled, but the number of persons over sixty-five years of age quadrupled. During this same period there has been a general movement of our people from the country to the city. In 1900 more than half of the population lived on farms but at mid-century this was true of only one fifth of our nation's inhabitants. These developments have important implications for our older citizens as well as for our society as a whole.

The three-generation family that typified our agricultural era has been supplanted by what sociologists term "the nuclear family."[1] This is a smaller, more streamlined, self-contained and flexible social unit, consisting of parents and nonadult children only. It is accepted that as the children of this modern family achieve maturity, they will leave home and establish independent residences of their own. The separation of grandparent from parent and parent from child has been stimulated by our more diversified economic organization, the bounty of an industrial society. The end result of this social atomization is that elderly parents are finding themselves more and more alone. In the city and by themselves the aged of today have become more dependent upon the extrafamily resources of the community itself.

In partial response to these developments more social benefits and services have been offered our senior citizens. Public assistance, old age insurance, and pensions for our aged veterans are but a few examples. An analysis of these programs reveals that they tend to be structured for the independently functioning individual. In illustration, public assistance is provided in the form of money payments to our needy aged. This procedure stresses and promotes the freedom and independence of the recipients. On the other hand, the money payment had tended to emphasize some facets

[1] Harold L. Wilensky, "Changing Patterns of Family Life," *Children*, III, No. 5 (September–October 1956), 165. (Washington: U.S. Government Printing Office.)

of environmental dependency. The money payment requires the capacity to plan and budget over a period of time. It makes the individual responsible for determining his own welfare. Although these are positive cultural values, they do not take into account the fact that many of our aged at some point find themselves psychologically and socially dependent. In order to truly enjoy their independence, they need services that are geared to their diminishing capacities.

A cultural lag is apparent. Recent findings from the field of geriatrics indicate that our approach to the care of the aged in our society is not oriented to the needs of our twentieth-century civilization. We view them as independently functioning individuals when in reality many of them are experiencing a lessened capacity for self-care.[2] A shift from relative independence of social functioning to relative dependence of social functioning is reported by Pollock[3] to be a normal component of the aging process.

The concept of self-determination that permeates our welfare programs is contrary to the changing capacities and abilities of many of our elderly. In one federal study it was found that many aged who were otherwise eligible for public assistance benefits were denied payments since, because of debilities of old age, they were deemed incapable of managing the funds properly.[4] It was ruled that certain applicants were not eligible for program benefits because they were unable to be self-determining in relation to the money payment. Moreover, in Los Angeles County an estimated two thousand recipients of Old Age Security are unable to function properly under this welfare principle, and the Department of Charities is concerned about their nonfinancial needs.[5] Guardianship has been considered as a resort but a lack of interest in their problems is evidenced by the fact that relatives, if any, were often unwilling to petition for guardianship, and the public guardian[6] would not accept referral unless property rights were involved. Consequently, in the absence of new ideas and services many aged are be-

[2] See the article by Richard Young, "Problems of an Aging Population," in *The Medical Clinics of North America* (Chicago: W. B. Saunders Co., 1956).

[3] Otto Pollock, *Social Adjustment in Old Age* (New York: Social Science Research Council, 1948).

[4] Federal Security Agency, Bureau of Public Assistance. *Sheltered Care and Home Services for Public Assistance Recipients* (Washington: U.S. Government Printing Office, 1944).

[5] Letter from the Bureau of Public Assistance, Los Angeles County, to the Policy Committee on Old Age Security, Welfare Planning Council, Los Angeles Region, dated September 14, 1955 (typewritten).

[6] A public official is permitted to petition to court letters of guardianship under a California Statute. See State of California, Welfare & Institutions Code, Section #5175.

ing institutionalized in our state hospitals and private facilities. In the period from 1920 to 1950, for example, there has been a 354 per cent jump in patients over sixty-five in our state institutions.[7]

These findings suggest that some service is needed to assist those aged persons who are individually unable to protect and implement their property rights, welfare benefits, and the right to be treated with respect and dignity regardless of age. Legal guardianship is the historic means society has utilized to fill these requirements. As now constituted, however, guardianship is not doing the job. A noted legal authority recently reported that no social reform is more urgently needed than the re-creation, development, and greatly extended use [8] of guardianship.

The author recently undertook a study of public assistance recipients under legal guardianship. One hundred and nine sample cases were systematically examined. It was found that the recipients of old age security under guardianship were largely persons residing in institutions. Case data indicated that the death of a marital partner had, in the absence of family, precipitated boarding home, sanitarium, or mental hospital placement. Unless there was property involved it was difficult to get people to accept responsibility as legal guardians. Legal guardianship, it was found, tended to focus on property rights rather than individual personal needs regardless of the type of guardianship, person and estate or person or estate, established by the court. This was largely due to the inability of the court to exercise proper supervision over the guardian–ward relationship and the passive role of the court whereby social wrongs traditionally must be brought to its attention. This approach prevents the court itself from exercising case-finding services. In other words, a welfare responsibility is involved in legal guardianship, but this function is not being implemented because of a lack of supportive social services.

The above suggests that the finding and making available of persons willing and competent to serve as guardians for selective elderly persons could constitute a desirable and proper function for a private or voluntary social welfare agency. In proposing or carrying out this function, there is no implication that the agency per se or its paid staff members would serve as guardians—any more than the employees of a child-placing agency care for the children in their own homes. Moreover, in respect to the proposal at hand, to have the agency, or agency staff members, serving in a guard-

---

[7] Mike Gorman, "The Major Need—Psychological Research on Senility," *New Channels for the Golden Years,* New York State Joint Legislative Committee on Problems of the Aging, Legislative Document (1956) No. 33, p. 67.

[8] A. Delafield Smith, *The Right to Life* (Chapel Hill: University of North Carolina Press, 1955), p. 136.

ianship role would be contrary to the spirit and purpose of the service. As envisaged, the aim of the service is to provide the elderly individual with a relationship to a community person interested in the implementation and the protection of the elderly on a friendly basis.

The agency would be responsible for these functions: It would interpret the need for persons to serve in guardianship capacities. The agency would have the task of finding, screening, and approving would-be guardians. Having accomplished these tasks, it would then have the responsibility of relating the would-be guardian with the elderly person in need of guardianship service. The agency would stand ready to furnish consultation service to the persons serving as guardian, including helping them disengage themselves should that become necessary. The relation of the agency to the elderly would depend on the total range of services that the agency might be providing in this area.

Insofar as the service would be limited to that of furnishing guardianship, the agency should be relatively small in administrative size. In terms of organizational structure, there should be a board of highly representative citizens interested in community services and protection of the elderly. The presence of such a board should be conducive to the obtaining of competent persons to serve as guardians. The employed staff would include an executive capable of contributing to community planning and one who would be able and psychologically willing to use medical and legal consultants whose services would be needed in making decisions as to the acceptance of cases and case planning. The social service staff would have among other duties the task of finding suitable guardians and of dealing with the elderly in their application-making.

Besides a professional interest in and a capacity to relate to elderly persons, the social service staff would need particularly to be oriented to law as a form of social protection. It should be to the point that they could confer with lawyers and judges in a comfortable and competent manner. In addition, it would be very important that there be at least part-time consultation service from lawyers, doctors (specializing in geriatrics), and psychiatrists. The availability of this part-time consultation service should make for a truly interdisciplinary approach, which is imperative if a competent service is to be developed in this welfare area.

The financing of the agency would be related to whether a fee was charged of clients using the service, and to whether the person serving as guardian was to be paid. Possibly an ideal, long-time goal would be that the agency should be so financed that it could pay persons serving as guardians if this were deemed necessary to recruit properly qualified individuals. Overtly, it would seem as sound to pay a person serving as a guardian competently as it is to pay foster mothers providing good placement care for children. Certainly the fact that a guardian believes he should be financially compensated for his service should not itself be construed as reflecting unfavorably upon his interest or qualifications to do the job.

To propose that this function of providing a guardianship service to the elderly be undertaken by a voluntary agency does not imply that it must all be done in this way. To propose this also does not constitute an assertion as to how this service might be administered—publicly or privately— in the distant future. Rather, the proposal that at least some of this service be under private auspices here and now is to recognize the reality of the situation. In effect, it is to capitalize upon the fact that in some instances voluntary welfare can be implemented more quickly and can be more administratively flexible in a formative period. There is, however, one aspect of the problem of providing guardianship service that argues rather specifically for private auspices. It is this: The aim of the service is to ensure that the elderly person will be protected in his rights to community services—economic and social—that have been set up in his behalf. A great number of these programs are already under public administration. Put negatively then, having the guardianship service—all of it—under public auspices would not seem to provide a "complementariness" or representativeness of interests that is desirable in a democracy. The bookkeeper should not also be the public accountant.

There are two other reasons why this function might properly be considered for private administrative auspices, at least at this time. First, the magnitude of the service should be controllable to the point that it could be financially limited to what a voluntary group would feel competent to undertake. Actually, if the guardians were not paid, and a sliding fee system were in effect for clients, the financial responsibility to a voluntary group should be a very modest one compared to many other programs now under private auspices. The second reason that argues for private auspices is that this particular program should provide a basis for interested community persons to gain a realistic picture of the problems of the elderly and the nature of the services currently available to them. Participation in this program, then, as a board member, or serving as a guardian, would mean that not only would such individuals learn the nature of the problem of aging but that they could become qualified interpreters of the need, and of the proper means of meeting the need, if they so will it.

3. Vocational Counseling of Older Workers

PAUL A. WILSON

Healthy, capable, willing workers who are unable to get or to retain jobs merely because of age constitute a serious economic and social problem in our modern society. Estimates of the number of older men and women in this category range from a few hundred thousand to two or three million. That the number is great enough to have far reaching consequences on institutions such as hospitals, clinics, relief and social work agencies, and many others, there can be no doubt even to the casual observer. Suitable work is one of the best guarantees for continued mental and physical health, for self-respect, and for continuing social participation. For the vast majority, work is a primary factor in giving meaning to life; without it life loses its attractiveness.

With this background of facts, and also because of the pressures engendered by an ever increasing number of older people ranging in age from forty to seventy, who clamored at the doors of private and public welfare agencies for help in finding jobs, the Vocational Guidance Bureau in Cleveland, Ohio, established a counseling service for older workers in October 1949. This Red Feather Agency, which has since become the Vocational Guidance and Rehabilitation Services, has continued the work without interruption to the present time. Such a service on the part of a private welfare agency was all but unique at that time. The only other agency known to have been doing such work on a full-time basis was the Federation Employment Service in New York City. Since that time the Jewish Vocational Services in Detroit, Cleveland, and possibly a few other cities have established special counseling services for older workers. There have also been part-time volunteer projects initiated in a number of large cities throughout the country. Needless to say, the Vocational Guidance Bureau in Cleveland has answered hundreds of queries about the service.

In its initial stages the Cleveland Foundation contributed heavily to the project, but within three years it had become an accepted part of the agency program.

The program as originally planned called for vocational counseling and placement of men and women between the ages of fifty and sixty-five who by reason of age and/or accumulated physical handicaps or chronic disabilities were no longer able to get or to retain suitable employment. Practical experience, however, soon proved that these limits were too narrow. Many men and women from forty up besieged the counselor for help. There have been times when the counseling calendar has been filled for three weeks in advance, and nearly always there has been a steady flow of referrals from other agencies as well as persons coming in on their own volition.

In the early stages, and from time to time since, newspapers, radio and television stations, and public and private agencies, have gladly cooperated in affording publicity. This publicity has been further aided by occasional talks to clubs and organizations by the director and the counselor.

A still further development as regards the age range of those applying for counseling has become apparent during the past two or three years. A changing labor market has made it somewhat easier for the group forty to sixty to find work, provided they possess some salable skills and are fairly fit physically. To offset this tendency the inflationary spiral has mounted to new heights with the result that those past sixty-five and eligible to social security benefits find that the forty-eight-cent dollars they receive will not meet their financial needs. Consequently, the caseload becomes weighted more and more heavily with men past sixty-five, many of them in their seventies, who desire part-time work to supplement their meager and ever shrinking monthly checks. Recent legislation will somewhat improve this situation in the future provided inflationary tendencies become stabilized, but there will probably continue to be a demand for part-time jobs to supplement benefits. Needless to say, part-time jobs are more difficult to find than full-time employment.

From the first, the chief emphasis in this program has been counseling, with placement secondary, for the reason that counseling has as its chief aim helping people to find themselves, and motivating them to utilize their dormant potentials. Yet, in view of the difficulty many older people were having in finding jobs of any sort, some effort was made by the counselor to locate openings by telephone solicitation, newspaper and radio appeals to employers, and visits to many types of commercial enterprises. Thus a clientele of employers was gradually built up, with the result that several jobs, for both men and women, are always listed with the agency. To further implement job listing, the counselor directed a pamphlet appeal to employers, which received wide distribution, and which made many aware of this new source of manpower.

Among the two thousand-odd clients who have been counseled thus far, there have been men and women from many walks of life, of all races and faiths, and of a wide variety of cultural backgrounds, education, and experience. There have been alcoholics, drug addicts, emotionally disturbed, severely handicapped minus legs, arms, or eyes, and chronically ill with severe heart, kidney, arthritic, or other disabilities. Those with multiple disabilities, to the extent of half a dozen, are not uncommon. There have been lawyers, professors, teachers, librarians, social workers, real estate and insurance salesmen, and ministers, as well as machinists, draftsmen, handymen, custodians, and common laborers. Among the groups most difficult to place have been displaced persons, severely handicapped, Negroes, former executives and administrators, and would-be factory or office workers.

The woman recently widowed in her mid-fifties or early sixties, along with the maiden ladies of uncertain age, constitute a special problem in placement. Many of these women once did office work, but have since grown rusty in their skills. Few of them can type well enough to secure work of that type. The counselor sweats blood trying to persuade these women that they must first secure refresher training in night school. A considerable number have taken such courses with very good results, but many hold out in the belief they can get a job as P.B.X. operator, filing, mail, or general clerk, or as receptionist or information clerk. These last may have to settle eventually for a job as retail clerk, dry cleaning store manager, cafeteria or mailing service worker, or even as nurse-companion or institutional worker. The last thing, with very few exceptions, that an older woman wants to consider is a job as nurse-companion, mother's helper, or an institutional live-in job. They do not want to care for sick people, or to be annoyed by other people's children, or to have their freedom taken away by long hours and confinement. Many will not consider giving up their present abode, their home, be it an apartment, or a house, or just a hall bedroom in a semi-slum neighborhood.

Counseling older people is not easy, but it is interesting to one who has had enough life experiences to understand the many problems involved, and to sympathize with the client. It is a job that requires unbounded patience, tact, friendliness, and an urge to help people in distress. The counselor must know something of psychology, of medical and psychiatric practices, and of rehabilitative measures. He must know a great deal of human nature, and be acquainted with the physical, mental, and spiritual changes that come with age. He must be a good listener and employ wisdom and judgment in formulating vocational plans for his clients.

Two points should be emphasized as of considerable importance in the counseling of this older group. The first is the time element involved. In most counseling agencies the initial interview consumes less than an hour. Indeed, in public employment services, it seldom lasts over ten or fifteen minutes. In this program the counselor has encouraged the client to "tell his story," with the result that initial interviews average two hours or longer. Many have lasted three hours. The older person moves at a slower pace, and he is inclined to explain his situation and his past experience in detail. He is often inclined to seek justification for his failures, to rationalize his present plight. This attempt not only enlightens the counselor, giving him a fuller idea of the client's needs, but the telling of one's life story to a sympathetic listener does wonders for the client. It gives him catharsis, inner satisfaction, and peace.

The second consideration concerns the type of person who acts as counselor. State employment service directors and some counseling agency heads are inclined to argue that any trained counselor can handle older people successfully. The program under discussion, however, has certain pretty well-established criteria for the selection of such counselors. To get empathy and rapport, the counselor had best be an older person himself. Not too old, of course, but old enough to understand the client's problems through the light of his own experiences—and old enough to command the respect of the counselee. The counselor must also possess many other attributes as well, but the man or woman with some gray in his hair and some facial wrinkles is more likely to win the respect and confidence of oldsters than would an inexperienced youngster fresh from college.

The counseling program in Cleveland is now seven years old. Of the over two thousand clients to date, more than 350 have been placed in jobs, and over twice that number have found some degree of employment after counseling. Many others have been guided to other community services such as medical clinics, rehabilitation services, recreational facilities such as golden age clubs, educational courses, home industry, small business, and hobbies and crafts.

As in all counseling programs, there have been some individuals who apparently got little or no help from the counseling interviews. A few have stalked out in anger, either because they were unwilling to give the necessary information about themselves or because the counselor was not in a position to refer them immediately to a job. Usually this takes time, to investigate references and to explore possibilities. A great many, however, have expressed gratitude for the help given, and the office records abound with success stories. Two women office workers, past seventy, have recently found employment, two widows in their sixties were recently placed in the offices of another agency, one man past seventy-six has been placed three times and is today successfully carrying on as a bank messenger and mail clerk. A sixty-year-old woman was encouraged to complete college work, an alcoholic is receiving treatment in a center. These are a few among many of the bright spots that encourage the counselor, now sixty-three years old himself, to attack each new day's work with vigor and faith.

Such a program as the one outlined here could be adapted to the needs of any large urban community that feels the need. The cost is not prohibitive, probably less than $6,000 a year. Part of the cost can be covered by fees; part of it can be absorbed by the use of volunteers who do contact work with industry, distribute literature, and find jobs. Two elderly men, both in their seventies, have been of considerable help in the Cleveland program. As to the question of need for such a service there can be no doubt. Neither is there any danger of duplication of services in most communities, since vocational counseling is so seldom provided for this older group.

4. Independent Residence Clubs

MRS. JAC L. EINSTEIN

Many years of volunteer service and board representation both locally and nationally in almost every field of social work, reading, study, attendance at national conferences—and most recently, active organizational participation in the field of geriatrics—have intensified my awareness of the importance and urgency for intelligent planning to meet the housing needs of our senior citizens.

Much progress has and is being made in providing housing for those who because of either financial, physical, or mental condition require sheltered care. In public housing projects too, special consideration and careful architectural planning for the aged is receiving increased attention. Great numbers of cooperative housing projects for the retired are operating successfully, particularly in the South and West, many of them sponsored by denominational groups.

We are geared to take care of the indigent and the dependent aging with ever increasing coverage and efficiency. There is the small group in our older population who still can buy, at a most prohibitive cost, the services they need to make their twilight years more safe and comfortable. But I am concerned with the vast number in between the two—those whose income will cover their shelter, food, clothing, and medical care but who have little or nothing left to meet the special needs that the limited physical ability of the aging so often requires.

This thesis will deal with the housing needs of that segment of our aging population and present a plan to meet that need. I propose to outline a program for careful architectural planning and organizational structure and for providing the central services that should enable the residents to prolong their years of independent living in the community.

The Residence Club here proposed is geared to serve people whose incomes are slightly above those eligible for public housing, but who could not afford to finance a comparable cooperative arrangement. It is planned for those with an approximate income of $3,000 and able to assume an average monthly rental of $85, which would include utilities and periodic heavy cleaning.

The plan does not presume to undertake total responsibility for the residents of the project. It would provide adequate economical housing plus the central services that would be particularly meaningful to the aging. Community services, whether to meet a health or casework service, should be available to the project residents just as they would be with the oldsters living elsewhere in the community.

With this background, I would propose the building of nonprofit, non-sectarian residence clubs to house approximately fifty to sixty units, that is individuals or couples. The expense of providing management and central services for a smaller group does not seem practical. Proximity to public transportation and to a shopping center is considered essential. Although apartment type or multiple-story construction might be considered, this plan is developed for construction of single-story dwellings in a garden type setting on a four- to five-acre tract of land. All units should have pullman kitchens, encouraging the preparation of some meals by the tenants. Dwellings would be architecturally planned to meet the needs of the aging with emphasis on comfort, convenience, the preservation of good health and strength, and the elimination of physical hazards. Consideration is given to three types of units.

1. Efficiency apartment—that is, one room and bath.
2. Living-bedroom, kitchen, and bath.
3. Living room, bedroom, kitchen, and bath.

There should be a central building, perhaps available on the site to be purchased, otherwise to be constructed, to house facilities for the central services—offices and living quarters for the personnel, to be in some way structurally connected with the individual units.

The key advantage in this kind of a facility is the ready availability of central services. There should be a recreation lounge with informal program geared to meet the desires of the residents, craft shops, and self-service dining room where good food could be provided at cost—and taken out, if necessary, with casserole service. Twenty-four-hour nurse coverage should be available to meet emergency needs—with a four-bed infirmary to meet emergency requirements. Laundry equipment should be available for use by the residents, and facilities should be established for service by barbers, beauticians, chiropodists, and so on, at certain times. The accessibility of these services would lessen the loneliness of old age, lighten many of the physical pressures of living and housekeeping, and relieve the anxiety of emergency health needs.

With the prevailing manpower shortage, adequate service is almost unobtainable even for the privileged few. Transportation and shopping grow increasingly difficult even for the young. These so-called aids to easy living would be a real blessing to our older persons, and those among the residents who could assist in any of these services would derive therapeutic benefits from their participation in the program and might receive appropriate compensation. Consideration might be given to the establishment of a token resident membership fee. This would encourage a feeling of some responsibility and participation by the group and could develop into a significant residents' council.

So much for what might be done. The next problem is how to do it. The time will come in the not too distant future, I am sure, when residence clubs for all economic groups will come into being.

Meanwhile their possibilities and values must be demonstrated. This plan endeavors to combine a self-supporting real estate venture with what might be called a new kind of social service. It does not equal the service given to those needing sheltered care. It does not assume responsibility for the residents but rather provides the services especially needed by the aging— that will enable them to prolong the years of their independent living.

The director, preferably a trained caseworker, should be familiar with the problems of the residents, and, when needed, would be expected to direct them to such community services as they require. For such a project an initial grant of from 10 to 20 per cent of the total capital cost would be needed and should be obtainable from foundations or individuals in the light of their expressed interest. A forty-year FHA guaranteed loan could be secured for the other 80 to 90 per cent.

With an estimated cost of from $500,000 to $600,000, depending on location (both land and building costs vary greatly in different communities), the $85 average rental that I propose would cover the cost of interest and amortization, utilities, and management; but to initiate and develop any such plan, a reputable, accredited sponsor is necessary. For philanthropic organizations, churches, unions, lodges, or clubs, this might be a challenging opportunity for service to their membership.

The sponsoring group would have a splendid opportunity for membership participation in the planning and in providing the volunteer services. It need not participate in the capital investment. It should, however, assume responsibility for the central services, including the recreation program, management of a self-sustaining food service operation, and the 24-hour-emergency nurse coverage.

Retired social workers, nurses, and others, on social security would find in such a Residence Club the opportunity to acquire living quarters plus income that would make this kind of limited service highly attractive.

The sponsoring group should have a majority of representation on an incorporated board of directors who would be responsible for the operation of the Residence Club. Other members of the board should be those in the community best qualified in the fields of health, welfare, geriatrics, and organizational planning, to help in the challenging development of such a project.

Social agency cooperation and consultation, if necessary on a remunerative basis, is most desirable, but because of the emphasis on independent living and the probable additional cost agency collaboration is an open question.

Construction estimates of an architect and contractor have enabled me to project the approximate building cost. Consultation with agency executives substantiates the thesis that this project would be of great benefit to a group in the $3,000 annual income bracket. Without this semicongregate living arrangement, the conveniences and advantages provided by the central services would most probably be beyond the means of persons with this limited income.

Except for the initial 10 or 20 per cent, which might be considered a subsidy, the rent should cover the actual cost of building maintenance, operation, and management.

There seems to be no question of the need for so-called Residence Clubs for our senior citizens, but imagination and dedicated leadership are needed to demonstrate what a real contribution they can be to the aging population of our generation.

5. Older People as Volunteers

FERN LONG

Two approaches might be made to the subject of extending voluntary activity and organization in the growing welfare field devoted to the aging. One of these approaches would concern the activity and organization that might result in attracting more volunteers in their younger years who would work with and for the older [1] people. The second approach would deal with voluntary activity and organization among the older people themselves, which would then be directed not only toward their own welfare, but outwards to include the welfare of the entire community of which they are a part.

It is with the latter approach that this essay will deal. Both observations and recommendations are based on the writer's firm conviction, resulting from the experience of working with older people, that first, much of the discontented passivity of old age is due to the destructive feeling on the part of older people that they are neither wanted nor needed; and second, that much ability, enthusiasm, and energy lie dormant within this older group and could be aroused and tapped for the greater good of the communities in which these older people live, and indeed, for the greater good of the entire nation.

To work toward activation of members of our older population as volunteers, two important first steps would be necessary. First of these would be a detailed survey of the welfare field in any given community with the specific objective of determining which volunteer needs could best be met by people in their later years. The second step would involve an equally detailed and careful survey of the older people themselves in that community, with the view of making an inventory of the unused talents that might be utilized by an agency needing those particular talents.

To return to consider in more detail the making of the first survey. Certainly it should be sponsored by all the welfare organizations of a community, and here the concept of welfare should be very broad, to include not only the health and welfare agencies that automatically come

---

[1] "Older," for the purposes of this essay, means over sixty.

to mind when the word "welfare" is mentioned, but also such educational agencies as exist for the welfare of a community's citizens: the libraries, the museums, the local colleges and universities, even the community theaters that are dedicated to developing one phase of cultural welfare. The initial impetus, however, would be given by whatever agency was chiefly and primarily concerned with community welfare. It would be the volunteer needs of all these community organizations that would be surveyed, and representatives of each of them would serve on the Committee Surveying Needs to be Met by Older Volunteers. These representatives could each be responsible for obtaining and providing the necessary survey information concerning his own agency. Certainly one phase of the survey should concern a detailing of what has already been done by any community organization in the field of making systematic use of the older volunteer.

The second of these first steps—that of surveying the older population with the objective of inventorying abilities and talents to be utilized in voluntary capacities—will be difficult in proportion to the size of the community, and in metropolitan areas a complete survey would probably be practically impossible. The activity here would be twofold: first its planning by a committee, and then its fulfillment by a corps of workers. This time the committee should be composed of representatives of organizations who are or will be in need of volunteers, but added to it should also be a fair number of older people themselves who might act as resources and in an advisory capacity. One of the functions of this Committee to Survey Talents and Abilities of Older Citizens would be to translate the needs listed by its sister committee into terms of types of people required to fill them.

The corps of workers making the survey could itself be composed of volunteers working under the direction of the committee, and possibly, in metropolitan areas, also under the direction of a trained staff member of an appropriate welfare organization. In a smaller community the information being sought would probably be fairly easily available. In a large urban center, limitations might have to be placed on the area to be surveyed: for example, only a certain geographic area, or only members of the given city's golden age clubs might be placed under survey in order to arrive at a limited inventory of talents and abilities of older people who might then be enlisted as volunteers.

With these first steps accomplished, a third and synthesizing process would be undertaken. It would consist of fitting persons uncovered in the second survey to the needs uncovered in the first. Although this step may be stated in very few words, it would actually be the most complex and difficult of all those outlined. Great skills and keen perceptions would be necessary to fit the persons to the needs, and certainly at first the effort should be limited experimentally to only a few older volunteers in a few agencies, or even to one or two in a single agency. Only in an exceptional case would any agency have only older volunteers; ideally, younger and older volunteers should work together, with no segregation based on age.

So far as I know, no community has yet undertaken recruitment of older volunteers on the scale suggested above. However, my own experience and observation lead me to believe that it would be a feasible operation.

For ten years I have directed, as part of my regular work, an educational project for men and women over sixty, and in addition have served on the committee on older persons of the local welfare federation, as well as being chairman of its subcommittee on education for older persons.

In both my professional and volunteer capacities I have observed the metamorphosis that has occurred when an older person assumes an active role after having been inactive for some time. For example, within the framework of the large educational program for older people that has been mentioned, there has grown up a voluntary choral group. Under the direction of a woman—a volunteer—who is eighty-two years of age, this has become an outstanding singing group, which has performed in hospitals, for other groups of older people, and for a variety of community organizations. The effect of this activity upon the participants has been astounding: voices have improved, appearances have changed, and a number of the members have become music students again after a lapse of many years. Although this may not be viewed as an orthodox voluntary activity, in my mind educational and cultural contributions should be thought of as a new kind of volunteer work, both *by* and *for* the older person, and certainly for the greater good of the community.

In this same large project another small group of volunteers meets faithfully to count sales tax stamps. The laws of our State make it possible to redeem these stamps for money, and our volunteers do the work preliminary to making that possible. Of course members of the entire group bring in these stamps in great numbers, and that in itself constitutes voluntary activity, motivated by the fact that all resulting funds are used for the enjoyment and welfare of the group.

The two activities just mentioned are organized, but in addition to that, small groups of volunteers have been formed spontaneously by some of the members, who have offered their services to local hospitals.

In connection with my own volunteer activities as a member of the committee on older persons, I have had the opportunity to observe the results of using older volunteers. For example, a retired automobile manufacturing executive put his mechanical skill at the disposal of a local hospital, and volunteered to clean needles used by doctors. In time he invented a new method of sharpening those needles that saved the hospital thousands of dollars a year. Before he died, he was provided with his own laboratory at the hospital in which to work, always as a volunteer. He himself said that these years of unpaid service were the happiest of his life.

These are isolated cases, and although similar ones could be recounted the fact is that at this point there are not very many of them. Only gradually is the realization beginning to grow that mental ability does not necessarily drain away as the years pile up, and that the older person can continue to make a valuable, and indeed, a unique, contribution to the ongoing life about him as long as he can remain physically and mentally active. Moreover, we are making some observations which might lead us to believe that both physical and mental activity are sharpened and prolonged if a keen interest exists in some enterprise in which the individual is deeply involved. Even though these examples of volunteers in the later years are not plentiful, still they are multiplying and I believe that they are straws in the wind indicating great, untapped human resources that may be put to use for the general welfare.

A group of older people in our city has taken the first step toward making these resources available for the greater good of the community. These are all men and women who have retired from responsible positions whose execution demanded a high degree of skill. They have organized themselves into a Senior Council, and are making their knowledge and skills available for use by the community. Already several educational and welfare organizations have availed themselves of this pool of resources. Again, this is still a voluntary activity by older people in a limited area, but nevertheless it is a signpost pointing the way to much more extensive areas of activity.

There is fairly widespread agreement that one of the greatest questions to be answered in our time is that arising from the increased life span of our citizens. Not only is life span increased, but the period of physical vigor is being extended—and at the same time working life is being summarily shortened by compulsory retirement. The great question is, what do we do with our lives after we are sixty-five? The proposal outlined in this essay is one small answer to that great question: it suggests a way whereby abilities, talents, and skills developed throughout decades of life need not be discarded after sixty-five, but may be put to work for the welfare of both the community and the individual.

13
Recreation

1. Family Recreation Centers

MRS. ADA BEIDLER BULL

Most of our so-called recreation (and character building) agencies were organized about three quarters of a century ago to meet needs particular to the mores of the era. Young men and young women were leaving their protected homes in the country and small towns following the Industrial Revolution to find employment in the cities. This called for centers where they might have a comfortable home feeling; where they might find the religious tenets of their parents' homes; and where they might be protected from the wiles and vices of the cities.

Hence we have associations for young men; also for young women. Besides, with the movement into the cities, the ancient lore of field and forest was unavailable to the displaced youngsters. Hence we have boys' and girls' organizations to help meet this lack; groups in which boys and girls are taught to experience, against a rather artificial background, the earth skills that our forebears used to learn at home.

Home? Yes, in this atomized method of meeting people's needs, the family seemed to be overlooked—or perhaps the family had not yet demonstrated its creeping weaknesses. You were either a young man, a young woman, a boy, or a girl (where were the old folks?). These agencies, formed to fill a partial, though particular, need, now have become jelled and the old term "vested interests" might be applicable. Have we done enough, or even what is good, by dividing people into age and sex groups?

My experience in the field of social work has been with public assistance, and then as executive of a Community Council in a small city. To its credit, public assistance has enabled families to stay together. When disaster and death hit, the mother does not have to farm out her children in different directions so that she can go to work. The aged do not have to separate and go to homes for the aged when their money is exhausted.

But from my position in Community Council I see that our various agencies do not seem to be functioning to hold the family together. Papa goes to the YM, mama goes to the YW, daughter goes to the Girl Scouts or Girls Club, son goes to the Boy Scouts—and Grandma? Is she forgotten, except in the few "Golden Age" groups?

I believe it is possible to look at people in their family setting, and set up *family* centers. My example is the famous Peckham Experiment of England. Although it was created in order to have a scientific control for the medical service rendered to the people, in actuality it was a center for families—including the older members. Certainly the agencies need not *assist* in the weakening of family ties by each one's making a bid for a separate member of the family, often on separate times of the week.

This is an age of mergers. Churches have "merger committees" whose business it is to keep an eye open for possible mergers with this or that church. Could not the Y's, Scouts, and others on a national and/or local level have merger committees, with a view to merging the family again into family centers? Or the communities themselves, through their councils or otherwise, might form merger committees, for it does not seem feasible to establish a family center that would compete with the existing agencies.

The Jewish Community Centers come closest in this country to a one-stop family center—and they tell me they have needed to form no golden age groups, because the older members have an accepted place among the adults in the centers. And yet the needs and interests of all ages and types are taken into account and planned for.

Besides strengthening the family, and therefore the individual, this plan has also financial advantages. The economy in overhead, buildings, and flexible use of personnel seems to be evident. These centers could be serving a particular area, with the economy of time and travel expenses.

Reading *The Peckham Experiment* [1] is an exciting adventure. The Experiment, located in South London, lasted four and a half years, until it was suspended in 1939 because of the inevitable· dispersion of the family unit in war conditions. Because the unit of living was found to be the family, and not the individual, the experiment was on the pattern of a family club, where member families would find equipment for the exercise of capacities for which there was little or no possible outlet in the ordinary circumstances of their lives. It was a social structure built with a new unit, not the individual but the family. The center was constituted so as to be ultimately sustained by membership subscriptions, in strong contrast to the prevailing trend in which the state or charitable societies assume for the public the responsibility for spending, unwittingly depriving the family of one of the primary opportunities for expression of the health and virility of its members.

[1] I. H. Pearse and L. H. Crocker, *The Peckham Experiment* (New Haven: Yale University Press, 1945).

Here was a center with a small staff but with a multitude of activities available. *And* the whole family was there, each member choosing spontaneously the thing he wanted to do, by joining a group he saw doing it. The center was so arranged that many of the activities could be seen as a new family registered, so that choices could readily be made.

The center engaged the whole person. It is difficult to know where to start in telling of it—with the baby, with the young folks, or with the young marrieds.

Much social poverty and social starvation was found because a young family was planted and left to grow in impoverished and barren social soil. Where can a young couple with a baby go evenings when the father is free? Because they had no social outlets, they grew stagnant, bored, and irritable. They joined the center (the more fortunate ones had joined with their families before they were married); evenings the baby was undressed, fed, and put to sleep wrapped in a shawl till in a deep sleep so that by 8 p.m. it could be picked up without waking, put in the pram, and brought to the night nursery. When taken home the baby was put straight to bed without being waked. Without some such routine, young parents are cut off from social life during the only hours of leisure they can spend together.

This couple found interests, active interests (which they had dropped at marriage), because there was always a group engaged in a particular activity. They made friends. They lost their compensating attachment to the baby. The weaning of the baby, including *skirt* weaning, was done at its proper time, because both baby and parents had interests that removed the need to cling. Because the center opened a very wide range of activities each member of the family could explore these opportunities spontaneously and make excursions into new fields. Life acquired a verve and a significance for them; they were no longer afraid of it. Heretofore the great potentiality of this family had failed to find expression for want of any natural flow in society; the sense of nesting and homemaking remained rudimentary; the appetite for it was not there; there were just barren spaces which should have become a live and functioning home.

The toddler, too, spontaneously found interests. The human being needs many and various opportunities in the environment, and practice in matching his knowledge with action evokes courage in him. But in most toddlers independent movement and initiative is reduced to a minimum.

The staff was small, because there were experts in most fields and activities among the members who taught their skills. Sometimes there would be shy grownups or young people who would stand and watch an activity without ever being able to take the first step to join the group.

The touchstone of the center seemed to be "Convert all situations into material for self-education of the members." Convert every chance you encounter into an opportunity for growing experience.

Only families could join, as families. The center became the social world for adolescence and was a mating and courting ground of salutary significance. The courting could take place, not under the surveillance of, but nevertheless within easy proximity of, the families.

The center provided cultural nutriment. Knowledge of how to go about things is gained above all from living in an environment in which the example of competent action is pervasive. General use of the building went with membership. This included the cafeteria and the main social hall with dance floor at all times when the center was open. Infants' Afternoon Nursery was open 2–6 p.m. daily, with use of gymnasium and infants' swimming pool. Mothers prepared nursery teas.

Available were:

Swimming	Woodwork shop
Table tennis	Billiard tables
Cards, chess	Darts
Workroom with sewing machine, cutting-out table, etc.	Equipment for boxing, fencing
	Bicycles
Roller skates	Puzzles
Badminton rackets	Drawing material
Books	Tap dancing shoes for learners
Typewriters	Water polo
Instruments for percussion band	Orchestra practice
Diving instruction	First-aid classes
Discussion circle	Demonstration courses on cooking, education of young child, etc.
Records	

2. Expanding Recreation Through the Library

DOROTHY T. MINNICK

With the tremendous competition of television, radio, and the movies, the library (especially in the small town) finds that its place in the social and family life of the community is one of continually lessening importance. Always darkened a number of hours in the week, now for many other hours libraries have become "museum-empty." Yet at the same time, volunteer social workers seeking to organize group recreation are faced with community facilities that are woefully inadequate, outdated, or even lacking entirely.

My plan to extend social welfare is to use existing library facilities for group recreation. I feel that this will not only promote social welfare and increase the library's usefulness to the community, but will tend to increase interest in books and reading. Last spring, as chairman of the Library Activities Committee for the Butler Memorial Library in Cambridge, Nebraska, I had an opportunity to test my plan and successfully did use library facilities for community recreation.

Cambridge, with a population of approximately 1,500, has community facilities of a schoolhouse, a library, a museum, and a swimming pool. The library has a meeting room twenty by forty feet. The only other community meeting place is the museum basement, which is dark, run down, usually dirty, and always depressing. Aside from school affairs, there are no community-sponsored social affairs that are not of a restrictive nature either on a religious ground or by club membership. Those without church affiliations or direct school connections have little if any constructive social life.

A number of attempts have been made to organize group recreation on a community-wide basis. They failed for various reasons that I will relate briefly.

1. A square dance enthusiast tried to organize community square dancing in the museum basement. The facilities were poor, *the basement itself*

was depressing, and after a first burst of enthusiasm, attendance dwindled. A small group survived, but they moved to private homes for their meetings.

2. The American Legion tried to promote community dances in their "hall" (a small wooden building). Their membership immediately divided into prohibitionists and nonprohibitionists, and a bitter debate developed as to *whether or not liquor should be served.* The nonprohibitionists won, but the prohibitionists made them so uncomfortable the dances were unsuccessful.

3. The Methodist Church built an annex and solicited funds from the entire community for this purpose by promising that the building would be used for the recreation of the entire community. After the building was completed, the Methodists made efforts to hold community skating parties and ping-pong tournaments, but non-Methodists were *reluctant to enter a church not of their faith,* and the Methodists stopped trying to include the community.

4. The Parent-Teachers Association tried to organize an adult minstrel group and later to sponsor teen-age dances. The first project was unable to attract unmarried or childless couples because of *the nature of the sponsorship* and the second ran into *conflicting school activities.* Both projects were short lived.

5. The library board appointed a five-member Activities Committee who in turn invited speakers and brought in art collections, but little interest was shown in either because these activities *did not invite community participation.*

The objective of the Activities Committee is to stimulate favorable community interest. I was appointed chairman of this committee last spring and after serious consideration felt that the library objective could easily be enlarged to include group recreation, thereby fulfilling its own objective and in addition making a substantial contribution to social welfare.

Since the spoken word bears such a close kinship to the written word, it seemed to me that the logical group activity for a library would be to present a play. No other library in Nebraska has conceived a similar project; consequently it was necessary to persuade the library board that it should lend the dignity of its sponsorship to a pioneering effort. They were won over when it was clearly understood that any profits resulting from our effort would go to the library. Library sponsorship has two distinct advantages:

1. It is nonsectarian and has no family restrictions, so that *it is easily identifiable as a community project.*
2. *It provides a cultural ideal* that is apart from and yet compatible with all church groups.

Other Little Theatre groups conceived a responsibility to themselves first. Ours differed in that it conceived a first responsibility to community social needs and a second responsibility to cultural standards of the library. This difference was brought home to me when I tried to find a guide to help us in organizing. I wrote to the National Academy of Theatrical Amateurs and to some Little Theatre groups in the hope that their organizations would serve as a pattern. However, all the groups I contacted considered the theatre their primary objective and were unable to give us any help.

I proceeded then more or less "blindly." Now I will relate the problems I encountered in the hope that my account may help others who may wish to repeat our experiment.

The knottiest (and this could be a pun) problem was the choice of the play itself, for few if any Broadway hits are written with the small-town church deacon in mind. A thorough understanding of the people in the community convinced me that I should put in abeyance plays with strong social problems or plays loaded with back alley words, for the success of the play (and the project) would be dictated by community prejudices and acceptances. I decided on *Arsenic and Old Lace,* and though it proved in the most part to be a happy choice I still met resistance to a few lines. It was a matter of minor annoyance that the actors themselves would have glibly rewritten the entire play, had I not firmly refused to sanction changing a single line. (They changed some anyway.)

The second problem was lining up a director, and I solicited the local high school English and dramatics teacher. Though married, she is childless and was very pleased at the prospect of some adult recreation.

To recruit actors, we made posters and ran a notice in the paper for tryouts at the library committee room. We had only three prospects. This did not particularly surprise us as the director had assured me that amateur actors prefer to be "asked." However I felt it was fundamentally necessary to our success to reiterate at every possible opportunity the open, unrestricted nature of our project. There were no dues, no prior experience necessary, in fact no restrictions of any kind. Anyone and everyone was invited to join. When the open invitation failed, the director and I "asked" and had no trouble recruiting the rest of the actors. They included a mortician, a jeweler, two farmers, one school teacher, two housewives, a newspaper editor, hardware store manager, garage mechanic, implements store owner, high school principal, and the owner of a lumber yard. Since we have no minority racial groups, they were all of the same race. The group did, however, represent different church and social factions. There were two single people, thirteen married; six had children in school, five had no children and two had children too young for school; there were five Congregationalists, three Methodists, three Catholics, and four without church affiliation; they ranged in age from twenty-two to fifty and in education from high school graduate to master's degree.

Meetings and preliminary rehearsals were held in the library, but it was obvious that we would need the school house auditorium to present the play. The use of existing buildings to advance community recreation is not new, and most of these plans revolve around the use of the school house. I am aware of two obstacles in this regard, conflicting engagements and the persisting prejudice that "the school house is for kids." When I asked the superintendent of schools, he advised me that there would be a charge for the use of the auditorium. I felt that if we accepted his ruling we would be establishing an unnecessary precedent; therefore I talked with members of the school board, explained our purposes, and pointed out that in the small community a city-supported library not only supplements the school library, it relieves the school district of considerable financial outlay in the way of books. The school board voted unanimously for the library's free use of the auditorium.

Community interest was aroused as soon as rehearsals began and we had no trouble getting volunteers for scenery, costumes, and ticket committees. I took sole responsibility for publicity as I felt I could best avoid any misunderstandings regarding our objectives.

In addition to desirable sponsorship and opening the way to use of other municipal buildings, the library can provide financial credit and a small fund for group recreation. Most libraries, like ours, have a fund that can be used at the discretion of the librarian or the library board. Our library advanced the money to buy the playbooks ($18); then we organized ticket committees and had an advance ticket sale to assure payment of royalty and printing charges. We made a net profit of $300. At our committee's suggestion, $50 was set aside to be used by future committees for a community project of a like nature. The State Library Association has given wide publicity to the success of our efforts in an attempt to persuade other communities to follow suit.

To me, the financial success and the librarian's pleasure were far overshadowed by the fact that for the first time since my residence here (eight years), the community had been enthusiastically united in a community recreation, and one that promises to continue. This year's Activities Committee plans to produce another play in the spring, and I have volunteered my "unofficial" cooperation and help.

In summary, the use of the library for social welfare in the area of recreation provides not only a building, but a dignified nonsectarian sponsorship, the reciprocal usage of other municipal buildings for special purposes, and lastly a small but secure financial starting point.

The Chinese have a proverb, "Books are for the very young and the very old." Americans could very easily add, ". . . but libraries are for everyone!"

3. Recreation Programs in Housing Developments

CLARA FOX

The Play Schools Association is a voluntary, nonprofit, nonsectarian private agency. The organization has more than thirty affiliated agencies in New York City and the immediate suburbs, and offers a field consultation service to these groups in the summer and a year-round service to a few selected agencies. It also conducts two laboratory centers which demonstrate the value of group play experiences for children at the school age levels.

During the past year the Association, through a small foundation grant, has been conducting a pilot project around parent-sponsored recreation and play programs in low middle-income cooperative housing developments. To date, this study has highlighted the importance of this work, which is directed toward developing the potential strengths and organizational abilities of large numbers of parent groups who are now operating low-cost, nonprofit programs for their children.

What do we mean by "middle income"? The emergence of a large middle-income group within the past decade is one of the most significant accomplishments of our American economy. The average earnings of the groups with which we are concerned are about $5,800 (according to latest government statistics). The average expenditures of this same group (using the same statistics) is approximately $5,576 for a family of four.

This middle-income strata consists mainly of white-collar workers, young professional and civil service employees, who have studied at our city colleges (many of them through the GI education bill) and have finally reached a standard of living higher than the economic levels of their birth. They have been inculcated with the democratic way of life. This way of life means equal opportunities for all, freedom from want and fear, and better educational advantages for their children, beginning in the years of early childhood education. This generation also includes a large number of women who worked or are working in secretarial or professional fields, and who have definite concerns about the kinds of life experiences that they wish their children to have as they grow. These concerns center around good housing, adequate medical care, increased educational opportunities (from the nursery years through college), sympathetic attitudes toward other racial and cultural groups, and, above all, economic security. Although these concerns and goals do not differ, in the essentials, from those that parents have always had for their children, the complexities of our changing society make special financial demands on middle-income families, since the cost of living is rising steadily.

Cooperative Housing

One of the most serious problems that arose in the decade following the war was the desperate need for adequate housing for this particular middle-income level, which was too high for public housing and too low for private home ownership. The purchase of cooperative apartments seemed to offer the soundest type of housing investment for these young families.

It is important to stress that the purchasers have to place a down payment on the apartment, which then makes them stockholders in the corporation and resident landlords. These payments range from $500 to as much as $3,500. Maintenance fees are lower than rentals of similar apartments elsewhere. The residents come from different economic and cultural backgrounds, and diversified city neighborhoods. They are plunged without preparation into an experiment of democratic living such as they had only read about in school textbooks before this.

Since almost all the cooperatives carry very large mortgages (through the FHA banks or private investment groups), the responsibility for meeting the carrying and maintenance charges, while keeping charges fixed, emerges as an overwhelming problem. One of the FHA stipulations is that each cooperative immediately elect a board of directors, who serve without pay, to assume the operation of the cooperative. Where the cooperative is large enough to sustain the cost, a resident manager is employed to deal with the day to day details. Smaller cooperatives usually employ a management company that handles several developments.

It is an unfortunate phenomenon that a board of directors is often composed of people who have had no previous experience in housing, and who accept the job unwillingly. It is not until residents of a community really get to know one another, and the problems of the cooperative, that more capable and understanding board members are elected. Thus, in the beginning there are numerous conflicts between the boards and the tenants that can divide and hamper the progress of development. To solve some of these conflicts, most cooperatives have established a "buffer group"—usually called "The Community Council," which is composed of tenant representation on a broader level, and acts as the intermediary between the board and the tenants. Where the boards give recognition to the councils better working relations have emerged, but where there is no cooperation, there is a continuous struggle for the status of the Community Councils. Since the latter groups are almost always responsible for community activities (the core of cooperative living), the importance of a strong council cannot be over-emphasized.

In our work with the cooperatives, we have always tried to affiliate with the Community Council and, through this work, have endeavored to forge the bond between the board and the council. This is far from simple since the boards of directors, particularly in the number 213 Cooperatives (these are the ones where the FHA has insured up to 90 per cent of the mortgage money) are faced with overwhelming maintenance problems, brought on by poor construction by many of the builders who built these cooperatives in the fastest and cheapest way without regard for the future carrying costs that this would involve. In one of the Queens cooperatives, hidden carrying costs and increased property taxes (which the tenant purchasers did not foresee) have raised charges more than 22 per cent in the past six years so that a four-and-a-half-room apartment that cost $88 in the beginning has now jumped to $117. Therefore, when the question of community activities comes to the fore, the boards do not, and often cannot, assume any cost for them.

Since these cooperatives have been constructed mainly on reclaimed lands in the more remote areas of New York City (to lower land costs), there are usually no resources available for recreation and play for children and teenagers. The public school is generally the only building in the area and immediately becomes overcrowded when hundreds (and sometimes thousands) of children move into a new neighborhood. The strain on this facility has resulted in two- or three-session schools so that the children spend much less than the legally required five hours in school. Nursery schools for preschool children are nonexistent, as are Y's or community centers where teenagers can gather. Serious delinquency problems are shaping up in many of the cooperatives because there is no healthy outlet for growing boys and girls in their free time.

It is a tribute to our American way of life, with its stress on the importance and growth of its children, that in many of these cooperatives parents assumed the responsibility themselves for organizing low-cost recreation programs which include activities such as nursery schools, after-school groups, day camps, teen-age centers, scouting programs, and others. A whole saga is unfolding around the valiant efforts that these parent groups are making every day, on a voluntary basis, to provide constructive experiences for their children. For the first time an indigenous, "grass-roots" leadership has arisen that tries to function on a democratic basis in such areas as program planning, fund raising, construction of fundamental equipment, and even in the conversion of barren space (such as storage and carriage rooms, garages, and so on) into playrooms.

However, they do need help, the kind of help that the Play Schools Association, through the consultation services made available by the grant, has been able to offer. For our principal aim in this work is to help parents help themselves. Our program is directed toward stabilizing these organizations so that they will continue to function independently with good, professional standards and consistent leadership drawn from the community itself. The growth of the groups that we have concentrated on during this experimental project is firm evidence that volunteer leadership can sustain itself, thus easing the burdens on public agencies that otherwise would have had to provide neighborhood resources for the large influx of new families and children.

I would like to describe our work in one of the areas to demonstrate how a cooperative developed from divided, hostile groups into a cohesive, integrated community.

The cooperative is located in the Borough of Queens, one of New York's fastest growing boroughs. It contains over 1,100 families and is set on eight square blocks, with an elementary public school and small adjoining Parks Department playground (which was the first achievement of the Community Council) in the center of these blocks. The surrounding neighborhood consists mainly of two-family private dwellings. There are no other neighborhood recreation resources. There are approximately one thousand children ranging from infancy to eighteen years of age; many of the women have had to go to work, part time, to supplement the family income because of sharply increased living costs. It is a very heterogeneous community and the leadership that has emerged from time to time is inexperienced and immature.

This cooperative has lived through every inequity that the 213's had to face in the six years of its existence, such as breakdowns in physical fixtures, litigation with the builder, tax rises, and increased rentals. It was built by three separate corporations and has three boards of directors. The first victory occurred when the three boards decided to function as a joint board with an over-all president, and employed an over-all manager. The cooperative constantly faces bankruptcy and is beset with financial burdens.

There is a Community Council, which had to fight for its existence from its inception. The council is organized on a membership basis and charges a membership fee of $2 a year which gives it a small fund for community activities.

There are eighteen buildings in the cooperative; each building has a "rumpus room," which the tenants themselves converted from storage space in the basement, so that some area could be available for meetings, social gatherings, and some activities for children. However, these rooms do not meet the local sanitary code requirements of the New York City Health Department for children under six, are inadequately lighted and heated, and have no washing or toilet facilities. Nevertheless, to the tenants who gave their money and time to paint the walls, install lighting and flooring, and furnish some equipment, these rooms are an expression of their co-operative effort to provide facilities for their leisure needs.

The recreational needs of the children in the cooperative had always been outstanding, and from time to time over a period of five years, parent groups had appealed to different professional groups to help them solve their dilemma. However, it was not until the Play Schools Association had received the foundation grant that enabled them to hire a consultative staff to work in the cooperatives, that the problems of this community could be fully tackled. Meanwhile, two groups had been functioning on a haphazard basis. One was a series of small unrelated play groups for pre-school children, who met mornings in the illegal rumpus rooms. These were organized by individual parent groups in each building and were poorly staffed and inadequately equipped. More than seventy-five children participated in these programs, which were a great concern to the Health Department because of their substandard level and violations of existing regulations. On this basis alone, it was felt that the pressure of a professional agency that would aim toward developing a licensed nursery school was very urgent.

On the other level was the teen-age canteen, also operated by a voluntary parents group, which served seventy-five teenagers from 15–18 years. This program was equally loose in structure, had an inexperienced leader, and was attracting neighborhood gangs who were disruptive and threatening to the community.

In March of last year, an accident in one of the rumpus rooms (unrelated to either of these activities) caused the board of directors to close all the rooms for one month because of insurance difficulties. At this point, all community activities collapsed and the Community Council was faced with a crisis and the realization that some source of help was needed to plan an over-all program that would have meaning and value for the children and adults in the cooperative. The Play Schools Association was called in to discuss the situation.

Numerous preliminary meetings were held with the parent groups of the preschool and teen-age groups. Finally, in May the Community Council voted to affiliate with the Association and a consultant was assigned to work with the council.

The consultant divided the work into two distinct areas—first, to reorganize the nursery school and the teen-age center on a substantial, professional level and to get them functioning as soon as possible; the other, to heal the split between the council and the board, to have the latter group assign the rumpus rooms to the council so that all community activities would have an over-all leadership and sponsoring agency. Neither goal was easy. Working with the small committees that were in existence, we began a program of parent and community education. The first task was to enlarge the committees so that they would become more representative of the community and iron out conflicts among the various tenants. For example, whenever a room was proposed for the nursery school in a specific building, the tenants of that building raised objections because of the noise, congregation, and so on. In the beginning, the board vetoed each proposed room as the objections were raised. This meant interpretation to individual board members until a large enough group became sympathetic enough to support the school. After seven months of this kind of plodding, the board of directors at a historic meeting voted to give an apartment to the school and some financial support through a decrease in the rent for this space. The nursery school is now ready to open with good, active parent leadership and over sixty children enrolled.

The teen-age program needed more interpretation, but here too much progress has been made. The program is now in operation with over seventy boys and girls involved and a group leader who is doing an excellent job. The Parents' Committee now consists of twenty able people who have assumed all of the costs for the program.

The Community Council has also made strides in its development, although the leadership still needs strengthening. They have just been allocated the rumpus rooms by the board and are now moving toward the development of their internal structure and planning extended services for children from six to twelve and a summer day camp. Each program will function on a self-sustaining cost basis, with its own leadership through committees. Most important is the new community spirit that pervades the community. Everyone feels confident that the needs of the children and adults will now be met as they arise. A special Youth Council is moving toward the groups in the neighborhood so that more planning can be done to make the entire area a model in community living and group relationship.

The experiences of the Play Schools Association in this cooperative proves that tremendous leadership reserves exist in each community and that, with professional help designed to stimulate this leadership, parents can "do it themselves." The need is still great for leadership training workshops for volunteers and professional supervision of these volunteers so that the gains are not lost. With a consultation service that is alert to these hidden strengths and recognizes their value, these gains are secured and perpetuated.

Some of the specific methods that we have used to stimulate this kind of planning and programing are:

1. A survey of the needs of the community in terms of numbers of children, age levels, and special interests.
2. The establishment of separate committees for each organized activity.
3. The establishment of subcommittees such as budgeting, fund-raising, equipment, enrollment, legal and publicity, housekeeping and maintenance, hiring, and parent education.
4. Large educational meetings with films, and discussants to inform and familiarize parents with prevailing educational philosophies and to answer the "whys and hows."
5. Collaboration with community councils (tenant representatives) to stimulate the formation of a recreation or youth committee within the council to be responsible for the community activities.
6. Interpretation of programing to the boards of directors so that they will assume their share of responsibility in community activities.
7. Leadership training workshops, from elementary procedures in running a meeting to the complexities of committee organization and functioning.
8. Workshop training for parent volunteer participants in actual teaching or group work situations.
9. Constant interpretation of the role of professional leaders and the need for these in order to operate a meaningful program for children.
10. Development of good relations between the cooperative and the rest of the neighborhood so that community tensions are lessened and the cooperative does not remain isolated.
11. The formation of a city-wide council of cooperatives affiliated with us in this pilot project so that there can be an exchange of ideas and program planning.
12. Interpretation of standards of licensing agencies within the city to ensure good physical facilities for these programs.
13. Publication of material, program guides, and organizational aids so that a permanent record of tested procedures may be drawn upon for future planning.

14
Special Financing Methods

1. The Promotion
of the Community Trust

GEORGE K. HERBERT

The lack of adequate financing for new and experimental ventures is becoming increasingly an impediment to the further development of voluntary social welfare. The days when a wealthy individual might be expected to sponsor each new charitable venture are fast disappearing. Although it is still possible to establish a new voluntary program through the beneficence of a wealthy individual, it is much more likely that a proposed new program today will look to a number of individual or corporate patrons, or will seek support from a local community fund or chest. If the approach is to a number of potential sponsors, there is frequently a severe testing of the patience and forbearance of the program's salesmen before sufficient support is found. If the approach is to the local community fund or chest, the program's salesmen very likely will find that established agencies and their programs have long-standing needs that all too frequently preclude the taking on of a new or untried program. Regardless of how initial financing is sought for a new development in voluntary social welfare, it is likely that the securing of adequate financing will be neither quick nor easy.

The one bright prospect for the furtherance of voluntary ventures in social welfare is found in contributions made by trust funds. Such funds, whether established by corporations or individuals, are frequently approachable for support of certain types of voluntary social welfare ventures. Very often, however, trustees will shy away from social welfare activities, or they may be interested only in ventures that will assure considerable favorable publicity for the founders of their trust. Still another limitation for any substantially large new venture in social welfare may be the limited size of local trusts from which support is sought. The proponents of such a program must then go to a number of trusts to seek contribution. It should suffice to say that the problem of initial support stands as an ever present deterrent to the translation of new ideas for the development of social welfare into active programs of research, prevention, or treatment.

Such is not the situation in a community having a substantial community trust. The community trust is not a new idea. For more than forty years community trusts have increased in number and grown in size. The scope of their activities and their impact on their respective communities provide a very interesting story in the potential for community betterment to be found in accumulations of wealth dedicated to the common good. Yet, the potential of the community trust has not been sufficiently realized by voluntary social welfare. Nor has the necessity for the further development of the community trust been a matter of sufficient concern to citizens with a broad interest in the promotion of voluntary social welfare organizations and activities.

The community trust in a major metropolitan community can do all of the following things during a single year: provide for the first year's operation of a new center on alcoholism; support a program designed to reach teen-age gangs with capable adult leaders; aid the trustees of a home for the aged to reorganize the home's program in order that it be consistent with modern standards of care; provide scholarships for several first- and second-year students in the local school of social work; provide part of the support for demonstration programs for the recruitment of qualified students to careers in professional social work and for the referral of the chronically ill to properly mobilized sources of treatment; support an experimental program to aid rural migrants to secure housing that will be adequate and not exploitative; underwrite the expansion of a group work agency staff so that more intensive service can be provided to small groups; replace all the equipment in the delivery room of a hospital for unwed mothers; support an experimental plan to aid youthful returnees from the state industrial school in finding suitable employment in the local community; and support a new program to provide vocational counseling for workers past age fifty and unemployed. Nor does this list include all the projects that can be sponsored in one year.

In some communities one or more of these activities might have been undertaken with the support of the community fund or chest. In some communities a group of hard-working citizens might have found multiple sponsorship for one or more of these projects. Few, if any, cities without a substantial community trust could have undertaken successfully this many new and experimental ventures within a single year.

The same tax laws that have been a major factor in diminishing the effect of the wealthy individual as a sponsor of new social welfare ventures have at the same time encouraged the development of trusts. The charitable trust as a means of preserving individual and corporate income from taxation has thrived in recent years, resulting in a proliferation of trusts both large and small. Each new listing of foundations and trusts is considerably lengthier than the one that preceded it. The giant foundations and trusts are well known for their enormous contributions to education, hospitals, research, and other undertakings that often challenge the imagination. Their peculiar contribution to the further development of our social institutions and to our understanding and control of sickness and disease seems to be determined in the broad undertakings they customarily sponsor. Such undertakings do not regularly include the sponsorship of programs of primarily local interest and concern. It is for the local trust or foundation generally to provide the financial stimulus for local voluntary social welfare programs.

Communities having no community trust very likely do have a number of trusts with varying amounts of principal and widely divergent purposes usually related in some way to the promotion of health, education, and welfare, and the relief of poverty within the community. These trusts may remain virtually dormant for a period of years, or appropriations may be made regularly by well-meaning trustees whose misguided zeal prompts them to devote trust funds to ventures not actually in the community's best interests. Both eventualities seem to be the product of a situation in which a comparatively large number of persons set out to "do good" without the benefit of coordination of effort. Unfortunately, uniform data on the yearly activities of charitable trusts are not available for communities. A summary of their achievements over a period of time would most likely be of interest to the community-minded citizen and to the legislator who has a continuing responsibility for statutes related to charitable trusts.

In contrast, the community blessed with a community trust can consciously follow the course of the trust's contribution to the promotion of the community's well-being. The community will have an annual accounting of the nature and extent of the year's contributions to worthwhile community projects. It will be able to assure itself that the best-informed and most capable citizens have been chosen as trustees. In short, such a community can see to it that funds devoted to a public purpose are properly applied and used to their very best advantage.

If community trusts can indeed provide the advantages here mentioned, it would seem a compelling necessity for responsible citizens to see to their establishment and growth in communities throughout the country. Some of the obstacles that stand in the way of the further development of community trusts can be identified. Often the selfish, and perhaps petty, interests of individuals in their bounty prevent a constructive community use. A general understanding of the greater good to be accomplished through a larger, broader trust is lacking. Restrictions and limitations on the use of trust funds frequently hamstring the efforts of trustees. There has been insufficient effort for the proper elevation of the community trust to its rightful place in the orderly development of voluntary activity and organization in social welfare.

Although selfish interests and the restrictions on poorly conceived trusts may continue to impede community-minded efforts, positive action can and should be taken to develop a better understanding of the community trust and its potential for community development. Because of the unique contribution the community trust can make in the development of local voluntary welfare projects and programs, it behooves the local leaders to take the initiative in their respective communities. More than that, *action must be taken on the national level by responsible leaders who recognize the special role of community trusts in the furtherance of voluntary social welfare programs and activities.* Leadership should be provided in the effective promotion of community trusts. Technical assistance should be made available to aid local groups in establishing and developing trusts for their respective communities. Ways and means should be found to help encourage the amalgamation of the increasing number of small charitable trusts for the accomplishment of a greater community purpose than can possibly be realized if present conditions continue. In brief, positive action should be taken that will at one time promote the development of community trusts, provide a substantial means of furthering voluntary social welfare, and help bring some order to the chaos that threatens the very existence of the charitable trust in our economy.

In summary, the financial support of voluntary social welfare efforts is presently characterized by the tremendous contributions of national foundations and trusts to major undertakings in education, research, and experimentation on a national level. In addition, the national health appeals provide funds for research, education, experimentation, and some treatment, again, mostly on a national level. Local community funds and chests provide substantial support for the operation of established programs in their localities. In addition, other contributions by individuals, corporations, and local trusts help to finance the capital needs of local voluntary organizations; these same sources may provide from time to time for the support of a new venture locally. *In the structure for financing national and local voluntary efforts in social welfare there is missing the cornerstone—the adequate financing of new and experimental ventures in the local community. The community trust is the appropriate vehicle to supply this cornerstone.*

2. Contracting for Social Services

WILLIAM H. WILSNACK

I propose that in a given community or area the voluntary social welfare organizations try a fundamentally new approach to their mission, one I shall call the "contract" approach. The essential idea is that a responsible social welfare organization shall specify the goals it seeks, and shall set out to attract specific plans for reaching these goals, ultimately accepting or "contracting" for the plan that appears most feasible.

This proposal assumes that voluntary social welfare organization is more privileged to experiment with such a new approach to our serious social welfare problems than many public organizations are. Public organizations, with policies and budgets generally attached to the maintenance of known services and to patterns generally acceptable to their constituents, often dare not risk charges of waste, extravagance, or experimentation against the administration and costs of these services; and this proposal might well entail that risk.

There are a number of circumstances that lie behind this "contract" proposal, as well as some clear-cut evidence that it can work and that it has worked in part or whole in other areas.

Progress in human affairs, whether social or material, should by definition be subject to some sort of measurement. Although the most objective forms of measurement do now and may always lie in the material sphere, advances in social philosophy and sociological technique make it possible to measure social progress as well. The simplest yet chief measurement is the extent to which our society meets the elementary needs of its members. Through evidences of education, employment, marriage and divorce, uses of leisure, illness, crime and delinquency, church membership, or birth and death, we have dependable guides to the satisfactions or lack thereof which our people are obtaining for their basic requirements. In addition we have more complex indices of attitude and opinion and changes in them that our social scientists have developed. Through all of these we now can measure social problems and their fluctuations.

We have developed a variety of successful techniques for resolving social problems. Better ways of communicating people's needs to those responsible to help fulfill them have been devised. We have the present-day group discussion techniques that permit two-way communication between the people and their agents or between different levels of authority. These techniques have been successfully applied in business and industry, labor and managment, politics, government, professional work, education, and, of course, social welfare.

Through improved knowledge in the areas of sociology, psychology, and physiology we can now treat individual, group, or community disorders with tested devices. For example, we can use neighborhood councils and the so-called "aggressive" casework as hedges against juvenile delinquency. We can offset economic dependency by social insurance plans, vocational training and rehabilitation, social casework services, and community organization for economic self-betterment. Mental illness can often be stopped in its tracks by the early provision of social, psychological, and medical services provided by the battery of professions that work under the banner of mental therapy.

Summarizing our social welfare situation today I would say it possesses available measuring devices of need, and valid techniques for meeting this need. It is what it lacks, however, that is crucial to my proposal.

The field of social welfare lacks clear objectives, and lacks imagination in the application of present knowledge and skill. Consider the ordinary situation in a community chest or united crusade area. A diversified group of services participate in joint financing, and, through a social agency council, in joint planning. The plans usually grow out of the individual patterns of service each agency already provides; and requests for increased budget are usually for more of same. The agency council is a referee against duplication and encroachments of function. It is rarely an integrator, and almost never a guarantor, of achievement. The agencies promise a continuation, improvement, or extension of services to the community during the fund-raising campaign, but do not promise specific results from these services.

For example, in my community a much-needed family service agency was started with a vague public understanding that it would fight delinquency. It has no specific program for this, and as a single agency it probably should not be expected to have one. Now the agency continues with another function, the maintenance and improvement of marital and parent–child relations. It is not expected, however, to set any goal in terms of increased family happiness in our community that can be measured as deriving from its services. Any objective measurement of its progress will probably be in the administrative terms of a decline in its own waiting list.

The "contract" plan would change all of this by using the essential pattern of our architectural and engineering progress. This progress is based on a simple set of steps:

1. The purchaser's determination of what he needs.
2. The purchaser's specifications or standards for having his needs met.
3. The putting out of these specifications for bid.
4. The study of the request by individuals and groups who have the technical ability to fulfill the request.
5. Preliminary designs, on a competitive basis. At this point the best available practical imagination of the technicians is drawn upon to design the most dependable and economic, that is, most feasible, plan for meeting the specifications of the request.
6. If the specifications call or attract radical new techniques that appear promising, preliminary grants by the purchaser for tests or demonstrations of their effectiveness.
7. The purchaser's final choice of bid.
8. The conclusion of the contract. This involves a measured, specified objective of definite standards, achieved by the techniques proposed within the indicated cost and within a definite period of time.
9. Fulfillment of the contract.
10. Inspection of the completed work by the purchaser, and its final acceptance by him.
11. Payment for the work.

Although voluntary social welfare organization would need to modify this approach slightly, I feel that its fundamentals can be usefully applied. For example, a community beset by a high rate of juvenile delinquency or a large public assistance caseload or serious problems presented by its homeless men might through its voluntary welfare organization determine what kind of reduction in the problem it would like to see take place in a given period of time, and what it could afford to spend in order to achieve this. Any individuals, groups, organizations, or combinations of these that could formulate and submit plans for meeting the objective would be encouraged to do this by a reasonable deadline. In the proposals of the bidders there would have to be stipulated the method, organization, staff, and budget required, and what results would be sought within the "contract" period. From such proposals the choice of plan could be ultimately made.

We know without detailed review that this method in American industry and public affairs has achieved tremendous advances and benefits in our material technology: buildings, bridges, aircraft, ships, pharmaceuticals, radio, telephone, and television. There are also some significant efforts in social welfare and related fields. In the voluntary social welfare field, the idea of using new ideas in a single community-wide venture has been a contribution to our work of Community Research Associates with its demonstrations and research concerning multi-problem families in such communities as St. Paul and San Mateo. This has provided the imagination and has spearheaded the funding, and results are not pre-set; but on the other hand measurements by which achievements would be gauged are predetermined, and the effort in each instance is a joint enterprise of several organizations.

Another and nationwide example may be seen in the polio vaccine program. Dr. Salk's vaccine was the accepted "bid." A wide plan of application was authorized, with a time schedule, and results will ultimately be measured by the decline of the disease. The actual experience in the anti-polio efforts shows how a plan of application and a time schedule can be altered by mutual agreement of the "contracting parties," whenever new circumstances warrant.

A somewhat different but no less conclusive or applicable example of the goal-centered basis of this approach lies in the activities of the League of Women Voters in my home community. One by one the league has undertaken the problems of combining city and county health services, improving county welfare administration, securing adequate juvenile probation services, and restoring equity to the county tax base. It has not specifically solicited plans except among its members. It has not put forth funds or "contracted" with other groups to achieve the results it desired because it is a do-it-ourselves organization. However, it has established time schedules for its own efforts to reach definite, pre-set objectives, and at the time of this writing it has seen the realization of three of these four goals.

My strongest conviction as to the workableness of this proposal comes from my own work experience. Although I work in a public agency at this time my particular area of responsibility permits the use of this type of approach. My colleagues and I began two years ago specifying a definite objective we sought in increasing a program of foster family care for convalescent mental patients from state hospitals. Our "funding base" was the number of community social workers we could assign to this task. Our technical experience up to that time justified our seeking places for 100 more family care patients in a year's time with the staff that was assigned. This task was "put out for bids" to our community offices and each office contracted for a part of it.

To our amazement the staff's dedication to this goal led them to nearly double it in the year.

We repeated this approach the next year. This time the staff was able to achieve only half of its "contract" objective. But the greater difficulty in this second year showed us how to improve our financing and staffing of the program so that this approach might be effectively continued in the future. Even when the best laid plans go slightly agley, this experience shows that one may still end with some net achievement plus improved knowledge for future application.

In my shop we are now tackling a more exciting endeavor, ways of social planning through which numbers of long-term State mental hospital patients can be returned to community life. We are now at the stage of inviting preliminary designs. We have had two very recent ones whose pilot trials have resulted in a remarkable amount of successful rehabilitation considering the time and staff involved. In one situation the combined equipment working time of less than one half of a professional worker resulted in the community rehabilitation of mental patients in one year whose total previous man-years of hospital care came to over 110. From such tests and measurements larger and even more hopeful social welfare enterprises with pre-set objectives can be fashioned.

An implicit defeatism may be found in many volunteer and professional people engaged in social welfare work today. Their personal experiences of too little and too late, at too dear a price of time and energy, tend to blind them to the real potentialities for social change that they possess. Much as they find their clients and patients to be victims of social circumstance, they too may be victims of a system that is not working. Replacing the faltering way of solving social problems by simply buying more social welfare talent with a "contract" pattern that invites our ingenuity and practicability would help voluntary social welfare pull itself and its communities out of the doldrums.

3. Fees for Service—
an Untapped Resource

MRS. MARGARET A. GOLTON

The expansion of voluntary social services can be considered from many points of view: the development of new services to meet newly identified needs, the expansion of established services to reach a wider clientele, the refinement of services within established functions to reflect new scientific knowledge, the establishment of new services as testing ground, and research.

Essential in each of these approaches is a constant alertness to the conditions about us, old and new, and the demands they make upon people, together with constant scrutiny of scientific findings for cues as to new approaches and methods of helping.

Social services have had their origin in the philanthropic impulse of man. Only recently, and at a very slow, halting pace, has it been recognized that the services that have been established for the improvident have validity for people in every stratum of society. One specific move in cognizance of this has been the establishment of fees for service. In the early days, some fifteen or twenty years ago, when a few venturesome souls suggested charging fees, there was skepticism and serious concern lest agencies, if they serve the affluent, become unavailable to the indigent; and lest there develop within agencies differentials in quality of service commensurate with the amount of the fee. Together with these objective concerns there was doubt as to whether social work could really demonstrate its worth if its services were assessed in dollars and cents per hour.

Progress has been made in the direction of social service being a service that is "For Sale"—somewhat less haltingly than at the beginning, but still gingerly and with much variation.

In agencies where fees have been established for specific and/or intangible services, rarely does one find these related to the cost of the service or to the "going rates" in the community for comparable service. Rarely does one find reflected in agency fee scales, for instance, what private practitioners, psychologists, and psychiatrists charge for personal counseling, or what physicians charge for office calls; what boarding schools and independent boarding homes charge for resident care of children; what commercially run day nurseries charge for part-time and full-time care (although few boarding schools, independent boarding homes, or commercially run day nurseries can compare in quality or range of services with the placement facilities made available through social agencies). There are still many agencies that look askance at fee charging in any form. For those who venture to view it, there are two major areas of concern: (1) that fee charging may reduce contributions to the Community Fund as people might resent paying twice, once to maintain a service and once to use it; and (2) that the service will be denied to people who cannot pay.

As one considers fee charging, one must reaffirm irrevocably that no one who is in need of the service, no matter how costly it may be, will be denied it if he cannot pay. The concept of service according to need is a part of American heritage and tradition; and we would do nothing to jeopardize this. Our aim is only to extend the concept of service-according-to-need to the "privileged" as well as the "underprivileged" and to make it psychologically available and acceptable to them.

In considering the effect of fee charging on fund raising, one may look to other fields for a frame of reference and rationale. For instance, in law there are the "retainer fee" and the fee for "extraordinary service"; in business, there are "capital cost" and "operating expenses." Both of these concepts carry elements of similarity to the "general contributions" and the "fee for service."

One thing that has become increasingly evident in recent years is that social ills and emotional maladjustments are not exclusive to any social or economic group. Newspapers carry more and more stories of antisocial acts by children from the highest social and economic strata. Institutions for emotionally disturbed children find an increasing proportion of their population from "intact" homes in the average and above average income range. If we looked into the student body of private boarding schools and military schools, what social and emotional deviations would we find?

We need to recognize that social services, traditionally structured and financed, are not psychologically available to individuals of higher income groups—first of all, because people who may contribute considerably toward the maintenance of social services cannot see themselves as recipients of those services and of the "charity" they help to maintain. There is added to this—and these elements are operative no matter what the economic group—the devaluation of free service and the question of whether one gets maximum assistance from the service without financial participation. The establishment of fees for service, therefore, not only extends the service to a wider range of the population, but it enhances the value of the service for all who avail themselves of it.

In addition to making social services available to a wider range of the population and enhancing its value for all, fee charging is a valid and important source of revenue. Through such additional revenue it would be possible to expand existing services, establish new services, refine established methods and skills, maintain and develop highly skilled staff, and carry on research. As we set our sights in these directions, we are less concerned with what will happen to our traditional "concept" of service, and more impressed with the urgency of this new perspective and approach.

The first step in the establishment of fees is the determination of the "cost of service." This should include rent, general operating costs, the cost of maintenance where maintenance is involved, and the cost of whatever specific professional skill is being offered. The translation of "cost" into an hourly, weekly, or a monthly charge depends largely on the nature of the service. Where it is counseling, the fee may be based on an hourly rate or a "unit of service," on a per interview or per week basis per individual or family. For instance, the fee for consultation for adoption can be considered a "unit of service" based on the number of interviews usually necessary to determine eligibility. This presumes, and as a matter of fact requires, a well-defined consultation procedure. The same principle can be applied in consultation for placement and in consultation for unmarried parents.

When a specific service such as adoption, placement, or day care, is involved, additional factors must be taken into account. For instance, in adoption it is important to take into account in setting the minimum fee what it would cost the family to have its own child. In full-time placement, similarly, the minimum fee should be related to what it would cost the family to have the child at home; and in day care, it should be related to the cost of the food the child receives at the nursery. In these last two areas, it is of utmost importance that having a child cared for out of the home is not less expensive for the family than having him at home—this for psychological and practical reasons as far as future planning is concerned. If a family is indigent and receiving public assistance, it may be possible that an allotment be made in the budget for such special services as day care, so that the family may have the psychological benefit of paying toward the cost of the service his child is receiving. Before one can approach the agency in such a plan, one must be convinced of the diagnostic necessity of the service per se, and of the importance of financial participation to the recipient.

The second step in planning for fee charging is to establish a sliding scale of fees, with the "minimum charge" and the "cost of the service" as the outer limits. What constitutes maximum financial participation without hardship to families in the various income levels requires careful analysis. It requires also a determination of what the agency and/or community recognizes as the standard of living necessary to health and welfare, and is willing to subsidize; what family obligations, and what expenses related to educational, cultural, and social activities take priority over the cost for social service; and what resources other than income can be considered in fee charging. A most helpful source of information is the United States Department of Labor statistics on the cost of living in each area of the country. The analysis of this is done annually, and is usually available at the public library.

For agencies that have traditionally served the underprivileged, the concept of fee charging related to the cost of the service and to the cost of comparable professional services in the community requires a major refocusing and philosophical reorientation. There needs to be less focus on budget, debts, and expenses for cultural advantages, and more consideration to how much the individual could and would pay a physician, an attorney, or a similar professional individual, for services he required. I am not suggesting, of course, that we impose hardship on the financially hard-pressed; only that we see our services commensurate with others of similar nature and caliber, and not as an "also ran" obligation, cautiously established, after we have considered all other obligations which the family considers primary.

Once we have established the standard of living to be maintained for each type of family—The Lone Individual; Both Parents at Home, One Working, Two Children at Home; Both Parents at Home, One Working, Two Children at Home, One in Placement; and the many other types— one must establish, arbitrarily, a scale range of income on which the variations in the fee will be based.

A relatively simple and reasonably equitable method for determining the fee within each established income bracket is to use a percentage tabulation. For instance, if one determines that a lone mother must have an income of $200 per month before she can pay the $30 per month minimum charge for her child in placement, one could establish as the first income bracket $200–$220. Thirty dollars per month represents fifteen per cent of $200. Establishing this as the base, the scale would be as follows:

Earnings	Percentage	Fee
$200–$220	15	$30.00
$220–$240	15.5	$34.10
$240–$260	16	$38.40
$260–$280	16.5	$43.20

As one proceeds up the income scale, one must give recognition to the variation in the standard of living as income increases: the increase in interpersonal obligations (for instance as a member of a staff) and of community responsibilities (contributions and others), as well as to the factor of incentive, so that there is net gain to the individual from an increase in earnings; as well as increased participation toward meeting the actual cost of the service he is receiving. In every income group, resources other than earnings should be taken into account. For maximum benefit to accrue to the individual and the community, psychologically and practically, from fees related to cost, it is important that every applicant be advised of the cost of the service irrespective of the amount he is able to pay. This places a dollar assessment on the service he is requesting and helps him recognize the extent to which his payment and the contribution of the community make the service possible.

As recently as September 1954 the Council of Jewish Federations and Welfare Funds, Inc., in its "Report No. I on Fee Charging" pointed out the wide variance among communities in income from fees.

In 1953 Hartford, Connecticut, and San Diego, California, reported $50 income (annual) from fees; the Jewish Family Service of New York reported $43,900 for the same period. Except for two New York agencies, however, where income from fees was reported to cover from 3 to 5 per cent of the budget, other New York agencies reported fees as a "negligible source of income." And only rarely throughout did fees approximate the cost of the service.

This same report lists four points under "Philosophy for Fee Charging" submitted by the agencies participating in the report: "(1) payment for services is an accepted pattern of American culture; (2) fees assist the therapeutic process by stimulating the client toward a more concentrated effort on his part; (3) a wider segment of the community will utilize social agencies if the 'stigma' of 'charitable' assistance is removed (statistics were presented by some agencies to validate this assumption); (4) the charging of fees for service gives casework a status on a par with other community professional services."

These points are pertinent and significant and may be helpful to agencies struggling to overcome the traditional concept of free service, the reluctance to assess social services in monetary terms, and our equally traditional underevaluation of the worth of our professional skills.

There is still another consideration that must be given attention. The profession of social service, which developed out of the needs of the underprivileged, in recent years has become an "underprivileged profession." When one compares today what engineers, for instance, are paid after a four-year college course with what social workers are paid after six years, one may become self-righteous and compare the business-for-profit against philanthropic service. Such a comparison, however, will not draw young people into the profession, or having drawn them into it, keep them there, as statistics on turnover well demonstrate.

We live in a competitive world and the "holier than thou ivory tower" of service *versus* profit is not likely to serve in manning our agencies and meeting the ever increasing needs in the human relations field. It is important that ways be found, therefore, not only to make our services available to all who need them, to develop and improve our services through the application of new scientific knowledge, but also to attract and develop qualified personnel to perform the many complex tasks in social service.

There are many new realities in the world of today that require scrutiny of the old established forms and procedures and a venturesomeness into new. Fee charging related to the cost of service and to the cost of equivalent services in the community, instead of having it related solely to budget and/or to the individual's ability to pay, affords an especial challenge in this direction. It provides a new frame of reference, a new psychological potential for recipient and practitioner, and a new source of revenue to agencies. It is an untapped resource which may well lead to a new, more vital, expanding and expansive role for social services in our communities.

15

The General Spirit
of Voluntarism

1. Early Education in Voluntary Welfare

HERBERT RUSALEM

The United States has a long tradition of voluntary association and community action in social welfare. These voluntary efforts have been a constructive expression of the neighborliness of our people and the sense of responsibility of localities for the social needs of their inhabitants. Recently, however, the assumption of responsibility for social problems by government has necessitated a reappraisal by voluntary social welfare of its role. More important, perhaps, has been a growing realization that social action by government is whittling away the functions of voluntary agencies.

Increasingly, our young people look to Washington, to their State Capitols, and their City Halls for leadership in social welfare. Many of our citizens hold the view that as government agencies assume leadership in greater degree, the need for voluntary service correspondingly declines. Eventually, it is felt in some quarters, the voluntary agencies will wither away, leaving the field of social welfare to official agencies.

In spite of increasing government concern for social problems, the role of private agencies has not declined. It has changed. It performs essential services in research, experimentation, initiation of new programs, stimulation of community interest, plugging the gaps left by government, offering flexibility of service and assisting local communities to meet their unique problems in ways that cannot be undertaken by centrally administered public services. In fact, the role of the private organization may have become even more important.

The development and expansion of this role depends upon a continued sense of responsibility on the part of the American citizen for others and a maintenance of the tradition of helping one's neighbor. Such sentiments are a part of our cultural heritage that, unfortunately, are becoming less prominent in the education of our children. In order that privately organized and administered social welfare movements may flourish, there must be a strong feeling within the American people in support of such efforts.

This feeling cannot be expected to emerge spontaneously or to appear in adult life without previous preparation. In essence, the attitudes toward private responsibility for social welfare rest upon how well we prepare our children to assume the responsibility and the leadership that are essential for its survival.

In our elementary and secondary schools, considerable emphasis is placed upon the contributions of government in social movements and social service. Such emphasis is highly desirable. However, little if any emphasis is placed upon the history, philosophy, goals, and activities of private social welfare groups in local communities. In a sense, children are isolated from this important force which pervades the community life around them. A child may become somewhat aware of private social service activity by reason of having received services from such organizations or having contributed to them. However, it is the thesis of this paper that an understanding of private social welfare hinges on planned teaching and not on incidental exposure. It is held that the way to extend voluntary activity and organization in social welfare is through making this area of study an integral part of our secondary education curriculum.

Curriculum building is a complex process involving joint activity and planning by parents, teachers, administrators, and children. Consequently, the function of this paper is not in the area of creating curriculum. On the contrary, it only suggests resources and areas for curriculum development.

In the first place, the purposes of a typical unit of study on social welfare for secondary students may be viewed as:

   a. To prepare students for adult roles in leadership and participation in local voluntary social welfare movements by introducing them to the history, philosophy, organization, administration, and contributions of such organizations.

   b. To assist students to find their most effective role in assisting local organizations in their efforts to solve problems, for since the whole community is concerned with its social problems and the means being used to solve them, students have a stake in this area.

   c. To use the energy, enthusiasm, and imagination of youth in the service of the community, thus promoting their emotional maturity and cooperative attitudes.

Perhaps a first step in developing curriculum in this area might be a survey of community resources and needs. With the help of student interviews with members of the community, published community surveys, if any, and consultations with public and private agencies, students may compile an index of local needs and local community resources established to satisfy some or all of these needs. Field trips to agencies, meetings with representatives of social welfare movements, and readings in the area of social problems may prepare students for the next phase—the identification of one or more problems which students may elect to study and solve. Problems may be selected in such fields as chronic illness, disability, child welfare, recreation, delinquency, and housing.

In the development and implementation of plans by student groups to solve selected community problems, social agencies have a crucial role. Central community chest agencies and councils may often contribute the fruits of their own studies in these areas. In some instances, these broad community planning groups may use the energies and manpower provided by interested youth in their own programs. Thus, students may develop cooperative programs with community chest agencies through which they make surveys and studies that fall into the over-all pattern of agency activity. In turn, the publications, library resources, and public education materials of agencies may be used as educational resources by students and teachers.

In accordance with the capacities of youth and the limits of responsibility that they may undertake, agencies may weave them into ongoing programs in various ways. Some of the roles students may fill are:

1. Volunteer readers for the blind
2. Recreation aides
3. Companions to the chronically ill
4. Assistants in public education
5. Guides in tours of some agency facilities
6. Tutors to home-bound and hospitalized children
7. Aides to the aged
8. Volunteer clerical assistants
9. Guides for blind persons
10. Information clerks

An encouraging trend is toward using secondary school age youth in community and school cooperative programs. Under such programs, the community activities of youth are made a part of the regular school curriculum. Thus activities may be selected by the school staff in consultation with community workers with a view to selecting jobs that are most suitable for the individual child and that contribute maximally to the community. Furthermore, school and social agency personnel jointly provide supervision and guidance. Finally, the student is encouraged to discuss his social welfare experiences in regular class sessions. Although these suggestions may be of great value from the point of view of providing youth with unique educational opportunities, this paper emphasizes particularly the consequences of such plans for extending social welfare activities. It is suggested that the following values may accrue for community welfare services:

Young people may develop a sensitivity for the contributions of private social action and a positive attitude toward its role in the American culture.

Students may contribute to the identification and solution of current problems, thus enhancing the effectiveness of social welfare in America.

The community leadership that is essential to the survival of private organized philanthropy may be nurtured and encouraged through student activities.

Through their services to clients and patients in the community, students may make a contribution to the health and welfare of American citizens.

The ideas expressed in this paper have been sketched lightly. There is need for extensive research in the means through which schools and community agencies may work best together. Furthermore, curriculum research is needed to prepare and distribute materials to the public schools and teachers to take positive steps toward developing dynamic educational programs in this area.

2. A State Drive for Increased Voluntarism

MILDRED G. BRANDON

Drops of sand will eventually build the beach. But why not build the beach first? Then if the wind scatters the drops of sand, and widens the beach, so much the better. This is what we decided in the Kansas State Department of Public Welfare.

By 1954 a few of the 105 counties in this public welfare program had, as in many other States, a volunteer project or two; or used a volunteer in a specific case situation. But this was not on an organized basis. In 1954 the Licensing Unit for Nursing Homes employed a trained group worker to start volunteer activities for the aged. This has been highly successful and will be reported elsewhere, but it reaches only a small segment of the public welfare caseload. It represents important little piles of sand, but has no resemblance to the beach.

The next year, our state director, Mr. Frank Long, appointed a staff committee "to explore the use of volunteers in our public welfare program." This committee did more than "explore." It visualized the beach, with lifeguards, umbrellas, booths, and all the other appurtenances. It visualized a volunteer program for the whole state, then wrote it up in the form of a guidebook for county directors, and recommended that a new position on the state staff, "Director of Community Resources," be established on the civil service register. This much has just been accomplished. We now seek a man to fill that position.

The Kansas State Department of Public Welfare is a recently "integrated service" program. All public welfare services, including Child Welfare, Services to the Blind, and Services to State Institutions, as well as Public Assistance, are administered through our operating unit, the Division of Field Services. Consequently it was necessary for the committee to approach its assignment on a broad front. Furthermore, the Kansas program is county-administered and State-supervised. In these two respects, it is different from the majority of other States.

The staff committee was composed of seven members, a representative each from the Child Welfare Division, Services to the Blind, Staff Development, and Licensing Unit in Public Assistance, and three members of the operating unit, the Division of Field Services. Before this committee really oriented itself, the legislature passed a law that within a few months all counties having a caseload of 500 persons or more *must* establish an Advisory Committee to the County Boards of Social Welfare and all other counties *may* establish such committees. This was a good-sized pile of sand. It represented thirty-nine counties. Since advisory committee members usually represent a community's best volunteer group, we decided to help start these citizen participants on the right foot. Within a six weeks' period, we developed two breast-pocket-size handbooks, one for county commissioners and county directors and one for Advisory Committee members. We covered such things as organization, selection of committee members, orientation, public relations, planning meetings, and suggesting projects.

One year later these committees are all functioning well and several counties have organized voluntary committees. From these groups all kinds of volunteer projects have sprung. One group is studying the needs of children in the community, bringing in all the organizations that have anything to do with child care; another has just completed a study of the county home and is putting it up to a vote of the taxpayers whether the county should levy taxes for a new home for the aged; some are studying boarding home rates and housing and rentals; another is looking into the causes of dependency in its aid to dependent children caseload; another is exploring state policies governing resources, and so on. As instruments of interpretation of public welfare these committees are unexcelled. Most of them have newspaper personnel as committee members, and wherever it has been possible a legislator. There has been much publicity in the press.

Since the 105 counties vary from quite small rural communities to large cities, it was necessary for the staff committee to think in terms of a very flexible program and one where all or parts of suggested material could be adapted if social welfare services were to be extended beyond the bounds of the State and county staffs. We began by tapping resources. We explored our idea with the Federal Social Security Agency, the National Social Welfare Assembly, the United Community Funds and Councils of America, Inc., the Junior League, American Red Cross, and Farm Bureaus. They were all helpful in sending materials and making suggestions. Also we wrote other States that we knew had a volunteer program in some form, although we learned none had attempted to set up a program on such a broad base. Many of our committee members had previous experience in working with volunteers in either public or private agencies, and this knowledge was utilized so that much of our material is original. When we pooled our material and our thoughts, we found we had a comprehensive outline. We believe the uniqueness of our guidebook lies in its completeness. We tried not to leave out one single idea that we thought might be helpful to a county.

Our contents began with "A Statement of Principles" drawn up and adopted by the Advisory Committee on Citizen Participation, sponsored by the National Social Welfare Assembly and United Community Funds and Councils of America, Inc. Then we tried to think of a starting point, where the counties could actually begin to explore the possibilities of utilizing volunteers in their agency. We wrote a brief section on "Determination of Need for Volunteers." This consisted of making a list of needs, a list of agencies or organizations that were already doing or should be doing some volunteer work, and then putting the two together. This seemed a simplified system and one any county could use regardless of its size.

We realized that unless the agency staff wanted to use volunteers and was really convinced of their worth, such a program would fail completely. Consequently we included some suggestions on "Motivation and Preparation of Agency Staff, Board Members, and Advisory Committees." We emphasized that the purpose of volunteers is to supplement, not supplant, the paid worker. This was to remove any threat to the staff. We described methods and sources for recruitment and gave one whole section to the screening process, including detailed pointers on how to interview prospective volunteer workers. We suggested a file be set up and showed sample filing cards in the appendix.

A completely original section was written on orientation, training, and supervision. We just thought how we would like to see it done and set it down. There are suggestions for the first meeting, including content. Volunteer–agency relations and purpose and continuity are stressed. Resources for training personnel are suggested, supervision is highlighted, and a plan for awards is presented. We considered this a very important item of the guidebook.

As a grand finale, and a device that we consider contributes to the completeness of our efforts, we compiled a full appendix. It consists of:

A. Code of Ethics for Volunteers
B. An Example of a Friendly Visiting Program
C. An Example of an ADC Project
D. List of Suggested Projects
E. Registration and Filing Procedures
F. Recognition and Awards

We have received permission from the United Funds and Councils of America, Inc., to join their national system for presenting recognition and awards. Although our top state job "Director of Community Resources" has not been filled, we have presented the guidebook to the executive committees of the County Commissioners' Association and the County Directors' Association. It has their full endorsement and various volunteer projects have been started throughout the State. The field representatives are giving help and direction. We have confidence it is a program that will grow. It can't miss! And this is how Kansas has found a way to extend voluntary activity and organization in social welfare.

3. Social Work Theory in the National Awards Competition

The National Awards Competition sought among other things to achieve a greater understanding of the working philosophy of the social work vocations. Who are the exponents of new directions in social welfare? What attitudes toward private welfare and voluntarism are found among social workers, both volunteer and professional? How do welfare workers go about organizing new activities; what social inventions are they producing?

The nature of the participants themselves gives some indication of the sources of energy in social work innovation. Entries in the National Awards Competition came from forty States, the District of Columbia, Puerto Rico, and Canada. They came from rural areas, small towns, and cities; fifty-six per cent originated in metropolises of a half-million or more persons. About half the essayists worked in private welfare agencies, and about forty per cent worked for public agencies. Fewer than twenty per cent were unpaid volunteers, although a number of professional workers did volunteer work too. Women entrants far outnumbered men.

From analysis of the papers, some estimate could be made of the number of years that the entrants had spent in welfare work. Probably no more than fifteen per cent had less than three years' experience; at least that many had sixteen or more years of experience. Confirmation that the entrants were on the whole a highly qualified group comes also from estimates of their educational level. It appears that over half of the authors had been educated beyond the college level in schools of social service or related disciplines.

A more detailed study was made of the background of those whose essays are published in this volume. (It should be recalled that the papers were judged anonymously and that all such information was compiled afterwards.) The published authors as a group have considerably more welfare experience, come even more frequently from the largest cities, and have had more professional education, than the average of *all* entrants. They

289

include far more men than the proportion of men among all entrants; more of them work in private agencies; and they tend to hold posts of higher responsibility in the welfare field. Their average age is forty-four. These characteristics of the authors of the leading essays are reported in Table 1.

Table 1. Background of Published Authors and Other
Entrants (National Awards Competition, 1956)

	Published Authors	Other Entrants
From metropolitan centers of over 500,000	73%	53%
Male	54	37
Work for a government	20	32
Work for a private agency	44	30
Work as unpaid volunteers	22	15
Professionally educated	97	57 *
Hold posts of high responsibility	61	23 *
Have spent seven or more years in welfare work ...	73	63 *
Have previous publications	63	†

* Estimated from essay contents.   † No information.

From the evidence thus far submitted, we gather that the published authors and the majority of entrants are experienced, competent people who know whereof they speak. They are a fair cross section of the grass-roots leaders of the social welfare field in America today. A high level of confidence and optimism permeates their work and writing; the very fact of their participation in the contest marks them as especially active persons.

We may inquire further now about the stance that they take toward private welfare work. In making this analysis, we must necessarily introduce a large measure of subjective judgment; not everyone would read the papers and derive the same conclusions as we have. Hence some reservations regarding our analysis are necessary.

Table 2 presents an estimate of the attitudes of the entrants with respect to private and public welfare as implied in their essays.

*Table 2. Attitudes Toward Private and Public Welfare ***

Complete and sole dedication to private welfare work	101
Dedication to private and tolerance of public welfare	158
Regards both equally	178
Dedication to public welfare and tolerance of private welfare ...	14
Complete and sole dedication to public welfare	4
Other	3

* This and subsequent tables are based on analysis of 458 essays.

In addition, an attempt was made to determine so far as possible from the contents what attitudes were held in the principal agencies discussed toward private welfare. (Over 550 agencies were discussed.) Table 3 presents an analysis.

Table 3. Motivation of Principal Agency Discussed Toward Private Welfare

Intensely and explicitly pro-private welfare 97
Pro-private welfare 244
Presumptively friendly to private welfare extension 88
Presumptively unfriendly to private welfare 12
Anti-private welfare 2
Strongly anti-private welfare 1
Not classifiable 14

Thus, at least so far as an analysis of content reveals, the entries collectively present an impressive array of dedicated efforts in private welfare and voluntarism. One must appreciate, however, that the attitudes of private agencies toward public welfare comprise a formidable topic for large-scale research and this is only the slightest hint of the nature of those attitudes.

The majority of entries present secular plans that do not call for an explicitly religious attitude. Twelve papers come from clerics or a religious order; 38 papers describe lay activities under religious sponsorship; 56 papers deal with secular activities and sponsors, but exhibit elements of religiousness in the entrants' attitudes; and 347 papers present ideas with no apparent explicit religious interest.

Several tables are required to present what were estimated to be the practical dimensions of the plans contained in the essays. First a general judgment was made regarding the practicality of the plans; the results are contained in Table 4.

Table 4. Practicality (but Not Attractiveness)

Practical 392
Practical but difficult 53
Of dubious practicality 2
Very impractical 0
Other 11

Next a judgment was made as to the readiness of each plan for initiation or support in the given locality or situation in which it is presently found. This is summarized in Table 5.

Table 5. State of Readiness of Each Plan for
Initiation or Support in Given Locality

Area receptive, and the better idea or novel idea
in operation already 255
Area receptive but plan needs initiation 49
Area unprepared and plan inoperative so that new
idea would have no ongoing base 136
Other 18

Then the plans were classified according to the degree of difficulty that would be encountered in extending them to other communities (excluding the vital question of availability of the seeding agent). Table 6 gives these estimates.

Table 6. State of Readiness Elsewhere in Parallel Situations
for Introduction of Discussed Change

Other areas receptive and better idea or novel idea in
operation already 64
Other areas receptive but plan needs initiation there 129
Other areas unprepared and inoperative so that new idea
would have no base 185
Other, unclassifiable 80

A distinction can be made between the practicality (or impracticality) of a plan and its conventionality (or its controversial character). The two are not necessarily or logically the same. Most of the plans (370) are conventional, with probable general acceptance if carried out. Some 70 are conventional, but might arouse public or strong private opposition. Only a half-dozen plans are unmistakably unconventional. This situation presents both good and bad features, good in that much work may be done without arousing costly public dispute, bad in that few remarkably new ideas are to be found in the essays.

There do not appear to be revolutionary ideas yet in the social welfare field; or if there are such ideas, they have not been put to any practical test, nor have they been accepted by the leaders in social welfare.

There were no plans for the decentralization or return to private hands of a whole government agency or activity. None proposed a plan for tax relief for increased charitable contributions. One writer suggested a way of educating the young to private, instead of public, welfare. Another author showed how private contracting of welfare services might be organized. Perhaps truly original and unconventional thoughts must come from an instructed minority who combine free imaginations with hard experience.

Or perhaps a competition directly seeking general plans, rather than re-warding accounts of specific experiences, would uncover more striking ideas. Little in the papers, or in the numerous contacts and voluminous correspondence connected with the Competition, could lead one to ex-pect major institutional or spiritual reforms from within the vast private and public welfare system as it is now constituted in America.

True, the dominant objective of 255 papers, within the limits of their category, is to present a new type of activity or organizational form for consideration and extension. However, in almost all cases a reformation, rather than a transformation, is the result. Ten papers are primarily con-cerned with bettering human relations, 14 with a new philosophical orienta-tion, and 167 with an improvement of an existing structure or organiza-tion. When the papers are studied to discover what obstacles appear to block the present realization of the idea being presented, only 27 suffer from a lack of precedent. The full list of obstacles put forward in all papers is displayed in Table 7. The three major obstacles are considered to be lack of motivated persons, lack of money, and the absence of an appro-priate organization.

Table 7. Number of Entrants Mentioning Various Major Obstacles to Carrying Out Their Plan *

Not enough motivated persons 132
Not enough trained persons 43
Lack of funds 91
Legal obstacles 4
Lack of public acceptance of the work 47
Organization lacking 32
Lack of precedent 90
Lack of knowledge 34
Other obstacles mentioned 27
No obstacles mentioned 114

* Total exceeds 458 because some papers referred to more than one major type of obstacle.

A number of essays describe a form of action and organization that com-bines both private and public agencies, or that joins a volunteer group to a public agency. In fact, the lines between public and private welfare are scarcely well drawn any longer in a number of important areas such as mental health, family services, and recreation. In some areas still private in theory it is becoming almost impossible to operate without coordinating with government agencies, both because of important technical advantages and because of the desire on all sides for such cooperation. This "close quarters" development should be thoroughly studied and evaluated by a private group; it may be a disastrous development or an unrealized opportunity to get reform from within.

We can say that the hundreds of essays show that voluntarism (and private welfare) is very much alive in America. Even granting that the entrants were self-selected and already concerned with private welfare, the Competition's results still attest to an astonishing free activity in our communities throughout the nation. The essays in this book alone might form the agenda of support for a number of smaller foundations and philanthropic individuals. One is tempted to say that our Competition reveals the existence of an unlimited reservoir of talents and activities in voluntary and private welfare, if there were a civic leadership willing to explore and exploit it. Yet one would be naïve to be carried away by these thoughts. Strong economic interests and ideological forces are also at work, repressing individual wills and engendering bureaucratic conformity.

Indeed, the many entries in the National Awards Competition, in their full and vivid detail, help one appreciate how mysterious the far-flung realm of social welfare in America is. Today in ten thousand places in America, we are experiencing at least two major political developments that are practically ignored by political theorists, educators, and civic leaders. One, already hinted at, is the development of multitudinous contacts between the private and public sectors of welfare. The other is the extension of the meaning of welfare work far beyond the bounds of providing subsistence to the poorest people and aid to the critically handicapped.

Most entries ventured plans that are well within or near the traditional bounds, but the greatest ambition characterizes other social work philosophy today. A direct quotation in the latter vein may be adduced:

> Social work has been defined as a "professional service rendered to people for the purpose of assisting them as individuals or in groups to attain satisfying relationships and standards of life in accordance with their particular wishes and capacities and in harmony with those of the community." Its objectives include not only the provision of material assistance to dependent or needy persons but also the rendering of help to people who have difficulties in making adjustments to their economic and social environments.[1]

We may wonder whether we have not here reached an absurd point, where whatever problem any normal person may possess in his capacity as a mortal man becomes the subject of a field of social welfare. Especially

---

[1] Clyde E. Murray, "Social Work as a Profession," in *Social Work Year Book, 1954*, p. 506, quoting J. P. Anderson, *Opportunities in Social Work*, 1952.

if, as is possible, the development of multitudinous contacts resolves into a rather complete determination of social welfare by public agencies, the second process could carry us far toward a social and political order in which there would be as many social workers as there now are pastors, Masons, and Boy Scouts, all armed with the power of the State. Under such conditions, voluntarism in the welfare field might be as much of an offense as it is in some communities today to lay one's own drainpipe. Even stranger events have happened in modern times.

Hence it may be in order to direct our theoretical and research energies along some new lines in social welfare research. Especially have we need of detailed and systematic investigation of the shifting and disintegrating line between private and public welfare work, and of the uncontrolled extension of the concept of "social welfare" through the medium of an ever expanding corps of professional workers. Trenchant descriptions of a multitude of local activities, such as are represented in the essays submitted to the National Awards Competition, are an important source of knowledge regarding facts and motives in welfare work today.

Appendix. Notes About
the Contributors

Virginia Banerjee (Second Award, The Blind) is Counselor for Blind Children with the Lake County Department of Public Welfare in Gary, Indiana. She attended Otterbein College in Ohio and is a graduate of the School of Social Service Administration of the University of Chicago. She has been a professional welfare worker for four years and is the mother of two children.

Mrs. Frank M. Barry (Second Award, The Aging) is currently employed as Director of the Department of Older Persons and Chronically Ill of the Welfare Federation of Cleveland, Ohio. Born in Canton, China, she attended Wooster College in Ohio and the School of Applied Social Sciences of Western Reserve University, where she is Assistant Professor of Community Organization. She has been in the field of welfare work for twenty years and is the author of several articles. Mrs. Barry has one child.

Mrs. Mildred G. Brandon (Honorable Mention) is Supervisor of Field Services in the Kansas Public Welfare Department at Topeka. She is a graduate of Texas' Baylor College and has an M.A. from Tulane University. She attended the University of Chicago and has spent about half of her twenty years' work in the welfare field with private agencies. Mrs. Brandon is a widow.

Thomas M. Brigham (Honorable Mention) is Coordinator of Social Work at Fresno State College. He attended the University of Cincinnati, The Citadel, Vanderbilt University, Colorado State College of Education, and San Francisco State College, and has done graduate work at the University of California. He has spent ten and a half years in welfare activities for various agencies, presently being a member of the boards of directors of three local private social agencies and consultant for public social agencies and advisory groups. Married, he is the father of four children.

Mrs. Ada Beidler Bull (Second Award, Recreation) has been a professional social worker for twenty years and has one child. She attended Lebanon Valley College in Pennsylvania and is a graduate of the New York School of Social Work of Columbia University. She is at present the Executive Secretary of the Bethlehem Community Council of Bethlehem, Pennsylvania, and is the author of the publication *How Can We Strengthen the American Family?* (Town Hall).

Byron B. Burnes (First Award, The Deaf), totally deaf since the age of fifteen, has devoted himself to welfare activity for the deaf for the past thirty years. He is Senior Teacher in the California School for the Deaf and President of the National Association of the Deaf, editing the monthly publications of those organizations. He has an A.B. from Gallaudet College in Washington, D.C., and an M.A. degree from the University of Chicago. He is married and has two step-children.

John L. Campbell (Second Award, Medical Care) is an Associate in Vocational Guidance with the Rehabilitation Teaching Program of Western Reserve University. He attended Muskingum College and received his M.A. from Western Reserve University in 1950. He has acted as a Consultant for the Society for the Blind and the Society for Crippled Children. He is married and has two children.

Anne Hawkins Cotton (Honorable Mention) attended the University of California at Berkeley and spent a year at the University of London. She has worked regularly as a volunteer for private agencies for about five years and is the author of one novel (Harper, 1949). A resident of Astoria, Oregon, she currently devotes time to the Myasthenia Gravis Foundation.

William James Davis (Second Award, Juvenile Delinquency) has been Executive Secretary of the University YMCA at Berkeley, California, for twenty-five years, except for time spent as assistant to the executive of the Berkeley Community Chest during 1936–38. He attended the University of California for two years of graduate work in law and education. He was President of the Berkeley Council of Social Agencies in 1942. Married, he is the father of two children.

Dr. Alfred de Grazia, President of the Foundation for Voluntary Welfare, is a Political Scientist at Stanford University. He has a Ph.D. from the University of Chicago and has taught at the University of Minnesota, Brown University, and Columbia University. As consultant to various governmental bodies, universities, foundations, and business concerns, he has developed programs for social research. His published works include *Public and Republic, The Elements of Political Science, The Western Public,* and *The American Way of Government.* He is married and has seven children.

Dr. Winfield G. Doyle (Honorable Mention) has been for six years Curator of Education at the Cleveland (Ohio) Health Museum, a privately supported agency. From 1940 to 1950 he was engaged in museum education at the American Museum of Natural History in New York City. He is a graduate of Oberlin College, has an M.A. from the University of Minnesota, and an Ed.D. from Columbia University; he is the author of various articles on museum and health education. He is married and has one daughter.

Mrs. Ruth Einstein (Honorable Mention), a widow with three children, has spent forty-five years in voluntary social work. An alumna of Western Reserve University and Cleveland College, she has over the years been active in a large number of volunteer organizations for family and child welfare in Cleveland. In both world wars she conducted programs for emergency child care and is at present working on plans for the establishment of residence clubs for older persons.

Mrs. Clara Fox (First Award, Recreation) is Field Consultant in Cooperative Housing Developments for Play Schools Association, Inc., of New York City. She has a B.A. and M.A. in the fields of sociology and psychology and has devoted twenty-two years to professional welfare activity. She was also director of a resident school for emotionally disturbed children and a member of the New York City Welfare and Health Council. Mrs. Fox is a widow with one child.

George H. Gibb (Honorable Mention) is a Department Representative with the Salvation Army in New York. He attended the Salvation Army Officers Training College and the Westchester State Teachers College. He did graduate work at the Yale University Summer School of Alcohol Studies. He has been in the welfare field for fourteen years, mainly with the Salvation Army, in which he ranks as a captain. He is married, with two children.

Mrs. Margaret A. Golton (Honorable Mention) is a casework supervisor in University Heights, Ohio. She attended Western Reserve University, where she received an M.S.W. in the School of Applied Social Sciences. She has spent ten of her almost twenty-five years in social work with a public agency and is the author of the Child Welfare League Bulletin No. 4145, "The Family."

Kenneth A. Green (Second Award, Alcoholism) is Counselor for Volunteers of America in Los Angeles. He was graduated from the University of California School of Social Work and has been a professional in the field for seven years. He is a member of the Southern California Group Psychotherapy Association, and is married and the father of three children.

Joseph Norman Heard (First Award, Child Welfare) is Librarian at Pan American College in Edinburg, Texas, and holds an M.A. in Library Sciences from the University of Texas. He is the author of an article "We Refused to Put Our Son Away" in *Extension Magazine* (1955), and of numerous articles in the fields of history, travel, and the library sciences. He is active in the National Association for Retarded Children. He is married and the father of a boy and a girl.

George K. Herbert (Honorable Mention) at present directs the Research Bureau of the Community Council in Houston, Texas. He attended the University of Louisville, and studied social work at the University of Chicago and law at the University of Houston and the Cleveland-Marshall Law School. He has been a professional welfare worker for six years and this essay is his first publication. Mr. Herbert was connected with the Welfare Federation of Cleveland and is a member of the National Association of Social Workers.

Walter Hall (Honorable Mention) is the pen name of a director of a school for the crippled and delicate in a western city.

Mrs. Charlotte S. Hirsch (Honorable Mention) has been active for a number of years as a professional worker in the field of mental health. She has been a board member of a family health agency, various mental health associations, PTA, and on coordinating and planning councils in her field. She is from Van Nuys, California.

Dr. Milton John Huber (Honorable Mention) is Executive Director of Boys' Republic in Farmington, Michigan. He has an A.B. from Western Maryland College and a Ph.D. from Boston University. He has also been Assistant Secretary of the Boys' Division of the Huntington YMCA in Boston and has published several articles on social welfare in professional or religious periodicals. Married, he has three children.

Miss Margaret Temperance Hutchinson (Second Award, Chronic Illness) has also been active in the fields of teaching, counseling, and the organization of small communities. She attended Muskingum College and did graduate work at Boston University, where she received an M.A., and at Columbia University and Union Theological Seminary. She is at present occupied with a family enterprise in Columbus, Ohio.

Milton A. Jahoda (First Award, The Blind) is Executive Director of the Allen County League for the Blind in Fort Wayne, Indiana. He attended Bard College and has an M.A. from the New York School of Social Work. A professional welfare worker for twelve years, he is a member of the Board of Directors of the Fort Wayne Community Chest and is the author of several articles on practices in agencies for the blind. He is married and the father of two children.

Mrs. Franklin H. Johnson (co-author, First Award, Rehabilitation) has been a volunteer in welfare activity for five years. She attended the University of Miami, is a board member of the Miami Junior League and the Dade County Council on Community Relations, and is Coordinator of the Coconut Grove Citizens' Committee.

Alfred H. Katz (Second Award, The Crippled) is Executive Director of the New York Chapter of the National Hemophilia Foundation. He was born in Auckland, New Zealand, and received both his B.A. and M.A. from the University of New Zealand. He also holds a Certificate in Social Work from the New York School of Social Work. He has been active as a volunteer worker and has published a large number of special studies in professional social work journals. He is married and has one child.

Mrs. Earl W. Kibby (First Award, The Crippled) is employed by the Department of Public Welfare of Pittsfield, Massachusetts, as a social worker. She attended North Adams State Teachers College (Mass.) and Hunter College in New York City. She has spent twenty-three years in public agency work, as well as doing volunteer work in connection with her church and with Visiting Nurse Clinics. She is the mother of six children.

Mrs. Raymond Kitchen (Honorable Mention) is a staff worker at the PTA wardrobe of Palo Alto, California, a voluntary activity supported by the Community Chest and started by Mrs. Kitchen about ten years ago. She spent a year in the San Diego County of Public Welfare and has been active in community work in Palo Alto. She is the mother of four children.

William H. Koch, Jr. (First Award, Migrant Workers) is State Director of Migrant Work with the Arizona Migrant Ministry, a church-sponsored agency. A graduate of Columbia University and Springfield College, where he received his B.S. and M.S., he has spent ten years in the fields of recreation, group work, and community organization, and is currently program chairman of the Arizona Conference of Social Work. He has written several magazine articles in the field of recreation. He is married and has two children.

Ralph M. Kramer (First Award, "General") is Executive Director of the West Contra Costa Community Chest and Welfare Council, a private agency in Richmond, California. He is a graduate of the University of California and the University of California School of Social Welfare. He is the author of over thirty articles and book reviews in professional journals and has been an Instructor at the University of California Extension. He is married and the father of three children.

Miss Dorthea M. Lane (First Grand Award, Mental Health) is currently employed as Assistant Chief of Social Work Service at the Veterans' Administration Neuropsychiatric Hospital in Los Angeles. She is a graduate of the University of Michigan and attended the University of Chicago School of Social Service Administration. Of her twenty-four years' service in the field of mental health, sixteen have been spent with various public agencies in Chicago and in Iowa. Her prize-winning essay is her first publication.

Miss Fern Long (Honorable Mention) attended Radcliffe College and has done graduate work at Charles University at Prague and at Western Reserve University Library School. She has had three years in professional welfare activities and at present is Supervisor in the Adult Education Department in Cleveland, which work results in frequent cooperative projects with the local Welfare Federation. She has had numerous articles published in professional library journals and is the author of two novels and one book of poems.

Charles W. McCann (First Award, The Aging) is Executive Director of the Community Planning Council of Pasadena, California. He attended San Diego State College and received an M.A. in Social Work from the School of Social Work of the University of Southern California, where he is a Lecturer on Social Work. He is the author of several other papers on the senior citizen. Married, he has two children.

Mrs. Dorothy T. Minnick (Honorable Mention), a housewife, is the mother of two children. She received her B.A. from the University of California at Los Angeles and has done graduate work at the University of Southern California School of Social Work. She has spent three years in social work with a public agency in Los Angeles County and is author of *With Rings on My Fingers,* published in 1948.

Dr. Albert Morris (First Award, Juvenile Delinquency) is Professor of Sociology and Chairman of the Department of Sociology and Anthropology at Boston University. He attended both Boston and Harvard Universities and has published extensively in the field of criminology. He has been on the boards of the United Prison Association, the Washingtonian Hospital, the Boston YMCA, and the Planned Parenthood Federation, among others. He is married and the father of two children.

Robert Plank (Second Award, Basic Medical Research) is a Psychiatric Social Worker with the Veterans' Administration in Cleveland, Ohio. Born in Vienna, Austria, he attended the University of Vienna and did graduate work at the University of California. Of his fourteen years in the social service field he has spent ten with public agencies and has published extensively in the field of psychiatry and epistomology. He is married.

David Roth (Second Award, Child Welfare) is Assistant Executive Director of the New York Jewish Child Care Council. He attended City College of New York and the University of Chicago, and has spent about half of his nine years in welfare activity with a public agency. He is a member of the National Conference of Social Welfare and the New York State Welfare Conference. This award-winning essay is his first publication. He is married, with one child.

Dr. Herbert Rusalem (Honorable Mention) is Director of Professional Training in the Industrial Home for the Blind in Brooklyn, N.Y. He is a graduate of Columbia University and is on the staffs of Columbia University and Hunter College. He has published in the *Journal of Rehabilitation* and the *Journal of Counseling Psychology.*

Tong G. Sam (First Award, Chronic Illness) is Supervisor of the Public Welfare Department in San Francisco. He attended San Francisco State College and Washington State College. He has been in the welfare field ten years, all but two with a public agency. He is a member of the California Welfare Directors' Association and this is his first published essay. He is married, with two children.

Marcella I. Schmoeger (Second Award, Mental Health) is Coordinator of Community Relations at Philadelphia's Fountain House, Inc., a private volunteer agency. She attended New York University and Temple University, as well as Iowa State and Packard Business School. She has published articles in the *Friends' Journal.*

Mrs. Mary Jean Shamlian (First Award, Basic Medical Research) of Soquel, California, does free-lance medical writing and is a part-time medical secretary. The mother of two boys, she has been active in Junior Red Cross, PTA, Cub Scouts, and the Community Chest. She is currently at work on a book concerning the problems of residence care for the elderly.

Barbara Sorensen (Second Award, The Deaf) is a fourth-grade teacher in the California School for the Deaf at Berkeley. She is a graduate of Ohio Wesleyan University and holds an M.A. in Special Education from Teachers' College of Columbia University and the Lexington School for the Deaf, as well as a Master's Degree in English from Middlebury College. She is the wife of Harry Roy Sorensen and the mother of one child.

Fred H. Steininger (Second Award, Rehabilitation) is Director of the Lake County Department of Public Welfare in Gary, Indiana. He has a B.A. from St. Joseph College in Indiana and an M.A. in social work from the University of Chicago. A welfare worker for seventeen years, he is Vice President of the American Public Welfare Association and teaches part-time at Valparaiso University. He is married and the father of two children.

Robert Stevenson (Second Grand Award, Alcoholism) is Secretary and Vice President of the Upper Midwest Foundation on Problem Drinking, Inc., in Minneapolis. He attended the University of Wisconsin and has been in the field of private welfare for fourteen years. He has been a feature writer for metropolitan newspapers on social welfare subjects and has written short stories and one-act plays on these topics. He is married and has one child.

Margaret B. Sweitzer (Second Award, "General") is a psychiatric social worker with a B.A. from Denison University and an M.A. from Western Reserve University. She has worked with YWCA committees and the Mental Health Association. She is at present a resident of Vero Beach, Florida, and the mother of five children. This is her first publication.

Mrs. Harry A. Talbott (Honorable Mention), a housewife and fruit rancher of Palisade, Colorado, is the mother of four children. She attended Mesa Junior College, Western State College, and the University of California at Berkeley, and has been a volunteer in welfare activity for eight years.

Stephen Thierman (Second Award, Migrant Workers) is Regional Secretary of the American Friends' Service Committee in San Francisco. He has a B.S. from Haverford College and a LL.B. from the University of Wisconsin Law School. With ten years in welfare activity, he has published a number of magazine articles on religion and welfare. He is on the Board of Directors of the Northern California Service League and the American Civil Liberties Union. Married, he is the father of four children.

Mrs. Carrie Turner (Honorable Mention) is a caseworker for The Society for the Blind in Cleveland. She attended Tuskegee Institute and Northwestern University and has spent nineteen years as a professional welfare worker, all with private agencies. Her previous publication was "Outlook for the Blind," a magazine article.

Mrs. Vladimir Virrick (co-author, First Award, Rehabilitation) has devoted eight years of voluntary work to the Coconut Grove Citizens' Committee for Slum Clearance. She is past president of the Cerebral Palsy Association and a member of the Urban League of Miami. She attended the University of Wisconsin, Columbia University, and the University of Miami. She has written a number of magazine articles and has one daughter.

Mrs. Alan Wiener (First Award, Medical Care) is Assistant to the Director of the Health and Welfare Council, a private agency in Philadelphia. An alumna of Temple University and the Pennsylvania School of Social Work, she has been a professional welfare worker for thirteen years and is connected with the newly established Association of Hospital Volunteer Directors. She has one child.

William H. Wilsnack (Honorable Mention) is Assistant Chief of Social Service in the State Department of Mental Hygiene at Sacramento, California. He is a graduate of the University of Michigan and has spent almost all of his twenty years of welfare activity with a public agency. He is married, with two children.

Paul A. Wilson (Honorable Mention) is Vocational Counselor for Older Workers with the Vocational Guidance and Rehabilitation Services in Cleveland, Ohio. He is a graduate of Oberlin College and New York University and has taught public school for twenty years. He is the author of "Suggestions for Workers over Fifty." Married, he is the father of two children.

OL

ELIOPF

De Grazia